THE DUTCH NAVY

William N. Still, Jr., Series Editor
STUDIES IN MARITIME HISTORY

Stoddert's War: Naval Operations During the Quasi-War with France, 1798-1801
by Michael A. Palmer

The British Navy and the American Revolution
by John A. Tilley

Iron Afloat: The Story of the Confederate Ironclads
by William N. Still, Jr.

A Maritime History of the United States: The Role of America's Seas and Waterways
by K. Jack Bauer

Confederate Shipbuilding
by William N. Still, Jr.

Raid on America: The Dutch Naval Campaign of 1672-1674
by Donald G. Shomette and Robert D. Haslach

Lifeline of the Confederacy: Blockade Running During the Civil War
by Stephen R. Wise

Admiral Harold R. Stark: Architect of Victory, 1939-1945
by B. Mitchell Simpson, III

History and the Sea: Essays on Maritime Strategies
by Clark G. Reynolds

Predators and Prizes: American Privateering and Imperial Warfare, 1739-1748
by Carl E. Swanson

Honolulu: Crossroads of the Pacific
by Edward D. Beechert

Wilmington: Port of North Carolina
by Alan D. Watson

Jacksonville: Riverport—Seaport
by George E. Buker

The Jeffersonian Gunboat Navy
by Spencer C. Tucker

The Dutch Navy of the Seventeenth and Eighteenth Centuries
by Jaap R. Bruijn

THE DUTCH NAVY
of the Seventeenth and Eighteenth Centuries

BY JAAP R. BRUIJN

UNIVERSITY OF SOUTH CAROLINA PRESS

Published in Columbia, South Carolina, by the
University of South Carolina Press

Manufactured in the United States of America

Library of Congress Cataloging-in-Publication Data

Bruijn, Jaap R., 1938–
The Dutch navy of the seventeenth and eighteenth centuries / by Jaap R. Bruijn.
p. cm. — (Studies in maritime history)
Includes bibliographical references and index.
ISBN 0–87249–875–1 (acid-free)
1. United Provinces of the Netherlands. Zeemacht—History.
I. Title. II. Series.
VA533.B78 1993 93-18700
359'.009492'0903—dc20 CIP

CONTENTS

ILLUSTRATIONS

Following page 110

MAPS

TABLES

FOREWORD

The United Provinces of the Netherlands dominated Western civilization in nearly every major respect throughout most of the seventeenth century. As such a presence, it played a key role in the shaping of the modern world. Politically, the seven Protestant Dutch provinces won their freedom from Catholic Spain in the late sixteenth century to forge a middle-class republic devoted to the principles of democracy. As the English diplomat Sir William Temple observed of the Dutch around 1670, "Men live together like Citizens of the World, associated by the common ties of Humanity, and by the bonds of Peace, under the impartial protection of indifferent laws, with equal encouragement of all Art and Industry and equal freedom of Speculation and Enquiry." Economically, this industry was manifested in such a dynamic and supreme mercantile trade that the Netherlands quickly became the first modern nation-state rooted in bourgeois capitalism. Culturally, free thought and high achievement in art—direct successors to forces active in the intellectual and creative climate in Italy during the preceding three centuries—established the Dutch Renaissance.

Dutch hegemony in Europe and across distant seas was made possible by fortuitous historical timing and strategic insularity. Not only were the Netherlands isolated by the natural water barriers of the North Sea and the estuaries and Maas, Rhine, Waal, and Lek Rivers to the south, but the Republic had little to fear from either the fragmented Germanic principalities to the east, the internally preoccupied countries of France and England, or the enfeebled Spanish Netherlands (modern Belgium) beyond the river barriers. Thus could a nation of fewer than two million people take to the seas with enough merchant ships—almost 2,000 at the peak—to capture the maritime trade of virtually all Europe and with the most formidable navy of the era to protect the concomitant prosperity.

It was the Dutch Republic that provided the precedent of a democratic free-enterprise maritime empire which would eventually be emulated by Great Britain in the eighteenth and nineteenth centuries and the United States in the twentieth century. The great Dutch jurist Hugo Grotius first articulated the principle of freedom of the seas (*Mare Liberum*) in 1609, laying the foundations of modern international law and justifying the policy of the Dutch East India Company to shatter and replace the Portuguese trading monopoly over the Indian Ocean and Southeast Asia. From the university town of Leiden, the English Pilgrims organized their voyage to America, via England, to what became New England in 1620, by which time Dutch explorers had already established the North American colony of New Netherlands with its seaport community of New Amsterdam—a town that was captured by the English in 1664 and renamed New York. To the Republic fled Protestant Huguenots and liberal English political philosophers like John Locke, and there flourished controversial thinkers like the Dutch Jew Baruch Spinoza and the Frenchman René Descartes. And the English Parliament turned to the stadholder of the Netherlands, William of Orange, and his English wife Mary to be king and queen of England after the so-called "Glorious Revolution" of 1688.

Why, then, have American and European scholars andstudents tended to ignore the Golden Age of the Netherlands? One reason is the fact that England ultimately triumphed at sea—with no small help from the Dutch in the process—to create the sprawling British Empire and its American offspring. Another is the distracting historical image of the Sun King of Versailles, Louis XIV, whose despotism brought France to great power status on the continent—but whose territorial ambitions where thwarted by allied armies, which were composed of a great many Dutch troops, in the wars that were waged from 1689 to 1713. But the main reason is the simple fact of language. Whereas French and English would encompass the globe, Dutch would be written, read and spoken only by the people of the Republic and its few overseas territories.

Only as Dutch historians like professor Jaap R. Bruijn, of the venerable University of Leiden, translate their considerable scholarly efforts into English can the Dutch achievement be fully appreciated by a wider reading audience. And no more crucial subject deserves attention than the mechanism by which the powerful Dutch navy guaranteed the successes of the United Provinces in the evolution of the Western world. This mechanism was the governing five admiralties of the seven provinces working in concert through the States General to insure Dutch naval supremacy and maritime hegemony.

From the Sea Beggars who harassed the Spanish Goliath in the 1570s and whose successors played a considerable role in helping England to frustrate the Spanish Armada in 1588, the admiralties emerged to forge the squadrons and fleets which humbled Spanish naval arms over the next half-century and battled pirates and freebooters from the Baltic to the Mediterranean to protect European trade. Dutch naval fortunes waxed and waned in the three sea wars with England—1652–1654, 1665–1667, and 1672–1674; in the last one, which involved France as well, conflict continued until the peace of 1678. Then the Anglo-Dutch alliance resulted in joint arms to defeat Louis XIV by 1713. Not until the United Provinces joined the coalition against Britain, which lost the war over America's independence in the 1780s, was the Netherlands' declining naval prowess overtly exposed, contributing to the final Dutch collapse to French revolutionary armies at the end of the century.

Thanks to this book, English-language readers can now learn the identities and the ingenious policies and social history of the men who made the Dutch miracle possible—and can understand how these naval institutions kept the flame alive even through the years of relative decline. The Dutch Republic of the seventeenth century was no minor power but rather *the* great force in the shaping of Europe during that era. This incisive study reveals just how important the admiralties were in helping to shape the Dutch achievement.

Clark G. Reynolds
College of Charleston
Charleston, SC

PREFACE

No serious study of early modern Europe can ignore the role played by the Dutch Republic throughout the seventeenth century as one of the leading world powers economically, politically, culturally, and militarily. An important factor in this success was the navy of the United Provinces. This force insured the safe passage of European seaborne trade against the fleets of Spain, Portugal, Sweden, Denmark, England, and France from the 1590s until the alliance with England after 1689. And even as a relatively minor force during the eighteenth century, the Dutch navy managed to hold its own until the eve of the French revolutionary conquest.

Dutch historians have undertaken studies of the navy of the Republic in the early nineteenth century. Their main interests, of course, were centered in the navy's heyday and focused on several specific episodes. Only three authors have written general surveys. J. C. de Jonge published the first and most extensive survey during the years from 1833 to 1848. The enlarged second edition of his *Geschiedenis van het Nederlandsche zeewezen* (*History of the Dutch Marine Affairs*), published in five volumes from 1858 through 1862, is still our most important source of factual information. Indeed, it is irreplaceable because of a disastrous fire in the Department of the Navy in 1844 which destroyed the archives of the former admiralties of the Republic. De Jonge had consulted them just in time. Collections of documents, privately kept by former naval administrators, later only partly filled the gaps in the badly decimated admiralty records. The two other surveys, published by J. J. Backer Dirks from 1865 to 1876 and by J. C. Mollema from 1939 to 1942, were mainly based on De Jonge's work, although they do deal, respectively, with the nineteenth and the early twentieth century. The contemporary four-volume *Maritieme geschiedenis van de Nederlanden* (*Maritime History of the Low Countries*)—published from 1976 to 1978, and edited and compiled by G. Asaert, Ph. M. Bosscher, W. J. van Hoboken, and J. R. Bruijn—is an analytical survey of the maritime as well as the naval history of both the Netherlands and Belgium from the Middle Ages to the late twentieth century.

Just as the study of history in general must always encompass new evidence and new ideas, so too must naval history. Unlike the nineteenth-and early twentieth-century historiographical focus on expeditions, battles, and ships, current historical scholarship reflects the influence of the social sciences. Naval historians all over the world have become interested in the common seaman and his officers as well as the administrative institutions that managed the navies. Since the 1960s, a growing number of studies on these subjects have been published, pioneered by the American naval historian D. A. Baugh's *British Naval Administration in the Age of Walpole* (1965). The history of the Dutch navy can also be approached along similar lines.

Although I realized long ago that no modern study of the Dutch navy in its glory years and their aftermath existed either in Dutch or in any language, my plans for writing such a study myself took time to mature. While teaching maritime and naval history at the University of Leiden, I intensified my research and reading, but I lacked the opportunity to write until 1990, when the Netherlands Institute for Advanced Study in the Humanities and Social Sciences (NIAS) at Wassenaar provided me with it, as it had done for previous projects of mine. Months of undisturbed work and the support of the NIAS staff, Mss. J. D. Young, S. Lepelaar and M. A. Simpson in particular, enabled me to write this book.

The book covers the two centuries between the 1590s, when the young Dutch Republic became a European power of some importance, and 1795, when the French revolutionary armies conquered the Netherlands and overturned the Republic. By way of background, the introduction presents information on the previous period and on the logic and illogic of the federal structure of the Republic and its system of five admiralties. Using 1652 and 1713 as watershed years, the three main parts of the book are each divided into four sections—the first of which deals with the naval activities of the era discussed, the second with the naval administration, the third with the officer corps, and the last with the men who comprised the crews. Part two has two additional sections dealing with the major changes around 1650 and the role of Grand Pensionary John de Witt.

Several of my friends and colleagues showed their interest when this study was in progress: at Leiden, C. A. Davids and S.

Groenveld; and overseas, N. A. M. Rodger (London), C. G. Reynolds (College of Charleston, Charleston, SC), and R. W. Unger (University of British Columbia, Vancouver). They provided invaluable advice and critical comment—including counsel on the grammar and style of a text written in a language that is not my mother tongue. I extend warm thanks to Gayle R. Swanson (Chapin, SC) who copyedited the manuscript, N. Kerkhoff (Vaassen) who kindly designed two maps, and R. B. Prud'homme van Reine (The Hague) who helped me sort out the illustrations. Staff members in archives, libraries, and maritime museums have also been very helpful, and many students over the years have given me inspiration and pieces of useful information. Above all, my deep appreciation goes to Clark Reynolds, Ann Simpson, and my wife, Elly.

Although this book, with all its shortcomings, is a one-man enterprise, it would never have been possible without so much support and advice. I am very grateful for this.

THE DUTCH NAVY

THE DUTCH REPUBLIC

INTRODUCTION

During the Middle Ages, a number of territories within the boundaries of the modern Netherlands, Belgium, and northern France each developed similar ruling institutions in the form of local parliaments or states. In the fifteenth century, the dukes of Burgundy succeeded in joining most of these territories together under a single ruler, but the tradition of provincial autonomy remained strong. At long last, the Habsburg emperor Charles V (who reigned 1515–1555) ruled all the territories, seventeen in number. The seat of the central government was established at Brussels, with the rights of the provincial institutions being largely oppressed in favor the Brussels's court. From 1556 onwards, however, Charles V's son and successor, King Philip II of Spain, and his governors rekindled the old spirit of provincial opposition against centralized rule by pursuing fierce religious and fiscal policies. The Protestant iconoclasm of 1566 shook the foundations of their power and caused Philip to install the duke of Alba as his military governor. Alba's high-handed and arbitrary rule subsequently provoked the Dutch revolt. In 1572, after some initial disturbances, the provincial ruling States of Holland and Zeeland, under the leadership of William of Orange (the Silent), launched a revolt against Alba that soon gained the support of other provinces. A long and fierce struggle ensued, finally to result in the birth of the Republic of the Seven United Provinces, comprising Holland, Zeeland, and the five other northern provinces of Utrecht, Gelderland, Overijssel, Groningen, and Friesland.[1] The kingdoms of France as well as of England all had their own interest in helping the rebellious provinces, which from about 1588 onwards became independent factors in international politics. But Spain waited until 1648 before it formally recognized the Republic as an independent state.

Charles V's seventeen provinces of the Low Countries belonged to the most prosperous and densely populated areas of early modern Europe. The degree of urbanization was high; a large number of cities and townships had spread over the country. In agriculture, farming and stockbreeding developed, providing sizeable commodities for commerce and trade. Local industry flourished likewise. Several small as well as large seaports became involved in international shipping. The most important trade center was Antwerp, situated along the Scheldt River. Functioning as the transit port for a broad array of products, from English cloth and French wines to American silver, it became the economic heart of the Low Countries. However, from the start of the disturbances of 1566 until it was recaptured by the Spanish army in 1585, Antwerp faced severe economic setbacks. The subsequent closure of the Scheldt River by the Dutch and their introduction of a system of licenses for trade fundamentally changed Antwerp's situation. The economic center of gravity moved northward to Amsterdam. Port cities like Middelburg and Flushing on the isle of Walcheren in Zeeland had traditionally held a great stake in Antwerp's trading activities, though most ships from overseas sailed directly to their final destinations. Hundreds of vessels from Scotland, England, France, the Iberian Peninsula, and the Mediterranean annually dropped anchor in the Walcheren roadstead. But Zeeland operated also as an economic center of its own.

The other major Dutch seaport was Amsterdam, located in the southwestern corner of the Zuyderzee. Much smaller than Antwerp, Amsterdam also had a different economic structure. It was oriented towards the Baltic, with many merchant vessels making it their homeport, and grain was its main commodity, either sold in the Low Countries or transported to more southerly areas. The three cities of Hoorn, Enkhuizen, and Medemblik in the north were only partly dependent on the economic activities in Amsterdam and had their own patterns of shipping and trade. In the course of the sixteenth century, Enkhuizen, for instance, became the leading port for the herring fishery. Vessels sailing from all these ports had to pass one or more of the many sandbars in the Zuyderzee before reaching the North Sea via outlets near the Wadden isles of Texel and Terschelling.

The Meuse and Rhine estuary, located halfway between Zeeland and Amsterdam, was the third shipping and trading center in the Low Countries. Less international in its commercial scope than Antwerp and Amsterdam, and concentrated mainly in fishing and the timber trade, the estuary was provided with a wide range of smaller and medium-sized port cities where an increasing number of vessels were homeported—most importantly Dordrecht, Rotterdam, Delfshaven (the port of the inland city of Delft), and Brielle. The entire area held great potential for growth.

The overall increase in the volume of shipping during the sixteenth century convinced the authorities in most port cities to consider enlarging their harbor facilities. Well before the Revolt of 1572, no fewer than eleven cities developed plans for new harbors, the most substantial at Middelburg, Dordrecht, and Enkhuizen. The biggest boom in harbor construction, however, took place after 1572; in a period of fifty years, thirty extensions of harbors were completed in sixteen Dutch cities. The city rulers of Rotterdam and Amsterdam were the most active in fostering construction. Such harbors not only were used for loading and unloading cargo, but also provided extensive facilities for the wintering of vessels.[2]

Shipping and fishing often required naval protection because armament on board a merchant vessel was not sufficient to guarantee safety at sea. In periods of international tension and war, or when privateers and pirates infested the seas, local magistrates in the port cities belonging to Holland, Zeeland, and Flanders joined forces and converted a number of big merchantmen into warships. Special taxes provided the necessary funds. The dukes of Burgundy and Charles V tried vigorously to establish one central and more permanent naval organization for the three provinces, with one admiral seated at Veere in Zeeland as central naval authority. These plans faced vigorous local opposition and never materialized, however. By 1572, no structure of an interprovincial naval administration existed, though some standing instructions for combined operations, notably maneuvering and signaling, had been issued and generally accepted. During the reign of Charles V, a number of concerted expeditions were made against France, the Hanseatics, and Denmark in order to safeguard shipping and herring fishing.

As a result of the political and religious turmoil after the rebellion of 1566, many inhabitants of the Low Countries fled abroad. A group banded together using a motley assortment of ships to become the renowned Sea Beggars, who operated against vessels belonging to the loyal followers of Philip II and the duke of Alba. William of Orange—from 1559, stadholder of Holland, Zeeland, and Utrecht—joined the insurgents and partly succeeded in controlling their organization and activities. In 1572 the Sea Beggars captured the city of Brielle by surprise, whereupon other cities such as Flushing and Veere in Zeeland and Enkhuizen and Hoorn in the north of Holland declared themselves free from Brussels. The Dutch revolt had begun.

The first phase of the struggle was filled with uncertainty for the insurgents. William and his followers came close to collapse several times, but they held out hope of uniting most of the seventeen provinces against Philip II. Although William was assassinated at Delft in 1584 at the instigation of the court at Madrid, the tide turned in favor of the Dutch soon thereafter.

In the first phase, the conflict raged on land and on inland waterways and lakes. The vessels involved were small and were commanded by local captains—as was the case in the relief of inland Leiden in 1574, in which, after a month-long siege, the defenders flooded the countryside, enabling a force of flat-bottomed vessels to come to their aid and chase off the Spanish. As a reward for its fierce resistance, Leiden was made the seat of the first university in the Netherlands. By clever strategy and sound tactics, Spanish commanders succeeded in occupying important parts of the rebellious provinces, thus splitting Holland into three or more pockets of resistance and separating it from Zeeland. Such circumstances, combined with the traditional Dutch predilection for local control, were instrumental in fostering the birth and growth of regional naval organizations. These were the admiralties located around Rotterdam and Amsterdam and further in the north of Holland. After 1588, however, when the continuing existence of the new independent country was virtually assured, and naval forces deployed more regularly in the open sea, the existence of separate admiralties made the hope of any substantial centralization even more unlikely than what had transpired under Charles V.

Clearly, then, the naval history of the Dutch Republic cannot be recounted as a straight narrative chronicle. The story has much logic to it, and yet much illogic as well. At its foundation lies five different admiralties, each organized in a similar fashion and sharing similar roles and missions.

The admiralties of the Netherlands in the seventeenth and eighteenth centuries provided the state's fighting arm at sea. A navy of sufficient battle force was the common concern of the seven Protestant Dutch provinces, assembled in the States General. Men-of-war had to be built, bought, or leased whenever the need arose. And the need was constant throughout the continuous wars of the seventeenth century: the struggle for independence from Spain from 1568 to 1648 (the so-called "Eighty Years' War"), the ongoing war with

Portugal until 1661, the three wars against England between 1652 and 1674, and finally the three conflicts against France from 1672 to 1713. Throughout this period, the Dutch Republic also played a role in several Scandinavian and Baltic crises.

The history of the Republic, as the above suggests, is one of provincial sovereignty and decentralization in a small country. As such, it is a history with medieval and sixteenth-century roots in the Republic of the Seven United Provinces. The Union of Utrecht of 1579—originally a defensive alliance between the rebellious provinces, but later used as a quasi-constitution—had stipulated that the sovereign partners would have common finances, one army and one navy, and coordinated foreign relations.

For such concerted action, the provinces delegated their sovereign powers to the States General at The Hague. The States General, in which the delegation of each province had one vote and in which unanimity was often required, was responsible for the centralized military and naval funding. One permanent source of income was allocated to the navy in 1582: the yield from the duties on incoming and outgoing ships and carts and their cargoes. For other sources, ad hoc decisions by the States General were required. A captain and admiral general was the commander of both the army and the navy; he was appointed by the States General. The command always went to the prince of Orange who was the stadholder of Holland, the wealthiest and therefore the most important province, and of several other provinces.[3]

After initial disputes over greater centralization, the Seven Provinces in 1597 decided to create five separate admiralties. Although this decision was considered only a temporary solution, it remained unchanged until the end of the Republic in 1795. The admiralties were located in the maritime provinces of Zeeland, Friesland, and Holland—the latter with three of the admiralties. The one at Rotterdam, also called the admiralty of the Maze (Meuse), held the right of seniority and always provided the flagship of the combined Dutch fleet. The most important of Holland's admiralties, however, was located at Amsterdam. The third one, that of the Noorderkwartier, had its seat in Hoorn and Enkhuizen, a quarterly rotation of the seat enacted to avoid jealousy between the two cities. The admiralty of Zeeland was established in the provincial capital Middelburg, that of Friesland first at Dokkum and after 1645 at Harlingen because the waterway to Dokkum had silted up. This decentralized naval administration, split up into five partly autonomous organizations, was the outcome of rivalries among the provinces and among cities in Holland.

Each admiralty was ruled by a board of councillors, appointed by the States General. Both Rotterdam and Amsterdam had twelve councillors, the admiralty of the Noorderkwartier eleven, Friesland ten, and Zeeland nine or ten. Nominated by the Provincial States, these councillors were either selected from the province in which the admiralty was located, or they represented one of the other provinces. An oath of allegiance to further the interest of the commonwealth (above that of their province or city) was required of them. Each councillor held his post for a certain number of years, although the periods varied greatly because a term could be prolonged.

An admiralty board met several mornings each week, the frequency of meetings depending on the amount of business to be settled. If urgent matters required its attention, the board could also meet on Sundays and even on Christian feast-days. In principle, the admiral general—the stadholder of Holland and Zeeland—would act as chairman of the board, but in fact he almost never did so. He could instruct his lieutenant admiral to represent him, and although this occasionally happened, in practice the councillors chaired their own meetings, using weekly rotations of the chairmanship. The meetings were held in the so-called "Prinsenhoven" (the temporary residences of the stadholders in the 1580s) of each admiralty.

The admiralties in the Dutch Republic were given a wide variety of tasks that lay in the realm of naval and merchant shipping and adjudication over the seizure of prizes and even embraced the actual collection of taxes. All these tasks were established at the formation of the Republic and in essence never changed. The organizational structures created in the sixteenth century lasted until the end of the eighteenth century and were thought to be permanent. At times, suggestions for reforms were discussed, but none was ever introduced.

Responsible for its own income, each admiralty levied taxes on incoming and outgoing commodities and means of transport (ships and carts) along the sea and the land borders of the Republic. The tariffs were issued by the States General in lists by commodity. It was a uniform system for the entire country.[4] The tariffs themselves were subjected to a number of changes over time as the result of war or peace or the need for economic reforms. The most important duties were so-called "convooien en licenten," the common duties already well-established in the late sixteenth century which functioned as import and export taxes. All other sources of revenue came later. Best known were the "lastgeld" of 1623 and the "veilgeld" of 1652, both fixed sums and percentages: an annual levy on the tonnage of each ship and a one or two percent levy on the total value of incoming or outgoing goods.

The revenues from these duties went to the admiralties. The collection, however, required a whole network of revenue offices at ports, along rivers, and in other places with border traffic. The territory of the Republic had been divided into five sections, in each of which the admiralty collected the duties. For example, the admiralty of Friesland controlled the economic traffic in its own province, in Groningen, and on the most eastern Wadden isles. Amsterdam was responsible for its own port, the isles of Texel and Vlieland, and the inland provinces of Utrecht and Gelderland. In addition to the one in Amsterdam, this admiralty had revenue offices in seven other places (Arnhem, Doesburg, Harderwijk, s'Heerenberg, Muiden, Vreeswijk, and Zutphen). The three remaining admiralties covered the rest of the country.

Each admiralty office was staffed with at least a collector, an administrator, and a controller, but more people were of course required in a big port like Amsterdam. All the revenues had to be forwarded to the collector-general of each admiralty, who stored the money in his office. When the Amsterdam collector-general Diederik Slicher died in 1729, his heirs handed over to his successor several coffers with money totaling one million guilders in cash, while another 450,000 guilders followed soon afterwards.[5]

In theory, the practice of making each admiralty responsible for its own income, and thereby stimulating it to collect as much money as possible within the set tariffs, was not an unsound one. In reality, however, there were some serious drawbacks because the financial potential of the different districts was not the same. Initially, Middelburg, Rotterdam, Hoorn, and Enkhuizen seemed to be expanding economic centers, attracting growing amounts of goods and ships. Yet this general prosperity proved to be transitory, and Amsterdam soon became the big economic metropolis, with Rotterdam following far behind and the others lagging even further back. Consequently, the admiralty of Amsterdam collected most of the common duties and thus enjoyed a far greater income. This discrepancy and the longstanding rivalries among the districts stimulated the weaker ones to apply the tariff lists less scrupulously in order to make themselves more attractive for merchants and shippers. When the Dutch economy began to stagnate, and overseas trade was mainly contracting into Amsterdam and to a certain degree into Rotterdam, the income of the three admiralties of Zeeland, Noorderkwartier, and Friesland dwindled so drastically that it was barely sufficient for the upkeep of the organizations.

In fact, the money was intended to be spent on the navy, the foremost responsibility of an admiralty. Specifically, the men-of-war were used to convoy the merchant fleet in peacetime—a sort of *quid pro quo*, a return on the taxes paid by the merchants. Convoys were provided on a number of traditional trading routes. The expenses for building, fitting out, and manning of convoy ships, mostly frigates later on, were paid from the admiralties' fiscal resources. And the receipts and costs for such items were entered into the ordinary bookkeeping. There was also a separate financial administration for dealing with non-permanent sources of income and expenditure.

Money for all the battle fleets and squadrons could not come from the normal import and export duties, which were not earmarked for this purpose and would not have been sufficient in any case. Instead, the States General voted special subsidies for wartime naval armaments, a practice which rendered the admiralties totally dependent on the efforts of the provinces to provide the funds. The ordinary revenue from the incoming and outgoing duties was, of course, always under the admiralties' own control.

The States General had at its disposal common sources of income collected and administered at The Hague. After the Union of Utrecht, the provinces successfully safeguarded their financial autonomy. The common budget of the Republic required the provinces' consent each year, and according to its economic and demographic resources, each province was allocated a certain share or quota for which it was responsible. In most cases the money was collected from taxes on consumer goods; the tariffs could vary with each province. The system of quotas assessed Holland for fifty-eight percent of the subsidies, Friesland nearly twelve percent, Zeeland a bit more than nine percent, and the four inland provinces between three and six percent each. The quotas changed only slightly during the course of the seventeenth and eighteenth centuries.

There was no guarantee that the admiralties would receive their part of the subsidies on time. Provinces were often in arrears with their installments, and there was no sanction imposed for non-payment of dues. The four inland provinces considered the army more important than the navy. During the eighteenth century, such preferences for paying subsidies to the army or the navy was a bone of contention between the provinces.[6] Most admiralties kept records of payments not received or long overdue . However, the five admiralties did not suffer equally from this problem. In practice, the three maritime provinces paid their quotas to the admiralties on their own territory. The quotas of the remaining four provinces were spread over the five admiralties according to a fixed distribution pattern. Hence Amsterdam, Rotterdam, and the Noorderkwartier were always assured that almost ninety percent of their subsidy would come from Holland, the most reliable subsidizer. The admiralties at Middelburg and Dokkum/Harlingen received fifty-five and seventy percent respectively from their "own" province. The remaining percentages had to be provided by the four inland provinces.[7] This meant that the Middelburg and Dokkum/Harlingen admiralties suffered most from the land provinces' payment delinquencies, a situation which rendered them less efficient because it resulted in their ships often putting to sea late or sometimes not even being fitted out for service. To ameliorate these conditions, the States General could decide at any given time to subsidize certain common naval activities out of ad hoc funds derived from well-defined levies on trade and shipping.

Not only were the admiralties responsible for convoys and the fighting fleet. They also employed privateers, commissions for whom were issued by the States General or the admiral general and distributed by the admiralties themselves. The commissions were of course valid only in wartime and automatically lapsed in peacetime. The admiralty boards had to ensure that privateering rules were observed, and most importantly, the boards acted as prize courts. The five local prize courts had to declare, as a result of an elaborate system of checks and controls, whether prizes taken by privateers and men-of-war were lawful or not. During many of the seventeenth-century wars, prize adjudication was a time-consuming and intricate business, especially for the councillors at Middelburg, in whose district most privateers were operating.[8]

The admiralties also had jurisdiction over merchant shippers and inland transporters who tried to avoid paying import and export duties. Further, the councillors were responsible for the administration of criminal justice in cases of offenses by any member of the admiralty's personnel, including those serving on naval ships. Disciplinary procedures were conducted by the commanders at sea.

For the proper execution of all these tasks, the admiralties had a number of facilities at their disposal. The center of each admiralty was the Prinsenhof mentioned above. The meeting place for the councillors, it housed the offices of the clerks and the financial administrators. Most admiralties also owned a number of storehouses. A dockyard with a number of stores and workshops was available for the construction, repair, and fitting out of men-of-war. The admiralties of Zeeland, Noorderkwartier, and Rotterdam had extra dockyard facilities in other areas—very expensive assets for relatively poor institutions. Each admiralty counted a number of building slips in its dockyards, which in the long run bore no relation to its financial resources. When the Republic was disbanded in 1795 and an inventory was made of the naval dockyard facilities, there were no fewer than nine dockyards with twenty-one slips. The only rationally organized admiralty was that at Amsterdam, with five slips in one dockyard. Rotterdam had three slips in the city and one at Hellevoetsluis, close to the sea. The admiralty of Zeeland had two dockyards—at Flushing and Veere—with three slips, and none at Middelburg itself. The Noorderkwartier administered three dockyards—at Hoorn, Enkhuizen, and Medemblik—with five slips. The Frisian admiralty barely existed at that time but still had a dockyard at Harlingen with four slips for construction and repair.[9]

The proliferation of facilities with their corresponding labor forces was the result of the great autonomy of the admiralties and the promotion of local interests. Naval administration was in principle the concern of all the provinces represented in the States General—a concern which was expressed in the composition of the board of councillors. In practice, however, matters did not work that way. Councillors from outside the province in which an admiralty was located were often considered to be interlopers and were not completely trusted, or they were more often absent because of the distance, though lodgings were available for them. The councillors from the local neighborhood—in the admiralty of Amsterdam, for example, from Gouda, Leiden, Haarlem, and Edam—together with the representative from the city of Amsterdam itself had the majority of votes in most meetings. The councillors representing Zeeland in the admiralty at Middelburg were at the same time the executives in their own provincial governing authority, a structure dating from the 1570s.[10] It is therefore no surprise that promotion of local interests was of prime concern to the councillors, a fact they demonstrated not least when staff had to be appointed. Local favoritism was strengthened by the fact that the three most important officials of each admiralty—the advocate fiscal, the secretary, and the collector general—were always chosen from the local class of regents. These officials were given life appointments and represented continuity in board decisions, which they prepared themselves and were responsible for executing.

This fragmented naval organization presented a gloomy picture in those periods of the Republic when centralized forces were lacking and few people took an interest in naval affairs. This was especially true of the eighteenth century. The States General could order the admiralty boards to send delegates to The Hague to receive instructions and discuss matters of common concern. From 1648 on, these meetings were called the "Haagse Besognes." The level of coordination reached at these gatherings depended on the power exerted by the States General and the gravity of the particular matter.

Such coordination was seldom a problem in the seventeenth century, during which Europe and the Republic were ravaged by wars and navies were thus extremely important assets. The grand pensionary of Holland in those times—particularly in the period from 1650 to 1672, when no stadholder, i.e., admiral general, was available—wielded great influence as leader of the delegation of Holland in the States General and as unofficial minister of foreign affairs. In cooperation with such distinguished lieutenant admirals as Maarten Harpertszoon Tromp (1598–1653) and Michiel Adriaanszoon de Ruyter (1607–1676), the grand pensionary achieved the highest level of coordination possible in the decentralized naval administration. Most famous in this respect was John de Witt (1625–1672), who once even piloted the fleet out to sea from the roadstead of Texel.[11]

Although the princes of Orange held the title of admiral general, they seldom played an active role in naval affairs. Their major interest was traditionally in the army, which they commanded in many campaigns. Although they never went to sea, at times they stimulated the coordination of naval activities. William III (1650–1702), the king-stadholder, took the greatest interest in the navy, which he needed in his great wars against France. Job de Wildt (1637–1704), secretary of the admiralty of Amsterdam, acted as coordinator on William's behalf. The later stadholders had their official representatives on the board of each admiralty, but they were never able to revitalize the organizational structure and impose cooperation and coordination.

This brief outline of the history of the five admiralties suggests great differences in the operations of Dutch naval administration over these two centuries. In this respect, Dutch involvement in

Europe's wars was important, but so were the changes in the social and economic background of the councillors. The tactics of naval warfare were altered drastically, as was the design of warships. Naval officers closed ranks to achieve a true professionalism, while shifts in the labor market altered the recruitment of ship's companies. The years 1652 and 1713 can be considered as clear watersheds. The "old" navy lasted until 1652, at which time a "new" navy was born. The year 1713 saw the end of the period of intensive warfare and the beginning of a long, seventy- to eighty-year period in which the navy was rarely of prime importance in either Dutch politics or daily life and was reduced to second-rate status.

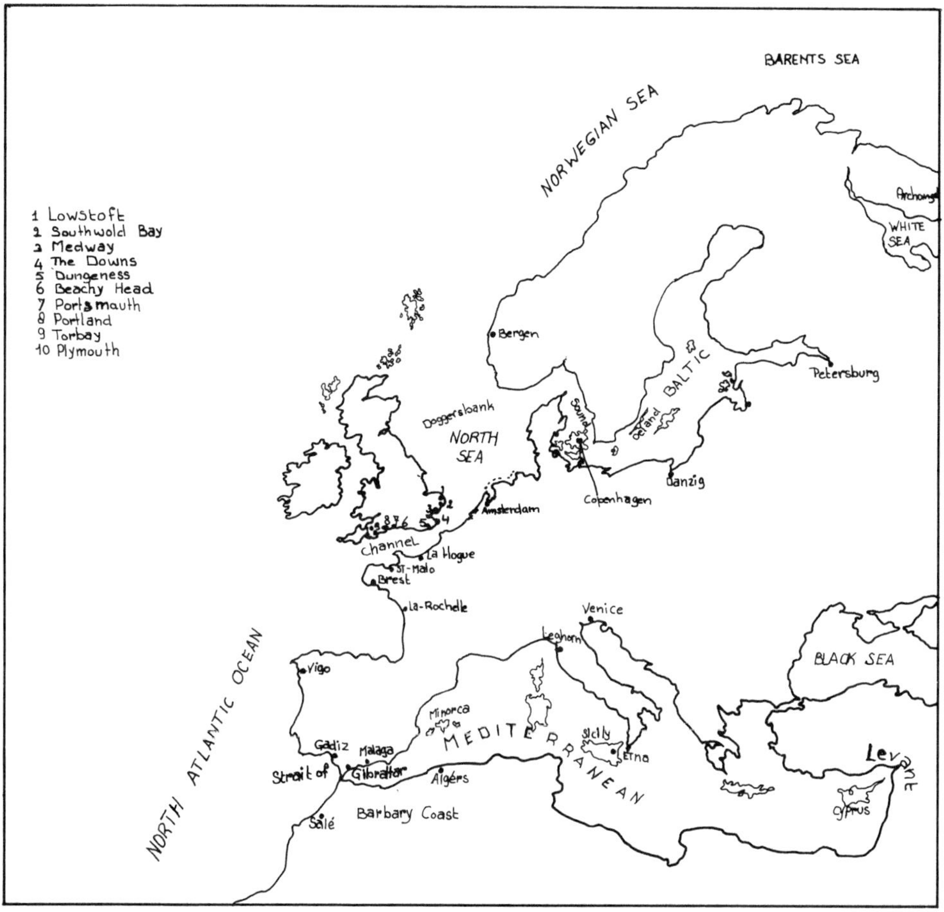

SITES OF DUTCH NAVAL ACTIVITY IN EUROPEAN WATERS

PART ONE

The "Old" Navy, Late 1500s–1652

During the last decade of the sixteenth century, the young Dutch Republic no longer had much to fear for its own existence. The Spanish Armada of 1588 had been defeated and dispersed; the duke of Parma's Spanish army had been blockaded and had then become involved in France's civil troubles. The Dutch army, commanded by Prince Maurice of Nassau (1567–1625), had taken the initiative. Through successful campaigns, it conquered a great number of territories containing cities of various sizes. The so-called "Dutch garden" was closed. The strong political leadership of Grand Pensionary Johan van Oldenbarnevelt (1547–1619) had provided the financial means and the required internal cohesion.

There were more reasons than one for nineteenth-century Dutch historian Robert Fruin to regard the 1590s as the "Ten Years of the Republic."[1] The economic breakthrough to world primacy was launched. Dutch merchants and skippers had traditionally held an important stake in the transport of cheap bulk commodities over large parts of Europe. At this time, however, they began to widen the scope of their ventures in other parts of Europe, notably western Russia and the Mediterranean area, and in West Africa, the West Indies, and Asia—thereby laying their hands on such "rich" trades as spices, sugar, caviar, and textiles.

As a result of this comprehensive role in world shipping and trade, Dutch industry could dispose of a great variety of raw materials to be refined into semi-manufactured and finished products. Traditional dairy exports were now supplemented by several high-grade commodities. A sophisticated banking system was also created. Thousands of immigrants from the Southern Netherlands (modern Belgium) and later from Germany crowded into Holland and Zeeland to stimulate a further new growth. The pace of commercial and industrial expansion was rapid, with the population increasing from some one and two-tenths million in

1550 to approximately one and a half million in 1600 and then to one and nine-tenths million in 1650.

War and politics had always had a great impact on the Dutch economy. Indeed, as interesting as the economic and political history of the Republic is, it was a nation almost continuously involved in a war of independence. Maritime activities could be hampered by political measures like embargoes or by hostile warfleets and privateers. As a consequence, the growth of shipping and trade varied during different periods and among different areas.[2] The Spanish embargoes in 1598 and 1621, plus raids by Dunkirk privateers, were serious obstacles to this growth. Spain and, after 1580, Portugal too were enemies on the very borders of the Republic, in the North Sea, the Channel, and the Mediterranean, and elsewhere in and outside Europe. The Twelve Years' Truce of 1609–1621 was the only break in a war which lasted eighty years (1568–1648). Nor could the new state avoid getting involved in the problems of the Thirty Years' War (1618–1648) in Germany and the Baltic region, because too many Dutch economic and political interests there were at risk. The United Provinces had no choice but constantly to maintain armed sea forces.

Naval Operations against Spain and the Dunkirk Privateers

Naval operations were initially concentrated in the Zuyderzee and on the estuaries and inlets of Zeeland. The campaigns of Prince Maurice had to be supported. The scope was widened when warships began to accompany the merchantmen, whereupon Dutch fleets appeared off the Iberian coast and even as far afield as the Mediterranean. This wider scope resulted in the Dutch increasingly stealing the initiative at sea from their Iberian opponents, for the States General felt strong enough to bring the war to the doorstep of Spain and Portugal and even to Spain's and Portugal's overseas territories.

The economic battle required a permanent blockade of the Flemish coast and the Scheldt River of the Spanish Netherlands. A great number of ships maintained this difficult and often boring vigil. The blockade was intensified whenever the enemy launched its most dangerous weapon, Flemish privateers in raids on Dutch merchant shipping.[3] Although these raids never became a decisive factor, they did cause sufficient damage to force the Dutch naval authorities to commit a major part of their forces to combat them. Strengthening the blockade and providing more escorts for convoys left only a few forces available for mounting expeditions against the Iberian Peninsula. The fight against the Spaniards and the Portuguese beyond European waters was entrusted mainly to the East India Company (known in the Republic as the VOC) after its creation in 1602 and to the West India Company (WIC), which was founded in 1621, the year the Twelve Years' Truce ended. The admiralties only occasionally participated in this global struggle.

Other naval activities resulted from the growth of merchant shipping in the Mediterranean and the Baltic Sea and from the increased political stature of the Republic. Shipping in the Mediterranean confronted the Barbary corsairs, who were countered by offensive raids as well as defensive convoys. In the Baltic, Dutch economic interests occasionally required a naval presence, often near the Danish Sound. Naval pressure was also used as a tool of diplomacy whenever a Dutch maritime presence existed.

LATE 1500s–1609

Following the defeat of the Spanish Armada in 1588, the Dutch admiralties undertook four different operations: (1) patrolling the rivers, inlets, estuaries, and the Zuyderzee; (2) cruising off the Flemish coast; (3) cruising in the North Sea and the Channel; and (4) sailing on convoy duties. Beginning in 1589, they developed an annual plan for these operations, with certain numbers of ships being allocated. For the inland service, an unfixed number of the smallest vessels sufficed. The total number of warships did not vary greatly from year to year, averaging about eighty. However, their functions changed during the period as independent cruising gave way to convoy escort, due not only to strategic needs, but also to the firm financial backing of the convoys by the commercial world.[4] Convoys were paid out of the admiralties' own resources, whereas blockading, cruising, and special expeditions fell under the purview of the States General.

Many routine operations were undertaken with small vessels. As long as parts of the eastern provinces were still in Spanish hands, the Zuyderzee and the Wadden Sea were unsafe for fishing and merchant shipping. The city of Steenwijk and the Eems estuary, for example, had to be blockaded and hostile raids prevented. Around 1590, captains like Jan Allertszoon of the admiralty of Amsterdam performed convoy duties in the Wadden Sea with vessels of fifty to eighty tons and even captured a privateer from Groningen. His colleague Gerrit de Witte in an even smaller vessel sailed on the IJssel River and assisted ground forces in recapturing the city of Deventer. As soon as they could be released from those duties, Allertszoon, De Witte, and others operated along the Flemish coast, escorted merchant vessels to the Thames or to Hamburg, or protected the herring fleet in the North Sea. Allertszoon gradually obtained ever larger ships, his 200-ton *Gulden Leeuw* carrying sixty hands and twelve guns in 1595.[5]

Service on the Flemish coast was not popular among the captains and their crews, for the blockade often had to be continued year round in all types of weather and amid dangerous sands. The Dunkirkers and other privateers proved ingenious in finding holes in the blockade, and their successful hit-and-run raids thoroughly demoralized their blockaders. But the blockade served the political and economic goal of sealing off the Spanish Netherlands from direct overseas trade and permitting only indirect commercial contacts with Zeeland, where the admiralty at Middelburg could profit from higher tax revenues.

Those basically defensive and blockading missions varied little during this period, except that the increasingly emboldened Republic also initiated expeditions further away. Many a naval captain enjoyed these opportunities and applied for commands in overseas expeditions. In 1594 one cruise of three men-of-war to Copenhagen was undertaken for diplomatic reasons, whereas fleets of no fewer than twenty-four ships mounted major raids. The alliance among England, France, and the Republic resulted in two notable raids on the Spanish coast in 1596 and 1597. Under the command of Admiral Johan van Duivenvoorde, the Dutch contingent joined ninety-six English vessels at Plymouth in 1596. The combined fleet took Cadiz by surprise, stayed a fortnight, and then sailed for home, laden with booty taken partly from Dutch merchant vessels anchored in the harbor. The following year, another Anglo-Dutch attack on the Iberian coast and the Azores was mounted, but with less success due to bad weather and quarrels between the commanders.[6]

These expeditions were only the harbingers of a much bolder exploit in 1599. An all-Dutch armada of seventy-three ships, some of which were dilapidated, with over 8,000 men on board and commanded by Admiral Pieter van der Does again attacked the Azores. Half of the force sailed into the Bay of Guinea in West Africa and there ransacked the island Sâo Tomé. But then tropical malaria struck, forcing the ships and their decimated crews to return home in early 1600. The loot did not compensate for the high costs, but the unsuccessful expedition became a landmark in Dutch naval history as the first purely Dutch naval initiative. The sheer scope of the expedition and size of the fleet had required careful advance planning, including nine months to victual the ships. Extra navigational instruction with regard to determining longitude had been given to a number of masters, who included De Witte in the raid of 1596 and Allertszoon in that of 1599.[7]

Although the Republic could not afford to fit out fleets of this size on a regular basis, it had definitively moved toward offensive operations, stimulated by private initiatives from many of the great entrepreneurs of Dutch commerce. The year before Van der Does had attacked Sâo Tomé, five naval vessels had been commissioned by the merchant Balthasar de Moucheron to seize the nearby island of Il Principe, although it had been quickly retaken by the Portuguese. A squadron of six men-of-war under the command of Paulus van Caerden was instructed in 1603 by the States General to build fortifications in Brazil and plunder Iberian shipping in the South Atlantic, but the mission was only minimally successful.[8] Again in 1606, two raids on the Spanish coast, commanded by Willem Haultain, failed—the second one ending in total disaster. All these overseas expeditions revealed that success was expensive, and the Republic tended to overrate its capacity to wage war covering vast distances. In particular, better and more uniformly equipped warships were required.

The last expedition before the Truce was concluded was of a slightly different kind. It was far better prepared for, and its object was not so much a raid as the annihilation of a Spanish fleet before that force could depart for either the Southern Netherlands or the Far East. Commanded by Jacob van Heemskerck, a fleet of twenty-six ships gained a resounding victory over an opponent with more guns on an almost equal number of ships. That dashing attack took place in the bay of Gibraltar on April 25, 1607, and succeeded in destroying all ten Spanish galleons, although Heemskerck himself was killed.

In contrast to these larger naval operations were the fights between galleys (rowing vessels) upon the Western Scheldt. In 1599, the Spanish had nestled at Sluys a number of galleys which constantly attacked Dutch shipping. In response to this unusual threat, five galleys were constructed in Dutch shipyards and manned partly by convicts. They proved quite effective in contributing to the recapture of Sluys five years later.[9]

The financial weakness of the five admiralties were evident throughout this period, while the provincial subsidies were often not paid on time, a flaw which would become a common practice. The authorities even went so far as to fit out certain expeditions during this period in the vain hope that plunder could fill their purses.[10]

The Truce of 1609 was financially a welcome event, if for no other reason than that the growing size and numbers of Dutch men-of-war had raised the operating expenses of the admiralties and the States General. In 1590, the ships had been no bigger than 80 to 160 tons. The overseas expeditions of 1596 and 1597, however, had required the use of much bigger warships, something the English ally took for granted. Three quarters of the twenty-four ships had had to be hired from private shipowners because the admiralties owned only a few vessels of 200 to 500 tons. The English alliance had sparked a brief flurry over the Dutch admiralties' constructing and purchasing a number of large and expensive "ships of force," some of 1,000 tons. Vessels of this size appeared to be very unwieldy and impractical in the shallow Dutch waters, and they were soon sold to the VOC or hired out to wealthy merchants.

After 1601, two other types of ships were favored by the councillors of the admiralties and the admirals: men-of-war of no more than 300 or 400 tons and the so-called "jacht," sharply built and equipped with oars. The jacht was a match for the Flemish privateers using the same type of vessel. Each admiralty owned a number of both types but had to rely on hired merchantmen in order to fulfill its naval commitments.[11]

THE TWELVE YEARS' TRUCE (1609–1621)

During the Truce, Dutch naval commitments naturally differed from the previous years. The blockade fleet was withdrawn from the Flemish coast, and great expeditions like that of 1607 were no longer needed. The admiralties could indeed afford to sell several good ships, to the king of France for example. The emphasis shifted to the protection of the merchant fleet. A great number of pirates, English and otherwise, roamed the seas from the Channel to the Straits of Gibraltar, while in and outside the Mediterranean, Barbary corsairs attacked Dutch vessels. The admiralties therefore commissioned more or less permanent cruising squadrons of two or three men-of-war to operate along the French and Portuguese coasts and in the Channel to protect convoys. Outward- and homeward-bound East Indiamen also began to rely on this service.[12] It was a genuinely new feature in Dutch maritime history and a tangible result of the Truce with Spain.

With the Republic now a leading commercial power, holding vested interests in the Iberian peninsula and the Mediterranean, the Barbary corsairs became a far more serious menace than the British, Irish, and other European pirates had been earlier. Barbary Algiers became the leading privateering state after Spain conquered Marmora on the Moroccan Atlantic coast in 1614. The Algerian fleet expanded rapidly, and the States General tried in vain to use diplomatic means to save Dutch ships from its attacks. Several Dutch ships were captured and their crews enslaved. Lengthy discussions in the Haagse Besogne and lobbying by merchants finally resulted in an expedition against Algiers in 1617.

No European power had ever considered such action before. A force of seven men-of-war had no effect, so a second expedition of nine ships was mounted under the command of the celebrated

Lambrecht Hendricksz Verhouven (nicknamed Moyen ["Handsome"] Lambert). This fleet, in cooperation with a Spanish squadron, succeeded in annihilating no fewer than eleven privateers near Gibraltar in June 1618. More expeditions followed, but none with lasting results. The end of the Truce in 1621 compelled the States General to cease special expeditions, but peace with Algiers could not be achieved, and the patrolling squadrons could not prevent the Algerians from capturing Dutch merchant vessels. The States General therefore decided to change the Mediterranean policy of several patrolling squadrons into one of regular convoy service, not only in the western Mediterranean but into the Levant as well. In close cooperation with representatives of the interested merchants, a convoy system was set up, in which twice a year (October and December) men-of-war would join merchantmen on their journeys to Italy and the Levant. This system was maintained until the end of the Republic.[13]

The rulers of the Republic displayed their growing self-confidence in other waters as well. Late in 1611, the States General ordered the admiralty at Amsterdam to send men-of-war to the Gold Coast. This fleet, under the command of Jacob Adriaensz Clantius, built the fortress Nassau at Moree in order to protect Dutch trading interests in West Africa. In 1624, the States General turned over the fortress to the WIC.[14] In the North Atlantic, the Dutch joined the English in developing a whaling trade, only to have its whalers chased off the whaling grounds by ships of the English Muscovy Company during 1612 and 1613. From 1614 onwards, however, Dutch escort ships made a show of force in protecting their compatriots near Spitsbergen and on the small island Jan Mayen against English and Danish competitors. Three to five men-of-war were often involved in these convoys, which lasted well into the 1620s.[15]

The Republic had even built up a reputation for having an arsenal of men-of-war and armed merchantmen available to assist other nations. The Venetian Republic, then at war with Ottoman Turkey, appealed for more warships in 1618, and through the close cooperation of the three admiralties in Holland and the leading merchant shipowners, the Republic was able to equip twelve fully armed and manned merchant vessels for Venice. These vessels were provisioned for ten months service and hired out to the Venetians for 840,000 guilders, a handsome profit for the increasingly assertive United Provinces.[16]

1621–1652

Hostilities at sea and on land resumed in 1621, the naval activities seemingly on the same scale as before the Truce. That very year, a force under Admiral Joachim Hendrickszoon Swartenhondt ("Black Dog") defeated a Spanish fleet again near Gibraltar, as did Moyen Lambert a Dunkirk force near Calais. With the founding of the West India Company that year as a sort of fighting arm in the South Atlantic, Prince Maurice and the States General made the decision to send a strong force via these waters into the Pacific to attack the Spaniards in South America. This so-called "Nassause vloot" (Nassau's fleet) consisted of ten men-of-war, among which were the five largest belonging to the three admiralties of Holland.[17]

Similar expeditions of about twenty vessels each attacked La Rochelle and Cadiz in 1625 and raided the Iberian coast in 1627, all the result of Dutch treaties with France and England. The Republic had agreed to give naval support during the French king's attack on the last Huguenot stronghold, a rather compromising activity for the Protestant Dutch authorities. The Anglo-Dutch raid on Cadiz was a failure, and when a second raid did not mature in 1627 as a result of English delays, the Dutch squadron of Laurens Reael could do no more than harass Iberian shipping and show the Dutch flag to Moroccan corsairs.[18]

The admiralties, however, could barely afford to continue spending money on ships, guns, and manpower for such activities because the Dunkirkers and other privateers in Flanders—particularly after 1626—resumed their operations with even more skill, energy, and resources than ever before. The port of Dunkirk, converted into an almost impregnable fortress, provided Spain with a base for twenty to thirty men-of-war, while local merchants and shipowners were more than willing to outfit privateering vessels in increasing numbers and sizes. The Dutch utterly failed to respond to this challenge, which had become a permanent threat to their herring fishery and merchant shipping.

Until Dunkirk was conquered from the landward side by a French army in 1646, the Flemish privateers and Spanish "king's ships" remained a permanent thorn in the Dutch side. Often this became a very dangerous thorn when combined with operations of the Spanish army under Ambroglo Spinola, who conquered the city of Breda in 1625. In 1631, Archduchess Isabella organized a fleet in Antwerp consisting mainly of small craft laden with soldiers and guns to invade the United Provinces. Only after sailing for several days through inland waters in Zeeland was the fleet stopped near the Slaak and annihilated by a Dutch force commanded by the renowned Vice Admiral Marinus Hollare.

Spain, still intent on reconquering the rebellious Northern provinces and on inflicting as much economic damage as possible, employed its Flemish squadron, privateers, and sometimes even large galleons of the Atlantic fleet annually to transfer troops and money to the Southern Netherlands. The inland route was used too until it was endangered in 1635 when war broke out between Spain and France. In 1638, it was completely blocked off. Dutch, and later also French squadrons, could seldom stop the Spanish transports. Then in 1639, a Dutch fleet commanded by the dynamic Admiral Maarten Harpertszoon Tromp intercepted in the Channel a huge Spanish and Flemish force of seventy-seven galleons carrying 24,000 troops under Admiral Don Antonio Oquendo. Following a fierce engagement in close combat, the heavily battered Spanish fleet took refuge at the Downs on the English coast, in spite of England's state of neutrality. Tromp blockaded the Spanish fleet there for five weeks, during which he strengthened his battle force from thirty-one to ninety-five ships. Tromp then attacked his demoralized enemies on October 21 and destroyed all but twelve Spanish ships in the Battle of the Downs. This crushing defeat forced Spain to drop all ideas of reconquest of the United Provinces. Tromp's epic victory earned the Dutch a reputation of being the leading naval power in Europe.[19]

The irony of this reputation becomes evident when one realizes that the victory was the result of a defensive strategy. Flemish and Spanish naval pressure had been so great that nearly all the Dutch naval forces had been required for the tedious and dangerous tasks of blockading and cruising in the Channel and the North Sea. Overseas expeditions were no longer mounted after 1627, so that the victory at the Downs was badly needed for Dutch morale. Although on occasion Flemish privateers were seized, sometimes after fierce battles, the plain fact was that losses of Dutch merchant ships and fishing boats could not be prevented, and even increased over time. The English historian Jonathan I. Israel clearly demonstrates that the second part of the Netherlands' long struggle against Spain was not at all a continuing commercial success story.[20] In the period from 1627 to 1635, for example, 423 Dutch merchant and fishing vessels were sunk and 1,606 captured by the Flemish squadron and privateers. Most of the captured ships were sold, often to their old owners. It was little better after the Downs victory: 495 ships were taken between 1642 and 1646.[21]

The business and shipping world complained bitterly about this state of affairs and demanded more protection. Escorts were provided on routes to France and the Mediterranean, but these were mainly small men-of-war and no match for "wolf packs" of privateers. The VOC was able to arrange in 1624 for its homeward-bound convoy to be accompanied by warships on the last leg of the voyage. But even this protection was insufficient, and from 1627 onward, the VOC was authorized to spend its revenues on equipping its own escort vessels. The losses reached their peak during the period 1628 to 1630. When all other protective measures had failed, the States General in 1631 was forced to accept the creation of private local navies by the cities of Amsterdam, Hoorn, Enkhuizen, Edam, Medemblik, and Harlingen for escorting shipping to and from the Baltic and Norway. The local "directies" (boards of directors) were ruled by burgomasters and merchants and began to fit out annually a number of heavily armed merchantmen. In 1645, for example, there were as many as fifteen such vessels, not unlike the longstanding annual convoy ships for the herring fleets.[22]

The "directie" ships also came under the authority of the admiralties with regard to captains' commissions, articles of war, and prizes. Expenses were covered by special duties placed on the merchantmen involved. Nevertheless, a second navy had come into being—one which lasted longer than was at first envisioned and which was badly needed. It even rallied in support of Tromp at the Downs in 1639. In 1632 and again in 1643, the States General decided also to stimulate more privateering ventures among the Dutch by offering higher premiums for the capture of hostile vessels. In Zeeland in particular, businessmen responded to this decision with enthusiasm and organized several large privateering companies.[23]

These private initiatives were symptomatic of the lack of success of the admiralties and the States General in their struggle with Spain. At certain times, the navy gave the distinct impression of being a demoralized and disorganized outfit, on shore as well as at sea. Some admiralties were affected by fraud and corruption, and local interests often weighed more heavily than common interests. In 1632 and 1636, Stadholder and Admiral General Frederick Henry (1584–1647) tried in vain to impose a more centralized structure for the struggle with Flanders. He wanted the admiralties to have responsibility only for convoys. Discipline was at times virtually nonexistent among the captains of the blockading fleet. Good leadership was lacking. The situation improved, however, with Tromp's appointment as lieutenant admiral in 1637, for he insisted on a return to discipline. And the overall morale soared after the victory over the Spanish-Flemish Armada in 1639.

Great as the internal problems were, and despite frequent failures in Flanders, one should not forget that the war had to be fought on two fronts: in the North Sea and near the Iberian peninsula. In addition, the merchant and herring fleets being defended were second to none in Europe and were continually expanding in numbers and size. By 1636 in Holland alone, these fleets were estimated to consist of some 1,750 merchant ships and 600 fishing vessels—a total which could never be protected sufficiently. But the image of Dutch naval power grew in 1644 and 1645 when Vice Admiral Witte Corneliszoon de With twice escorted hundreds of Dutch merchantmen to and through the Sound, exacting from the Danish king more favorable conditions for the payment of the Sound tolls. On the second occasion, his force consisted of forty-seven men-of-war with 4,300 men on board. Merchants and shipowners paid for these expeditions through an extra levy on Baltic and Norwegian shipping. People boasted that the "keys of the Sound" rested at Amsterdam! At the same time, Holland and Zeeland equipped a naval force of thirty-three ships for Sweden.[24]

In spite of the growing Dutch naval forces, the French conquest of Dunkirk in 1646 was a great relief to everyone concerned, especially the Dutch. Flemish and Spanish naval activities ceased almost overnight. Ongoing negotiations resulted in a lasting peace with Spain in 1648. It was hoped that those years of peace would cure the financial ills of the admiralties, since henceforth no more than forty convoy ships would be required. The peace also freed some ships for an expeditionary force to Brazil, commanded by Witte de With and paid out of provincial subsidies. The fleet arrived too late to help turn the tide in the victorious Portuguese struggle with the WIC, however.[25]

Tromp's flagship *Aemilia* was sold, and the construction of a new one was deemed unnecessary by the councillors of the admiralty at Rotterdam. But the decision to disarm proved premature because neither the North Sea nor the Channel became the safe shipping lanes as hoped. These waters remained infested with privateers, now mainly coming from the British Isles and taking part in the intricate English Civil War.[26]

The Boards of the Admiralties at Work

About fifty councillors comprised the boards of the five admiralties. They represented all seven provinces of the Republic and were supposed to operate collectively in the governing of an admiralty. For them to carry out this latter regulation, their continuous attendance at the meetings would have been required, and it was something that rarely happened. Councillors from the inland provinces tended to be absent more often than their colleagues from the maritime provinces. Severe weather conditions prevented some from traveling long distances to attend meetings, and the lack of good fellowship amongst the councillors could have had the same effect on attendance levels. Another reason for their not attending could have been that councillors were commissioned elsewhere on behalf of the admiralty.

Minutes, which were always taken at these meetings, are the historian's most valuable source of information on the councillors' activities. Among the most complete minutes which have survived are those of the meetings at Rotterdam, for example, in 1625. The councillors met in the Prinsenhof almost daily, even on Sundays. On one Sunday, June 15, the councillors met twice, first at 7 A.M., then again after church at 11 A.M. Five members were present. The States General and Prince Frederick Henry wanted the board to speed up the equipping of some men-of-war and the nomination of its captains. Such demands could force a board to meet daily for weeks in a row—a fact which suggests that a councillorship was certainly no sinecure. Only rarely did fewer than three members appear, but full boards are also mentioned in the minutes. Decisions carried by a majority of votes were rare exceptions, but this does not mean that all other decisions were taken unanimously. The few abstainers or dissenters were simply not recorded. It is interesting, however, that on January 18, 1625, the secretary noted with obvious satisfaction that the whole board had decided to cease entertaining themselves at inns and the Prinsenhof at admiralty cost.[27]

The agenda always contained a great variety of topics, often ten or more, as a consequence of the many-sided tasks with which admiralties had been burdened. Foremost were the matters resulting from the collection, administration, and adjudication of the fiscal duties and from the land warfare, with its constantly shifting battle lines. Agendas therefore dealt with a variety of problems. A cargo of sugar boxes was confiscated in Delfshaven. Permission was asked for the export of empty casks to Ireland. It was unclear whether figs and raisins should be considered as food and were therefore not to be exported to the enemy. Permission was asked for the duty-free export of a small box with red coral beads to Antwerp, a topic which appeared twice on the agenda. A man in a village near Bois-le-Duc was permitted to collect milk to be used in his bleaching business. Stricter instructions on behalf of the States General were issued with regard to the export of masts, pitch, and tar to neutral countries. Vacancies on the staff of the revenue offices were filled. Some widows were given on request a continuation of their late husbands' salaries for five or six months.

The naval side of the councillors' agenda included a mix of trivial and important items, in no particular order. For example, a group of merchants complained about the behavior of the captain of an escort vessel to Rouen. Jan Salomonszoon van den Tempel, the master shipwright, was asked for his opinion about a new yacht for Prince Maurice. The regulation against private repair work at the dockyard was lifted when a highly placed nobleman wanted these privileges. The transport of troops was arranged. Escort ships were provided for the herring fleet and for the coastal fishery; by tradition, escort was the special concern of this admiralty, although the fishing trade took care of the finances and the manning. Bordeaux merchants wanted extra convoy. The States General asked for information about the equipment of ships for the blockade fleet and announced an expedition to the Spanish coast. And in the same meeting, it was decided to pay the master's wife for washing and cleaning the linen and pewter on board the admiralty yacht in which councillors traveled. Two councillors, at The Hague for consultations with their colleagues in the other admiralties, deemed it unnecessary to attend the funeral of Vice Admiral Moyen Lambert in the Great Church of Rotterdam on March 21. Seventy-five years old and almost forty years on the payroll of the admiralty, Lambert was one of the famous admirals of his day; a few months before his death, he had captured a Dunkirk flagship.

Board meetings could never have been very dull. It was an old custom to let people present their cases in person. They were permitted to stand in front of the bar, behind which the councillors were seated at a table, while ushers kept a careful eye on their behavior. Captain Jan Janszoon van de Kerckhof, on one occasion dissatisfied with a certain command, called the councillors liars and left the room with much noise and shouting. The board was also often confronted with the misery resulting from the activities of the Dunkirk privateers. Wives of seamen who were in prison in Dunkirk or who had been killed in action complained about their poverty and their husbands' fates; they always demanded that something be done. An exchange for a number of Dunkirk prisoners held at Rotterdam was discussed with the burgomasters and with the States General. Seamen's wives also came to claim their husbands' back wages. More quietly discussed items on the agenda must have been the requests for pensions by an old sailor and a steward and the request for an allowance by someone who had lost his sight in one eye.

Relations with the city government could always be touchy. An admiralty was an institution of the Seven Provinces as a whole. General and local interests could conflict, especially with regard to the custom duties.[28] Presiding councillor Jan Jansz. Calff, representing the city of Rotterdam in the admiralty, was invited to the town hall to listen to complaints from masters and merchants about the arrogant and ill-mannered behavior of one of the clerks at the revenue office. One burgomaster had overheard this man at an inn slandering his admiralty superiors. Though the case itself was not important, of particular note is the fact that the board did not consider it wise policy to invite this burgomaster for questioning at the Prinsenhof. It was thought better to hold the meeting at the town hall instead.

The other admiralties faced the same sorts of problems and issues. During the spring, most men-of-war had to be fitted out and crews recruited. In late summer and early autumn, many a ship returned and the crews had to be paid off, although the necessary wages might not always be available. One or two councillors were then commissioned to pay the ratings, or enlisted men, while the captains had to wait. Though the nature of agenda topics could be diverse, not much variation occurred as long as the United Provinces remained engaged in wars. In 1638, for instance, the shortage of money at Rotterdam was much more severe than in 1625, as was the problem of getting the ships properly manned. In July 1638, the dearth of sailors became so great that only one out of three convoy ships could be manned. The three captains had to draw lots over who would sail with the available hands, leaving the other two ashore. Another factor that set the year 1638 apart was the occasional attendance at the meetings of Tromp, the newly appointed lieutenant admiral, as the representative of Prince Frederick Henry. He urged the councillors to be more active in the struggle with the Dunkirk privateers.[29]

On the board of the admiralty of Amsterdam, that city was always represented by one of its foremost elder burgomasters. Close relatives of city council members occupied the permanent positions of secretary, advocate fiscal, and collector general. The relations between city and admiralty were usually harmonious. When in financial difficulty, the admiralty was sometimes supported by money from the city. In 1625, for example, the admiralty of Amsterdam received the large sum of 397,000 guilders in five installments.

Wives and other relatives of seamen occasionally disturbed the decorum of the meetings, as was the case 1641 when Black Anna, Zealand Maayken, and some other women ended up receiving notice to keep away from the Prinsenhof. The councillors were more tolerant and even helpful with regard to licenses for the illegal export of guns and ammunition, not least to the enemy Spain. Interventions by the States General on this issue around 1640 were not at all effective. Such licenses continued to be given. Neither did the board take action when it had to solve the problem that most admiralty suppliers strongly preferred to be paid in the office of secretary Elbert Spiegel and not in the usual office, about which hints had been made as to the practice of illegal payments. Neither at Rotterdam nor at Amsterdam was it thought inappropriate to leave vacancies unfilled or occupied by substitutes. Secretary Spiegel at Amsterdam was succeeded by his first clerk David de Wildt in 1641. De Wildt was permitted to dispose of his clerkship, and he had it temporarily held by an outsider[30] to enable his son Job to finish school and graduate from the university. In 1652, when he was fifteen years old, Job was appointed first-clerk, and in 1659 he joined his father in the secretariat and later became Stadholder William III's right-hand man in naval affairs.

It is clear, then, that the admiralties were not free of malpractice and corruption at the top end of their administration. The history of each admiralty provides a number of such examples. At Amsterdam, the collector general was in charge of great sums of money, often more than needed for the admiralty itself. Surplus money was regularly spent by the States General on non-maritime matters—for instance, on the salary of the sculptor of the tomb of William the Silent in the New Church at Delft. But this was perfectly legal.

In 1616, the States General permitted the Grand Elector of Brandenburg to borrow 248,000 guilders on the Dutch credit market, and they instructed Pieter Martensz. Hoeffijser, the collector general at Amsterdam, to help the resident of Brandenburg (his brother-in-law) by offering him the admiralty's income from the convooien and licenten as a surety for interest and repayment of the borrowed money. But this arrangement would be for one year only. The Grand Elector, however, did not pay back his debt, and the admiralty had to sign bonds for the required interest. This situation continued for years, and Hoeffijser became very heavily involved in the affair but not in a positive way, since he seemed unable to refrain from malpractice. His name had already been indirectly mentioned in 1619 in a case involving the forgery of coins by his brother-in-law (both men were married to daughters of a burgomaster of Deventer and former councillor on the Amsterdam admiralty board). From 1632 to 1635, a number of naval captains accused Hoeffijser of extortion. In 1638 a son-in-law was given a high position in Hoeffijser's office. The next year, the limit was reached. The admiralty board decided no longer to sign the Brandenburg loan bonds. An official inspection of Hoeffijser's books was announced, and early in 1641, he fled from Amsterdam, destroying most of his administrative records. It was discovered that he had embezzled at least 200,000 guilders of the admiralty's cash and had not acknowledged a substantial repayment of the debt by Brandenburg.In the wake of this investigation, Secretary Spiegel's practices were also revealed, but no charges were pressed, and Spiegel succeeded Hoeffijser as collector general.[31]

A totally different example of malfeasance can be cited with regard to the Zeeland admiralty. In the matter of the collection of certain duties between the provinces of Holland and Zeeland, Holland could prove from internal Zeeland correspondence in 1648 that the city of Middelburg had promised certain groups of merchants a reduction of two thirds on the tariffs for convooien and licenten. Middelburg wanted to attract more business within its walls, even at the expense of neighboring cities. Instances of the bribery of admiralty officials were not prosecuted. And even worse, Holland revealed that the accounts of 1645-1648 were incomplete, although these revelations came to nothing. Apparently it had become normal practice on the board of Zeeland for the councillors from the other provinces not to convene when the local councillors thought it better to discuss certain topics only amongst themselves. Their colleagues in Holland considered this kind of privacy to be "not decent."[32]

Several lesser and greater scandals resulted in much public discussion about the admiralties during the 1620s and 1630s. The financial administration of Rotterdam and Amsterdam was examined in 1621 at the instigation of the Provincial States of Holland.[33] In 1626, the people of The Hague were treated to the spectacle of four councillors, the advocate fiscal, and the auctioneer of the admiralty at Rotterdam, chained two to two, leaving the famous jail Gevangenpoort and arriving in court. They were sentenced to imprisonment and fined sums from fl.15,000 to fl.91,000. This case was kept as secret as possible and was not mentioned in any minutes, probably from considerations of decency because such high-ranking persons were involved. The six were found guilty of fraud and embezzlement of the worst kind. They had made fictitious bills, then endorsed and cashed them themselves. The group regularly met in two local inns at Rotterdam. The incriminating documents had been burned in time, but how shamefully the "gang of six" had operated is illustrated by a board decision of July 25, 1625. At that meeting, the almost-complete board promised under oath not to accept any gifts or to abuse the admiralty's funds.[34]

The borderline between acceptable self-interest and corruption or malpractice can be an indistinct one. And yet while it is obvious that the appropriation of public funds for one's own profit is wholly unacceptable, Spiegel's behavior was not questioned. Neither was that of Rotterdam councillor Joost Adriaansz. van Coulster in 1625 when he stipulated that he wanted priority of payment for his delivery of beer to the navy.[35] Nor was it considered a conflict of interest when in 1586 the admiralty at Amsterdam hired a merchant vessel of which councillor Egbert Pietersz. Vinck was an important part-owner, and when, two years later, he suggested increasing the rental fee.[36]

Councillors were members of the ruling "regent" class in the United Provinces. They and their colleagues in the city governments and in the Provincial States and States General were often involved in business as well as in setting rules. They were active tradesmen, merchants, shipowners, or investors in old or newly reclaimed land. They were still *homines economici* who possessed all sorts of practical experience and knowledge, although their situation began to change in the 1630s and 1640s.

A few examples characterize the admiralty councillor of the "old navy," though there were several hundred such councillors functioning at the time. Pieter Jansz. Liorne (1562–1620) of Hoorn sat on the board of the admiralty of the Noorderkwartier in 1612 and 1613. He was a Mennonite, and despite the policy of having only members of the Dutch Reformed Church in the ruling class, Liorne became an alderman ("schepen") in 1597 and a city councillor in 1599. Liorne had begun his career as a merchant and shipwright, and he had become famous in 1595 with his design of the fluyt, the bulk carrier of the Dutch merchant marine. Utilized for his expertise by the States General and the admiralties as an advisor for new types of warships, he also explained to the master shipwrights of the admiralties at Hoorn how galleys could be best constructed to counter the threat by Spinola around 1600. For several months in 1601, Liorne was aboard the flagship of the blockading fleet near Dunkirk and, with two others, rendered advice to the vice admiral. Later he had a house built as a school for instruction in the art of navigation, run by the renowned teacher and free-thinker Robbert Robbertsz. Le Canu. Liorne served as an alderman for four other terms until 1611 and was also councillor of the Hoorn chamber of the East India Company. In the year he was appointed admiralty councillor, he became a member of the Reformed Church, by which action he was released from the Mennonite principle of nonviolence. He brought a tremendous amount of maritime knowledge and experience to the admiralty board, though he served for only for two years. In 1614 he became burgomaster of Hoorn and was so named again in 1615 and 1618. In his final year, he was removed from office by Prince Maurice as a result of political changes, which ended tense religious troubles in the province of Holland.[37]

Jacob van Neck (1564–1638) was born in Amsterdam, son of a leading soap-boiler. He became a merchant and supplied cargoes for a number of ships before being appointed admiral of the second expedition to Asia in 1598, after the first had discovered the profitable seaway to Asia. This expedition was such a financial success that Van Neck was asked to command yet another in 1600. At its completion, he married the daughter of an Amsterdam alderman. In 1609, Van Neck began what was to be a distinguished political career both in Amsterdam and on the national level; the fact that some years passed before he could make his mark was probably due to the bankruptcy of his father-in-law. In 1620, Van Neck became a councillor in the admiralty at Zeeland, the city of Amsterdam always being entitled to nominate a candidate for this seat on behalf of the province of Holland. But he never attended meetings at Middelburg on a regular basis. Indeed, soon after becoming a member of the city council of Amsterdam, he was elected one of the four burgomasters in 1622 for a term of two years.

Nevertheless, Van Neck proved useful to the admiralty of Zeeland by arranging at Amsterdam the delivery of all sorts of shipbuilding material and armaments, more abundant there than in Zeeland. In 1624, he assisted the Zeeland vice admiral in the purchase of a new man-of-war from a private shipwright at Amsterdam. The following year, Van Neck was solely responsible for selecting two other ships for Zeeland and supervised some alterations to other vessels. He also assisted the captains who had to pick up the vessels and who needed seamen to man their ships in Asian waters. The sixty-year-old former admiral managed to combine the two jobs, and in 1625, he even accepted a second term as burgomaster of Amsterdam. Because of his frequent absence from Middelburg, he may not have even noticed that his Zeeland colleagues kept some business away from him and the other councillors. His term in the admiralty lasted until the end of 1625.

But Van Neck's public life was not yet finished, for he was made a member of the Council of State at The Hague in 1627. He was involved in negotiations with England and mediated in troubles between some of the admiralties. The increasing interest the city of Amsterdam was taking in its local admiralty was revealed in 1628 when top-regent Van Neck first entered the Prinsenhof meeting room. He would remain in office until 1637, his term being twice renewed, in 1631 and 1634. He took part in all the activities of the board, regularly fulfilled commissions to the Texel roadstead in order to supervise the departure and arrival of warships, bought materials for the dockyard, and at the appropriate times gave voice to the traditional interests of his city. He also visited The Hague frequently and discussed matters of naval policy with members of the States of Holland and States General and with colleagues in the Haagse Besogne. Van Neck was one of the three hundred wealthiest citizens of Amsterdam when he died in 1638, shortly after he had started a second term on the Council of State.[38]

Not all admiralty board members could claim such a distinguished maritime and political career as Van Neck. More typical were Jan Teding van Berkhout (1549–1633) and Joost Adriaansz. van Coulster (†1649). Van Berkhout was a member of the city council of Monnickendam and burgomaster for several years. He frequently represented his city in the States of Holland, and around 1600 he was councillor of the admiralty of the Noorderkwartier. His father had been a member of the ruling class, with the son continuing his father's business in grain, dairy, and shipowning activities as well as starting a local brewery at Monnickendam.[39] Van Coulster, by contrast, was not born into the ruling class. Born at Schiedam, he moved to Rotterdam and became master of a merchant vessel, developed commercial activities, and also started the brewery "De Oranjeboom." In 1624, he entered the city council of Rotterdam and was elected alderman. The next year, he exchanged the town hall for the Prinsenhof. In the following twenty-five years, he would commute between both buildings—serving on the admiralty board from 1625 to 1628, 1631 to 1634, 1640 to 1643, and in 1649, and as burgomaster in 1629, 1630, 1635, 1636, 1645, and 1646. He also held some minor city offices during these years, living fashionably in the center of the harbor district and continuing his shipowning and other business activities. In 1625, Van Coulster succeeded his fellow-townsman Jan Jansz. Calff on the admiralty board. Calff's timely death that October forestalled his being sentenced to prison in the case of fraud and embezzlement discussed above.

In this context, Van Coulster's business operations, which appeared regularly on the admiralty agenda, are interesting. When he asked for permission to export some rope to London, an injunction against his son's vessel, laden with timber, was withdrawn (only Van Coulster and one other councillor were present during the Sunday evening meeting). That same year, 1625, and again in early 1627, Van Coulster was financially interested in two ships that had imported mineral soil from Davis Strait (west of Greenland). He boldly claimed that this soil should be considered as ballast and be exempted from incoming duties. His claim was accepted. The second time, Van Coulster told his colleagues that he was part-owner of the ship and left the room before a positive vote for him was taken. But ballast which filled most of the ship's cargo space could hardly have been a very convincing argument for tax exemption.[40]

The five admiralties in the United Provinces were responsible for an almost incredible variety of tasks, and everything from the most trivial subjects to supplying Admiral Tromp's blockade of the Spanish fleet at The Downs had to be discussed. It is important, however, to keep in mind that most issues of national interest were prepared and discussed at a central level, at The Hague by the stadholder, the States General, the grand pensionary, and the Haagse Besogne. And letters from those bodies and officials forced the councillors at Middelburg, Harlingen, or Rotterdam to pay close attention to these issues.

Admiralty councillors were no different from the rulers at large in the Republic. Membership on an admiralty board was common during the career of many a regent. The next job could be burgomaster, member of the Council of State or the Provincial States, or board member of one of the six chambers of the VOC. Apart from these public offices, most regents were also actively involved in business and were well aware of prices and practices on the freight-and-commodity market and in the industries. The labor market for seamen was not a closed world to either Van Coulster or Van Neck. This situation tended, however, to change, and a process of aristocratizing began when the group of regents closed their ranks at the end of this period. It then became much more difficult for *homines novi* such as Van Coulster to enter a city council, which had become the very heart of the Dutch regent world.

The gap between admiralty work and a man's own private business could be very narrow. At times, councillors had to go almost daily to the Prinsenhof, and a delivery of rope, timber, or beer could often be organized as well and as quickly by the councillors themselves or their relatives as by an outsider. Fraud went almost unnoticed, as one's colleagues had the same kind of interests. But in 1633, Van Coulster went too far in the opinion of two of his colleagues, and they voted against hiring his merchant vessels, which he had offered at an excessively high price.[41] Many hundreds of transactions had to be arranged and bills paid or cashed. For instance, in 1645 the income from only the convooien and licenten amounted in Amsterdam to more than one million guilders and at Middelburg to nearly half that amount. The risks of fraudulence or corruption were amply compensated by the profits coming from business acumen and timely deliveries of goods. All this was inherent in the political structure of the United Provinces. Later, when most regents had withdrawn from active business pursuits, corruption would shift to include mainly the sale of offices.

The admirals general, Stadholders Prince Maurice and Frederick Henry, never kept a tight grip on the operations of the admiralty boards. They could exert pressure on the boards to fit out ships, urge more cooperation, and affect certain minor decisions, but they were never able, and did not often try, to bring about basic changes in the admiralties' administration. Frederick Henry tried but failed completely during the 1630s. Disenchanted by the admiralties' failure to control the Dunkirk privateers and by the huge losses of merchant vessels, he wanted the admiralties to be responsible only for the convoys and to make the blockading and cruising fleets the responsibility of a small group of the most experienced admiralty councillors, located at The Hague, who would spend the provincial naval subsidies. He considered it essential that the ships of these fleets be assembled and fitted out at one central base, at Hellevoetsluis and that the whole system of provisioning be centralized there.

However sensible Frederick Henry's plans may have been, they did not work because too many interests were at stake. No admiralty wanted to restrict itself to just small numbers of escort vessels because the other ships guaranteed major activities in the city and at the dockyard and brought in more orders for food, hemp, guns, etc. And as we have seen, many a councillor profited from these arrangements and furthermore considered himself something of an expert on broader naval matters. It is difficult, however, to discover whether personal interests ever prevailed over national interests in the struggle to prevent effective operations by the Dunkirkers. Zeeland hardly reacted to Frederick Henry's plans, while others made objections and refused to agree to the changes. With the city of Amsterdam itself leading the opposition against reform, Frederick Henry's plans finally had to be withdrawn in 1639.[42]

Amsterdam's stern stand in this affair confirmed a new situation. The governments of the cities in which an admiralty was established now considered that institution to be an important asset. Local influence on the board and the administration consequently expanded. In 1628, for instance, Amsterdam had one of its leading politicians on the board, Jacob van Neck, and in 1637 its most famous burgomaster, Andries Bicker. Frederick Henry's plans were the last attempt to impose more centralization on the naval administration. Under the guidance of Amsterdam, this effort resulted instead in the growth of local influence. At the same time, the process of aristocratization of the regent class had progressed so far that the merchant-councillor began to disappear.

The Slow Birth of a Naval Officers' Corps

A few hundred naval officers served the admiralties at any one time. Little has been written about them as a group, and only a few biographical works about the most famous ones exist. The ordinary officer is not known at all, and even the image of the average naval captain remains vague.

No special training or education was required to become a naval officer. Candidates were supposed to be qualified to belong to the captain's staff and to supervise and give orders to the crew via the petty officers. It is hard to separate the reasons why one young man might have become an officer and another only as an ordinary enlisted seaman. Social background or sometimes a natural aptitude for leadership were usually the determining factors for selection into the officer class.[43] During the period of the "old navy," the officers' ranks were not actually closed to men from the lower strata of society, but they were always wide open to those from the higher classes. And the mixture of ship types—real men-of-war, hired merchantmen, and the so-called "directie-schepen" —with their different kinds of officers confuses the picture even more.

Since the days of the Sea Beggars (ca. 1570), it had not been uncommon for noblemen to command warships. At least one quarter of the Sea Beggars' captains belonged to the nobility, most of them having taken refuge among the Sea Beggars to escape Spanish religious persecution. The same can be said about an almost equal number of merchants and high officials.[44] Part of them continued their new seafaring occupation and may have set the trend for other generations of noblemen and sons of upper class burghers to enter into a naval career. Warfare at sea was considered mainly a military affair, in which a "soldier" should command, not a "seaman." Such "soldier" commanders were advised by ships' masters and mates on aspects of navigation. The nobility enjoyed a natural superiority over subordinate officers and crew.

Sea Beggar captain Willem Bloys van Treslong (ca. 1529–1594) had served in the navy of Charles V and Philip II of Spain. Born at Brielle into the lower nobility, he distinguished himself in 1571 and 1572 and was appointed lieutenant admiral of Holland in 1573 and, three years later, of Zeeland, becoming the prototype of the flag officer of future decades. Quite remarkable was his suggestion to launch an attack against the Spanish coast in 1578, eighteen years before such a plan was actually carried out. Capture of the Spanish treasure fleet from America was another of his objectives.[45]

The highest naval position in the province of Holland—lieutenant admiral—was held for almost half a century by the high noble family Van Duivenvoorde-Van Wassenaer. Johan van Duivenvoorde, heer van Warmond (1547–1610) succeeded Bloys van Treslong in 1576 and held the post until 1603, when he resigned because of age. He was followed by his cousin Jacob van Wassenaer, heer van Obdam (1574–1623). Johan van Duivenvoorde was a fine example of a leading aristocrat, diplomat, and politician while following his career as a naval commander. Well versed in naval affairs, he was active on the Scheldt in 1585 when Parma besieged Antwerp; he also operated on the coast of Groningen, commanded blockading squadrons off Ostend and Dunkirk, and led the expeditions against Spain in 1596 and 1597. Though a Roman Catholic, he represented the nobility of Holland in the Provincial States and was often a delegate to the States General. Managing to escape prosecution for manslaughter in early 1588, Van Duivenvoorde attended board meetings of admiralties, some of whose members were godfathers to his children. In spite of his long association with the navy, his name is not connected with any sort of innovation. Such ideas came from more practical-minded people like his second-in-command, Jan Gerbrandszoon from Enkhuizen, a reformer in ship design with Liorne.[46]

Unlike Van Duivenvoorde, the captains who served the admiralty at Amsterdam during the 1590s did not belong to the nobility. They were a motley group, some of whom entered the navy directly as captains, while others were first appointed midshipmen and swiftly promoted to lieutenants; it generally took a year or two for them to reach the rank of captain. Mobility in the higher ranks was considerable because of the growing numbers of ships and the high mortality rates. Many a captain died on board his ship during skirmishes and fights with the enemy or from diseases and storms. Naval careers did not last long.

A captain might previously have been a merchant skipper, a younger son of a burgomaster of Haarlem, or an almost bankrupt tax-farmer. Nearly all owned private houses in Amsterdam and were married. Family bonds also existed: Joachim Pieterszoon Cleynsorghe's brother was also a naval captain, with two of his brothers-in-law serving as his lieutenants in 1592. Captains and their officers were always in close contact with the people. When they were accompanying their disbanded crew from Texel roadstead to Amsterdam, they could easily get involved in incidents arising at inns with local people, or be sued for unpaid bills at such establishments. They were also tempted to evade the rules concerning smuggling and to try to embezzle goods aboard their prize-ships.[47]

Captain Jan Claesz. Spiegel (ca. 1540–1599) had an extremely varied career. This son of an Amsterdam merchant was a stubborn Calvinist who became one of the important Sea Beggar captains. Later he operated an inn on the Dam at Amsterdam, where he welcomed many a captain of the admiralty. His brother, a grain and gunpowder merchant, became a member of the city council in 1591. For some unknown reason, Spiegel came out of retirement to resume his seafaring profession in 1593 as a fifty-year-old midshipman on a convoy vessel to Brittany. He finished his second naval career as a captain in the expedition of 1599, dying on the isle of Sâo Tomé. He had never sold his inn, "In the Prince of Orange"; it was run by his wife, herself an inn-keeper's daughter, until it was bought by Jochem Hendriksz. Swartenhondt (1566–1627) in 1606.[48]

Swartenhondt changed the inn's name to that of his own surname and ran it as a first-class establishment, entertaining guests from the city council, nobles, and artists. Swartenhondt had also been a seafarer since childhood and could pride himself on having lived a most adventurous life, one that included his being imprisoned in Spain. He had served for some years in Prince Maurice's army before finally becoming a naval captain in 1596. He took part in several overseas expeditions, including one with Van Caerden to Brazil in 1603, after which he lived ashore as the distinguished inn-keeper. Swartenhondt returned to sea only once, in late 1620, when a fleet of war was fitted out for the Mediterranean with a Zeeland nobleman in command. An experienced captain was required to serve as second-in-command. Several captains were approached by the admiralty and the States

General, and each asked high remuneration. Swartenhondt got the job and defeated a Spanish fleet off Gibraltar. When he died, he was indeed a man of some means.[49]

The fact of the varied backgrounds of Dutch naval captains around 1600 and the mobility of the social classes is no better illustrated than by the example of Evert Hendrikszoon (†1601) of the admiralty of Zeeland. Born in a small village on the isle of Walcheren and probably a fisherman, Hendrikszoon moved to Flushing in 1572, joined the Sea Beggars, and soon commanded a vessel against the Spaniards. He was to become one of the few captains employed almost annually by his admiralty. His fellow officers would have preferred him instead of Bloys van Treslong as lieutenant admiral, but he lacked an adequate pedigree. No daring exploits are known of him, though in 1590 his admiralty offered him a nicely engraved silver plate. Because of age, he asked to retire in 1600. He had been so greatly appreciated that he was awarded a pension of fl.200 per year, while his eldest and blind son received an annual allowance. Evert Hendrikszoon was the founding-father of the renowned family Evertsen, which in its next three generations would provide the admiralty of Zeeland with many captains and flag officers. Evert's second son Jan (†1617) was a captain too, and one of his daughters married a member of the Flushing city council. Five grandsons—still teenagers when their father was killed in an action against a French pirate—followed in the family footsteps. Out of consideration to their father, the admiralty appointed the five sons lieutenants; two would later become captains and two lieutenant admirals. Naval service, courage, and contempt for danger became the hallmark of the Evertsens. Although there were other similar seagoing families, the Evertsens' record was the most impressive one.[50]

As varied as the backgrounds and careers of the Dutch captains were, it is evident that most generally remained in naval service upon reaching the rank of captain and did not switch over to other seafaring occupations in the merchant fleet or VOC. At the start of the Twelve Years' Truce in 1609, however, most captains were dismissed by the parsimonious admiralties. The admiralties could easily take such drastic action because, apart from a few flag officers, no captains, let alone the lower ranking officers, had permanent positions. By 1617, however, the demands for their talents led many former captains and officers to be invited to rejoin the navy.

Nevertheless, it was an unsatisfactory state of affairs that no system existed in which good and experienced officers were encouraged to remain in the naval service. Nor was there any rule requiring officers to pass tests covering their navigational and military knowledge, although a few regulations in that direction were implemented by some of the admiralties. In 1618, for example, Zeeland ordered its captains to keep a log during the voyages, and Amsterdam required an inspection of observations made by the mates. The Amsterdam chamber of the VOC appointed an official examiner in 1619.[51] And it was only after the resumption of the Eighty Years' War in 1621 that the admiralties introduced guarantees of permanent employment for their captains, unable any longer to escape such fixed expenses. Vice Admiral Moyen Lambert's experience is the most shocking example of how an admiralty could treat its personnel. He had served the councillors of the Maze as one of their most reliable officers for almost forty years, but he had never been granted a permanent income nor the official rank of vice admiral because it was considered too expensive. At long last, in 1624, Moyen Lambert received an official appointment at the age of seventy-four. By then, he had become a popular figure; verses about his ventures were exceeded only by the lengthy eulogy on his tomb.[52]

A permanent corps of captains was introduced in 1626. The five admiralties together appointed sixty captains for life. Only the best captains were given this privilege; they were called captains "ordinares." Younger captains ("extraordinares") would command convoy ships while the others would serve with the blockading and cruising squadrons. From then on, the "ordinares" captains were appointed by the Admiral-General, who could choose from two nominees given him by the admiralty with a vacancy. The captain's monthly salary was fixed at thirty guilders.[53]

The arrangement of 1626 had important log run implications for the navy. Each admiralty would have a fixed, at times adjusted, number of captains on its payroll. At the time of this regulation's introduction, however, the naval administration was suffering from financial problems, fraudulence, and corruption, all of which received considerable publicity. The payment of a captain's wages was often far in arrears. The continuing success of the Dunkirk privateers and the Spanish king's ships demoralized many captains, and they were often accused of cowardly and disorderly behavior in the face of the enemy, or of malingering by staying safely in port. The situation became even more confused when the so-called "directieschepen" appeared on the scene and took part in naval operations. Their masters, like the masters of hired merchantmen, were often uncontrollable when they were without the direction of inspiring and experienced squadron commanders.

Good leadership was lacking at the top of the officers' corps during the 1620s and 1630s. The earlier practice of appointing high noblemen as the lieutenant admirals no longer worked. The policy had been to have two lieutenant admirals, one for Holland and one for Zeeland, who would guarantee leadership and superiority over unruly captains. Four vice admirals appointed by the admiralties of Zeeland, the Maze, Amsterdam, and the Noorderkwartier would compensate for the likely shortage of practical seamanship during the campaigns.[54] The navy, however, was unlucky with the admirals appointed after the Truce.

The situation in Zeeland was no better than in Holland. Willem de Zoete van Laecke, heer van Haulthain (†1637) was a nobleman from the Spanish Netherlands. He had succeeded an illegitimate son of William the Silent as lieutenant admiral in 1601, but his leadership was often criticized as particularly weak. Jonker Philips van Dorp (1587–1652) took over in 1627, after having served as a rather unpopular vice admiral. Though Van Dorp was officially appointed by Frederick Henry in early 1629, the States of Zeeland dismissed him at the end of an unsuccessful winter campaign against the Dunkirkers. The stadholder did not appoint a successor; he had other plans in association with the situation in Holland.

The lieutenant admiralship of the most important province was regularly vacant in this period. Jacob van Wassenaer died in 1623, but Maurice's illegitimate son, young Willem van Nassau, heer van der Leck had to wait for his appointment until 1625. He was soon killed in action, not at sea but during the siege of the city of Grol in Gelderland in 1627. Only three new vice admirals in Holland were sworn in during the following year. The lack of good top-ranking leaders became an issue taken up by the citizens of the port cities. The self-confidence of many good captains had increased. Many felt qualified for leadership at the top, particularly those whose parents or other relatives belonged to the ruling class. Frederick Henry surprised almost everyone by appointing Piet Pietersz. Heyn lieutenant admiral of Holland in March 1629.

Piet Heyn was certainly not of noble birth. To those in an inner circle, however, it had been evident that a change in policy with regard to the lieutenant admiralship was in the air. Two months after the death of Willem van Nassau in 1627, some members of the States of Holland had mentioned the names of six candidates at the request of the Prince: there were two noblemen, a former governor-general of the VOC, a distinguished diplomat and naval commander (Laurens Reael), an army general, and two officers of the WIC (Piet Heyn and Jan Dirksz. 't Lam). The choice had not been made in 1627, but by 1629, Piet Heyn was by far the most popular seaman in the United Provinces.[55] In mid-January he had returned from the West Indies, having captured the Spanish Mexican-treasure fleet at Matanzas Bay in Cuba in September 1628—the first and only time that an entire fleet fell to an enemy, striking a terrific blow to the royal Spanish treasury and filling the coffers of the WIC and Frederick Henry with a net profit of seven million guilders. A few days after he had been mentioned for the lieutenant admiralship in October 1627, Piet Heyn came home from another looting expedition near Brazil, having captured thirty-eight Spanish and Portuguese vessels. Here was just the type of man to inspire the admiralties, the captains and their crews in their desperate struggle against the Dunkirk privateers.

Piet Heyn was the first lieutenant admiral to be selected for professional qualities only. It is wrong, however, to consider him just an ordinary sailor roaming the seas. Born in 1577 at Delftshaven—the port of Delft, adjacent to Rotterdam—he joined his father, who was skipper of a merchant vessel, and had an adventurous youth. Imprisoned probably three times by the Spanish (in Spain, the Southern Netherlands, and the West Indies), he was, with his father, forced to row in Spanish galleys. In 1607 Piet Heyn entered the service of the VOC and five years later returned home as master of an East Indiaman. He then married the widow of one of his colleagues and settled in Rotterdam. Like his father, he became a master in the merchant marine, operating in the European trades and in the Mediterranean, and was soon one of the rich citizens of Rotterdam. He was elected city alderman in April 1622. A few months after he had completed the customary one year term of that office, he was asked to be the second-in-command of a WIC expedition to Brazil. It was the start of a career which made him dreaded by Spaniards and Portuguese in America as well as in Angola.

Early in 1627, admiralty councillors in the Haagse Besogne referred to Piet Heyn as a good candidate for a vice admiralship. Yet only after Piet Heyn's unsuccessful negotiations with the WIC for a better contract could Frederick Henry entice him away to the navy. His naval service did not last long, however. The Prince and the States General had hoped that this very popular and strict commander would be able to implement the new regulations enforcing observation of the articles of war. On May 29, 1629, Piet Heyn left Hellevoetsluis, organized the blockade of Dunkirk, and chased a squadron of Ostend privateers. He caught up with them and was killed by a bullet in the ensuing fight. He was buried with great pomp inside the Old Church of Delft, his grave being covered by an ostentatious tomb.[56]

Piet Heyn's death created something of a vacuum, and all the good plans for the navy were reduced to ruin. Strangely enough, no decision could be taken about a new lieutenant admiral, neither for Holland nor for Zeeland. Van Dorp's offer in 1630 to return to the post in Zeeland was declined. This period of indecision lasted until 1632, when the stadholder finally decided to appoint Van Dorp—this time as lieutenant admiral of Holland—and to leave that position in Zeeland open. It was a choice made in despair. Van Dorp lacked authority as a leader and had no capacity for organization. He even seemed to find his way ashore at the most inconvenient moment.

As it turned out, the Flemish privateers and the Spanish ships mostly had their own way. Van Dorp's high-handed behavior lost him any sympathy he had among his peers in the nobility and the States of Holland. His half-hearted offer to resign, made in October 1637, was immediately accepted. It is almost incredible that the rulers did not intervene earlier—not the least Frederick Henry, who already in 1635 had declared that something had to be done or otherwise the navy would deteriorate further. But Van Dorp would return once again to the navy: as a councillor in the Rotterdam admiralty, representing the nobility of Holland, where he used the opportunity to express his disregard for his successor.[57]

There was no hesitation about that successor. Although, again, he was no nobleman or former governor-general of the VOC, Maarten Harpertszoon Tromp had given ample evidence of his seafaring qualities and the gift of leadership. He was a born seaman. The States of Holland had been in contact with Tromp since 1635. And, interestingly, his service as Piet Heyn's flag captain in 1629 was recommendation enough in the opinion of the jurist Hugo Grotius's family. Tromp's lieutenant admiralship bore many of the fruits expected from it. His speedy victory over the Spanish Armada in 1639 gave him a worldwide reputation, and popular opinion placed him on the same footing as Piet Heyn. Here was a great seaman who was also acceptable in the highest social circles at The Hague. In 1640 he married into one of the most notable families of The Hague, taking twenty-six-year-old Cornelia Teding van Berkhout as his third wife. They moved to one of the most stylish streets in the government center of the Dutch Republic.[58]

Tromp's naval and social success does not imply that the naval officer suddenly became a fashionable person in high society and that regents started to send their younger sons to the navy. Nothing could be further from the truth. The navy would indeed attract many regents' sons, together with youngsters and adults from several other groups of the population, though very rarely from the lowest strata. It is a mistake to think of Dutch naval captains only as "tarpaulins" or to ignore the great mobility between the middle and upper classes in early seventeenth-century Dutch society. The city councils were not yet closed shops. A successful sailmaker or brewer could be elected just as well as a former VOC official or a merchant master, unlike practices later in the century. The oft-quoted Joost van Coulster, during the 1630s and 1640s one of the most influential burgomasters of Rotterdam, in 1634 married as his third wife Moyen Lambert's daughter, the widow of a local sailmaker and alderman. In 1629 he procured a captain's post for his eldest son Willem and saw his second daughter in 1636 married to Captain Jan Jacobsz. van Nes—who had been since his youth, from 1614 onwards, on the payroll of the Maze.

Other examples of high society in the officers' ranks were the two sons of the admiralty councillor Jan Teding van Berkhout, who became members of the city council of Monnickendam; they were also the uncles of Cornelia, who married Tromp in 1640. Though not rich, Van Berkhout's sons still belonged to the local elite, fathering altogether eleven sons of their own, plus a number of daughters who were married off to local peers. Only two of Jan's grandsons were destined to enter local politics. The navy offered respectable employment for five others, all of whom became captains. Two of them were active in the 1630s and 1640s, the remaining three in the 1670s, 1680s, and 1690s.

Twenty-year-old Gideon de Wildt became a captain at Amsterdam in 1644. His father was a regent in Haarlem and had been a member of the Amsterdam admiralty in Jacob van Neck's days, and, perhaps equally important, his brother was secretary of the admiralty from 1641. Captains Dionys and Jacob Troncquoy were sons of a lower-ranking admiralty official. Wemmer van Berchem (1585–1653), from an old family in Gelderland, had been entrusted with high positions in Asia before he was appointed captain at Amsterdam.[59]

In Zeeland, the situation was no different. The leading seaport cities of Middelburg, Flushing, and Veere on the isle of Walcheren give perhaps the best examples of the involvement at any one time of several families in ruling, trade, shipping, and the navy. Naval captains' daughters made fashionable brides for the sons of regents and high officials. Three families in particular come to mind: De Moor, Evertsen, and Banckert. Sons of a vice admiral, the De Moors were, respectively, a burgomaster, a captain, and a surveyor of the navy dockyard. The Banckert family counted no less than eleven naval officers among its members.[60] As far as the admiralty was concerned, the different generations of cousins or nephews who were on active service at the same time could be distinguished only by the addition to their names of "the Old," "the Young," or "the Youngest," or by nicknames like "Oude en Jonge Boer [Farmer] Jaap" as was the case at Rotterdam concerning the family Van Nes. Not a few members of these families reached the then-available top ranks in the officer corps. Two Evertsens of the third generation (Johan and Cornelis the Old) would become lieutenant admirals in the 1660s. Like others, they married daughters of colleagues. These two brothers were both killed in 1666 during the Second Anglo-Dutch War; they were born seamen who did not marry rich women and who had to live mainly from their naval earnings. They were certainly not wealthy. Widower Cornelis the Old could declare in his marriage contract of 1659 that in addition to his eight small children he could only provide his new bride with fl.42,000—nevertheless a considerable amount of money at a time when Cornelis's able seamen earned only about fl.13 per month.[61]

The financial aspect of a career as a naval officer has seldom been given much attention in historical literature, and no substantial research into this subject as pertains to the seventeenth century has ever been done before. The monthly wage of thirty guilders was not a captain's most important source of income. But such would have been the case for a lieutenant if a convoy trip or a season of blockading the Flemish coast had been uneventful, and if no privateer or other hostile ship had been successfully attacked and captured. In the event of the capture of hostile shipping, prize money was distributed afterwards by the admiralty. How often this took place and what amounts of money were involved has not been studied. One may assume, however, that considerable sums were regularly allocated to all crew members, the highest portion going to the captain. Flag officers, however, profited most from prize money, a fact which partly explains why such a position was so much sought after. On board a flagship a lieutenant admiral received four times the prize money of a captain, a vice admiral twice as much—and they were entitled to remuneration for all prize ships and goods taken by any captain in their admiralty region.[62]

The captain and crew would receive a special remuneration for enemy ships captured, brought into Dutch ports, and auctioned off. The admiralty and the Provincial or General States could reward squadron commanders with silver or golden chains, the value of which was always expressed in guilders; such chains were often melted down by the owner or his descendents. Silver boatswain whistles were common rewards for captains.

By far the most important source of income for captains and flag officers were the so-called "kostpenningen," the provisioning pennies. Perhaps from time immemorial, a strange system existed with regard to the provisioning of men-of-war, a task which was the responsibility not of the admiralty but of the captain and the flag officer for each ship. The admiralties paid them a fixed allowance per man per day. The allowance, which increased over the period from five to seven stuivers, was supposed to be higher than was necessary to cover the expenses of the prescribed rations. Any surplus was considered a legitimate source of income for a captain or a flag officer. Hence a command was financially very attractive, and the bigger the ship and crew and the longer the journey, the higher the earnings.[63]

This system of provisioning brought the navy into the center of public life in cities and villages where captains and flag officers lived and organized their purchase of peas, salted beef, and beer, as well as firewood for the galley's oven. Most commanders felt personally responsible and arranged the purchase and transportation of provisions together with their wives or, if unmarried, with their mothers or sisters. These women were first contacted by an admiralty board and invited to come to the Prinsenhof when an expedition or a convoy trip might possibly last longer than expected. The extra provisions were then the sole responsibility of these women. Problems often arose when a commander died at sea and it was not possible for his successor to make adequate arrangements for provisioning the ship. The deceased captain's wife would then ask the board to intervene. Thus it is no surprise that officers' wives at times figured prominently in the admiralties minutes. Some widows were granted a small pension for a couple of years or even for the rest of their lives—for instance, Cornelia Teding van Berkhout in 1653.[64]

There was, however, one important snag in this financially attractive arrangement of "kostpenningen." The captains and commanders could never be sure that the provisioning pennies would be paid immediately upon their return. When the admiralty coffers were empty, or almost empty, the payment of this money was always regarded as the last priority. This happened regularly, and part of the profits then dwindled away in the interest to be paid to the suppliers of the goods. One may safely deduce that such delays could be a reason for commanders' not adhering too strictly to their instructions. Maarten Harpertsz. Tromp cannot be accused of such behavior, though he had to wait several years for a sum of more than 14,000 guilders. In 1635 he urgently requested to receive half of the sum in cash and the rest in bonds issued by the province of Holland, but only 2,000 guilders were given to him in the first installment.[65]

Tromp's financial position, shortly after his 1639 Armada victory and at the moment of his marriage to Cornelia in 1640, made him the most successful officer of the "old" navy. This most popular admiral, who was given the paternal nickname of Bestevaer ("dear father"), was born at Brielle in 1598. His father, Harpert, served in the navy and in 1606 moved to Rotterdam, where he could afford to buy a house, having been appointed a naval captain. Dismissed soon after the Truce of 1609 began, Harpert wanted to take part in the risky Guinea trade, but in 1611 his ship was captured by Moroccan privateers. Harpert was killed during the fight, and young Maarten, who had joined his father in 1607, became a slave on board privateering ships for more than two years. During the Truce, he could not select a naval career and switched between merchant vessels and Moyen Lambrecht's flagship, fighting the Barbary corsairs in 1618 and 1619. He then rose to the position of master, a petty officer's rank in the navy. After another spell in prison (in Tunisia), he returned to Rotterdam in 1622 and decided to become a naval officer like his father.

After Tromp served had two years as a lieutenant, Prince Maurice appointed him captain in 1624. In the same year, he married the daughter of one of his merchant masters, and ten years later as a widower he married the daughter of a former collector of taxes at Brielle. Well respected by his colleagues, superiors, and subordinates, he was feared by his Spanish and Flemish adversaries. Tromp's antipathy against Lieutenant Admiral Van Dorp and the prevailing disorder became so intense that he decided to stay ashore in 1634 and live from his own means while serving the Reformed Church of Rotterdam as a deacon. But his "retirement" lasted no longer than two years. After he had declined an offer to succeed Van Dorp the previous year, in 1636 he accepted a position in Frederick Henry's unpopular scheme for a more centralized system of fitting out and provisioning warships. A second offer to take over Van Dorp's post was made in late 1637, which he accepted. When his second wife died in April 1639, Maarten was left with three sons and a daughter.[66]

Prior to his remarriage, Tromp had all his belongings inventoried—as required by the "rights of succession" because of the children from his earlier marriages. These documents have been preserved and date from January 1640, just before the February 1st wedding took place at The Hague in a spacious house placed at his disposal by the States General. Tromp's total belongings were valued at nearly 90,000 guilders. This sum included fl.13,800 prize money still owed to him, fl.10,000 from prizes taken at the Downs, and the rest from other prizes, from which he was entitled to receive the lieutenant admiral's portion. About fl.33,000 was invested in annuity bonds, fl.20,000 in different houses (seven at Brielle), and fl.2,500 in three merchant vessels (two were quarter shares, and one was a thirty-second share). His cash on hand was fl.14,352. In view of his earlier merchant shipping ventures, it is remarkable that Tromp had hardly invested in merchant shipping.

The money was badly needed, inasmuch as the wedding was extravagantly expensive for this former galley slave on the Barbary coast. The costs were specified at no less than fl.15,960, including two pearl necklaces of fl.5,062 and a pair of earrings and twenty diamonds at fl.320 for the bride. The bridegroom himself spent more than fl.1000 on his own wardrobe; his shoemaker at Rotterdam billed him for fl.45, and the Rhine wine drunk during the festivities cost fl.900. It is not surprising that Tromp's wedding was mocked in a pamphlet.[67] The actual social ascent of Tromp was not unique, although the way it occurred was. A great many of his colleagues were incorporated into the circles of regents and merchant princes after they had started at a seemingly lower level. Others already belonged to those circles, while others would never climb the social ladder significantly. It was possible in the "old" navy to pass through almost all the ranks aboard a warship and reach the top, although the progress of Willem van Coulster in 1629, his fifteen-year-old son Joost in 1646, Gideon de Wildt in 1644, and Tromp's nineteen-year-old son Cornelis in 1649 proved that well-placed relations were useful in getting an early captain's commission. This system was partly in line with the process of aristocratization of the ruling class.

But until the navy was more professionally organized in the 1650s and 1660s, Tromp and his fellow flag officers were still often confronted with captains who did not fully obey their orders and avoided engaging in battle. These captains' ships had been hired by the admiralties, and their owners had no interest in risking their property. This type of captain—or more realistically, the master—was accustomed to following his own ideas on seamanship and not to keeping in line with other ships. The contrast between the professional naval officer—especially after the formation of the captains' corps in 1626 and the coming of Tromp's leadership—and the remnant of the old order in the form of merchant skippers on hired warships would reach its sad climax in the first clash between England and the United Provinces in 1652. An excellent demonstration of this situation was when Vice Admiral Johan Evertsen refused to bear responsibility for a disastrously organized fleet. While he remained ashore at Flushing in October, a "directieschip" of which he was a shareholder fought badly at Kentish Knock, a fact for which its captain was court-martialed. Even David de Wildt, secretary of the admiralty at Amsterdam, owned a share in one of the ships taking part in that battle.[68]

Truly International Crews

The common seaman has always been elusive for historians. Usually, the most one can discover about him is his name, birthplace, and monthly wage as registered on the ship's muster roll. Every ship in the merchant marine and the navy had a roll compiled for each voyage, but only a few of those hundreds of thousands of muster rolls from the seventeenth and eighteenth centuries have survived. The admiralties took better care with the so-called "payrolls," in which a complete financial record on each crew member was kept; many of them from the second half of the eighteenth century still exist. The financial documents of the admiralty of Zeeland's administration have survived in their entirety, providing our sole source of information about the origins and wages of sailors in the "old" navy.[69] Because these sources have not yet been thoroughly studied, however, a few examples must suffice.

The Zeeland payrolls immediately prove that any idea of a national navy was entirely alien to the Dutch Republic. A naval vessel's crew was invariably a mixture of nationalities, a situation no different from that on board merchant ships. The Dutch Republic was an open society into which immigrants from the surrounding countries were continuously crowding. Expanding maritime and naval activities created a high demand on the labor market, making the seaman's occupation international by its very nature. Even among the Sea Beggars (ca. 1570) the proportion of foreigners was probably twenty-five to thirty percent, mostly Englishmen, Germans, and Frenchmen.[70]

Only a handful of people originating from Zeeland had joined the Sea Beggars. More did enlist with their admiralty but never in overwhelming numbers, although its board always spoke in glowing terms of the provincial interest in the navy. From a sample of 422 enlisted men around 1600, only one third of the petty officers and ordinary seamen were living in Zeeland. The navy must have been very popular among the people of Flushing, for its eighty-seven enlistees formed by far the greatest contingent; the rest of Zeeland had no more than fifty-five. Much larger Middelburg was homeport for only eight. The other six provinces provided seventy-one men, which suggests that just half of the crew were Dutch. The remainder came from abroad. Of the non-Dutch half of the crew, the seamen from the Spanish Netherlands were quite prominent—there were even seven from Dunkirk—but this was not very surprising at a time in which borders were not yet settled. More interesting are the numbers of Englishmen and Scots (see Table 1), who later became scarce on board Dutch ships. Even one of the captains was from Oudenaerde in the Spanish Netherlands—Michiel van Trappen, also called Banckert.

Table 1
Geographical Origins of Petty Officers and Men aboard Zeeland Men-of-War around 1600

	petty officers	*men*	*total*	*percent*
Flushing	15	72	87	21
rest of Zeeland	15	40	55	13
Holland	11	32	43	10
rest of the Netherlands	9	19	28	7
Spanish Netherlands	21	40	61	14
England	6	30	36	8½
Scotland	2	25	27	6
Germany	7	29	36	8½
Scandinavia/Baltic	8	24	32	8
rest	1	3	4	1
unknown, but foreign	4	9	13	3
total	99	323	422	100

SOURCE: Middelburg, State Archives in Zeeland, Rekenkamer Archives 636, payrolls of the *Tonijn* and the *Zeeland.*

One may safely assume that the picture of the other four admiralties with regard to their crews did not substantially differ from this Zeeland sample. The proportions between the contingents were of course never the same, but Germans, Scandinavians, Frenchmen, people from the Southern Netherlands, the British Isles, and the Baltic regions in all ranks worked closely together with Dutchmen.

The navy's demand for seamen fluctuated constantly, depending upon the number and the size of the ships to be fitted out. The admiralties were compelled by the Flemish blockade to keep their ships more or less in continuous service, even during the winter. The end of this blockade meant that naval service was from then on restricted mainly to the period from late spring to early autumn, except when ships took part in an expedition to the Mediterranean. Actual figures on the seamen employed annually are not available, but if one takes the numbers of ships fitted out as a starting point for making calculations, some reasonable guesses are possible. The expedition to the Azores in 1599 alone required over 8,000 men, while during the Truce in 1615, hardly 2,000 men were enrolled. But in 1628, for instance, there were at least 8,500, and fourteen years later, in 1642, about 11,000 men.[71]

It was the captain's task to recruit his own crew. As soon as his ship had been allocated to him and the sailing date fixed, he could start recruiting. He had already received the names of the required number of officers, and usually a few signed on quickly, probably men who knew him from a previous voyage. Those, particularly the ship's clerk together with the officers, would help with the rest of the recruitment, though it is impossible to be precise about their actual methods. In any case, force was not used. It was the established custom in the port concerned and in nearby towns and villages to call people together by "beat of drum" to serve with the particular captain. Placards were also posted.

The greatest labor pool of seamen existed at Amsterdam, in which city the average wage level of sailors was generally lower than anywhere else. The admiralties always tried to stick to uniform wages for each rank, but a shortage of labor sometimes compelled them to pay extra money or to engage recruiting agents in Amsterdam. As noted above, councillor Jacob van Neck was active in this respect for the Zeeland admiralty. When in mid-summer 1625 an extra expedition against Spain had to be organized, all the available hands in Zeeland were already at sea, while a persistent plague ravaged in Rotterdam. Most of the 700 seamen needed by these two admiralties had to be recruited at Amsterdam and Enkhuizen. Another complicating factor could be the competing activities of the "directies." From 1631 onwards, these municipal officials often offered higher wages and better victualing and guaranteed prompt payment.[72] By and large, however, there were no signs of a general lack of seamen for the navy during this period. Shortages, if they existed, were only local and always temporary.

Little is known about the level of wages for seventeenth-century Dutch seamen. The navy, like the VOC, had the reputation for paying less than the merchant marine, the whaling trade, and the privateers. It was a set policy of the government to prevent the navy from increasing the general wage level. The difference in wages among the positions on board was rather small. What counted for a petty officer's enlistment was practical experience, not any sort of education. Also significant was the system on board of having mates connected with petty officers (e.g., boatswains or carpenter's mates), which provided the mates with a sort of training and education. And although the admiralty of Amsterdam tried to improve the art of navigation on board its ships, the navy at large could not pride itself on the general application by its mates of the estimated determination of longitude or the distance run. The determination of the latitude was more generally noted in the logbooks. The situation was no different in the merchant marine, though the East India Company was more sophisticated.[73] An example of the ranks and the related monthly wages on board ships of the Zeeland admiralty is given in Table 2. They had been fixed on March 13, 1621, at Middelburg.

The 1621 level of wages was rather low and would be increased for most ranks by twenty to thirty-five percent, but no more. The wage of course included board and lodging. A few petty officers had functions which provided legitimate subsidiary earnings. The provost, for instance, had a right to a proportion of the fines he could exact for certain breaches in the standing orders. The ship's clerk had the most opportunities for extra earnings. Not only was he paid for private writing jobs for his comrades, but it was also accepted as normal that for advance wage-payments on board, he made a charge. Advance payments were continually being requested, as many seamen came on board penniless and wanted to buy all sorts of things on the voyage or in a roadstead from bum boats. Opportunities for making extra money were also available to the ship's surgeon, who was paid for the treatments he rendered.

The literature describes crews of the "old" navy as rude, given to debauchery, and mutinous. And it can be taken for granted that patriotic feelings were absent amongst such heterogeneous groups of people, unless profitable looting lay in the offing. Cowardly behavior brought regular complaints. The period ca. 1600–1615 was known for piracy on a grand scale in western and southwestern European waters. Many a seaman in western Europe switched over from a regular seaman's life to a supposedly

Table 2
Ranks and Monthly Wages on Ships of the Admiralty of Zeeland in 1621

master	fl.24
mate	fl.24
clerk/purser	fl.12
boatswain	fl.14
boatswain's mate	fl.10
second boatswain	fl.12
second boatswain's mate	fl.10
quartermaster	fl.12
surgeon	fl.15
trumpeter	fl.14
carpenter	fl.16
steward	fl.12
steward's mate	fl.10
master gunner	fl.13
gunner's mate	fl.10
cook	fl.12
cook's mate	fl.10
provost/master at arms	fl.12
gunner/able seaman	fl. 8
ordinary seaman	fl. 6
boy	fl. 3

Source: Middelburg, State Archives in Zeeland, Rekenkamer Archives 654, "acquitten van de ontvangst."

more adventurous life as a pirate or privateer off northern Africa. Only strong and strict captains could keep their men under control during this period. In 1612, for example, a conspiracy to run off with a naval vessel to North Africa was discovered just in time to prevent it. Irresponsible or incompetent conduct by captains in confrontations with enemies, a regular occurrence, did not inspire a better standard of behavior from their subordinates.[74]

The ongoing struggle with Dunkirk also had a great impact upon the behavior of seamen, in the navy as well as the merchant marine and fishing fleets. Dunkirk, in Flanders, popularly called the Algiers of Christianity, was considered "the scourge of the seaman's existence," and those on board captured vessels were often known to be cast overboard. Though such barbarous practices were probably less common than has been suggested, official Dunkirk sources do mention that from the beginning of seventeenth century, the Dunkirkers locked sailors in their own holds and sank these vessels, or they let them decide by lot which of them should be cast into the sea—the so-called "voeten spoelen" (washing of the feet). The government at Brussels and the States General at The Hague both officially forbade the taking of prisoners, a brutal form of terror which continued well into the 1620s. When Dutch captains began to refuse to obey orders to throw captured Dunkirkers overboard, the government in 1628 finally ceased such retaliatory measures, which had cost many hundreds of seamen's lives.[75]

Another aspect of the struggle with Dunkirk was the fate of those brought into Dunkirk itself. Roman Catholics were often freed, others got the chance to serve with the privateers, but those who refused were thrown into dungeons and put up for ransom. For sailors too poor to raise the ransom at home, the prospect of release was almost nonexistent. The self-interest of the owners of the privateers, however, did often encourage them to take the initiative, for they wanted to get the average ransom of fifty to sixty guilders per prisoner and had their well-established agents at Amsterdam or Zeeland negotiate with a prisoner's relatives or superiors. After 1621, prisoners could also be exchanged. The Dutch also took Dunkirk and Ostend prisoners, although the costs of their board and lodging could weigh heavily upon the budget of the local magistrates in whose prisons they were kept.

A numerical basis for the exchange could be used, but it presented obvious problems. On whose side lay the numerical advantage? In 1636, the Republic felt powerful when Johan Evertsen returned with the Dunkirk admiral Jacques Colaert and 200 of his men. Strong feelings were at stake in 1629 when an exchange was discussed, one which would include those Flemings who were guilty of the death of Admiral Piet Heyn. In the meantime, their opposite numbers in Dunkirk had to wait. From the Dutch point of view, overlong delays could be dangerous, stimulating the prisoners at last to join an enemy renowned for its handsome rewards. The numbers of prisoners involved were high; in 1630, for instance, 434 were held in Dunkirk. The Dutch attitude towards Dunkirk prisoners became more humane. In 1642, for example, two Dunkirk vessels were taken and brought to Hellevoetsluis, where their crews were imprisoned but the young boys sent home to their parents.[76]

This risk of imprisonment at Dunkirk was great for men and boys in all branches of seafaring, as well as for those on board naval vessels. If arrangements for an exchange or ransom took too long, the sailors' wives and loved ones would rally and campaign for their release. Grand Pensionary Jacob Cats in 1640 suffered such a demonstration in front of his house, the women shouting that he had left their men folk to rot in the dungeons "in stink and filth."[77]

Seamen's wives were often active and did not hesitate to make vocal protests against other perceived wrongs. Quite regularly, their demonstrations succeeded in obtaining the payment of wages in arrears. During the First Anglo-Dutch War in June 1653, naval seamen's wives in Alkmaar threatened to plunder the house of the city of Alkmaar's representative in the admiralty of the Noorderkwartier. They would refrain from doing so only if he promised to call back their husbands and sons from a ship which they considered unseaworthy.[78] These women were often well aware of conditions on board their loved ones' ships. It was common practice that wives, including the captain's, joined their men on board, not only when still in port but also in the Texel roadstead. But before departure to sea, the women were required to go ashore and to take the excess belongings of their husbands, friends, and sons with them.[79]

The troubles around Dunkirk lasted until 1646, but the problems with unseaworthy, under-armed, and inadequately manned naval vessels would continue and reach their zenith during the First Anglo-Dutch War. Naval warfare in the 1640s required more manpower than before, and more ships were fitted out by the admiralties and the "directies." Qualified captains in sufficient numbers were seldom available. What could be expected from a sixteen-year-old captain on an expedition to Brazil in 1647? This was the incredible responsibility foisted on the young shoulders of Joost van Coulster's grandson. In 1641 a squadron of twenty men-of-war, sent in support of Portugal (which in the previous year had regained independence from Spain), was commanded by three "flag officers" who had never served before in the navy. The admiral was Artus Gijsels, a former merchant and governor of the VOC, whose sole experience with ships had been the nominal command of two homeward-bound East India fleets. The second-in-command was a harbormaster of Curacao. The third had been a master in the merchant marine—none other than Michiel Adriaanszoon de Ruyter. The whole naval force consisted of twenty hired merchantmen. The fitting out of this force had taken place after all naval vessels had already been given an allocation. It was only De Ruyter's leadership and tactical insight, until then unrecognized, that saved the squadron from disaster in a battle against a combined Spanish-Dunkirk force near Cape Vincent on the Portuguese coast. Most commanders did not behave as promised when they received their commissions, reported De Ruyter diplomatically.[80] Any sailor who had taken part in the Brazilian expedition of 1641 would have needed some explanations about the logic of foreign policy when he was required to fight the Portuguese six years later. This expedition experienced all kinds of difficulties which were beyond the authority of Vice Admiral Witte de With. When the ships had to stay much longer in tropical waters than planned, the situation changed from bad to worse. Sufficient provisions were lacking, and some ships deteriorated so badly that parts of their oaken hulls looked like honeycombs from the rot. The sailors became discontented and wanted to return home. Aboard the *Dolfijn* in May 1649, the situation got out of hand. Captain Job Forant, born in France, was justly accused of bad provisioning in favor of his own profit. He lost authority on board, as one of his lieutenants, a former pirate, conspired against him. A mutiny finally broke out, and though without any orders to sail home, the overwhelmed *Dolfijn* did just that. All crew members escaped punishment; only Forant was brought to trial, the verdict being dismissal and banishment from the Republic.[81]

The background of the *Dolfijn* story goes much further than a corrupt captain and bad planning by the authorities. This and other examples demonstrate that the "old" naval administration had become very much out of date in many respects. What the admiralties needed was a larger and more professional corps of standing captains and officers and a more regular pattern of recruitment by which interested seamen would know when they were going to be enlisted. It was not unusual for ships to be fitted out at haphazard moments the whole year round. The competition created by the "directies" and their higher wages was detrimental to the admiralties, though one should keep in mind that these city officials did jobs the admiralties were not able to do. More frequent and more direct control of the navy's activities by the authorities at The Hague would also have been an improvement. Such alterations in the naval administration were beginning to be introduced by the 1650s. Higher and more promptly paid subsidies, however, would remain a continuing goal of each board of admiralty. One very important change that was made in Dutch naval policy had to be imposed from abroad: very soon after the peace with Spain in 1648, it became evident that the navy had to cease using hired merchant vessels for naval operations.

The admiralties had indeed followed trends in naval warfare throughout Europe but had not stimulated any innovations in warship design. Those inducements had mainly come from Flanders, where in the cities of Dunkirk and Ostend, light and fast sailing frigates were being constructed from about 1626 onward. The frigate could easily escape the Dutch blockading and cruising ships. In the 1620s, the Dutch navy was still composed of a very heterogeneous mixture of ships in type and size: in 1629, for instance, there were no less than nineteen different kinds of vessels. The biggest and most successful ship was the *Groene Draak*, 500 tons, launched in 1628 at the Rotterdam admiralty dockyard. It was Piet Heyn's flagship in 1629. Its length was about thirty-five meters, with the armament consisting of twenty-six guns. One of its commanders called the *Groene Draak* "maneuverable as a top, sailing like a fish and stiff as a dike." Flag officers quarreled about who would be allowed to command the ship. A pilot's error caused the *Groene Draak* to be lost on the sands off Flushing in November 1631. Yet this fate is what prevented the vessel from falling into disgrace, for the admiralties had decided to change their ships' design. The States General took the initiative around 1630. Some high-placed persons had sarcastically observed that "cows did seldom catch hares" (for which last, read Dunkirkers).[82]

From 1632 onward, the man-of-war with a high fore-and-aft castle went out of fashion. Though each admiralty shipwright followed his own ideas with regard to the proportions of length, width, and draught, all new ships were now "frigatized," which meant that their structure was more lightly built, that the decks went through from stem to stern, and that there was a low forecastle and quarterdeck. The ships became more slender, the length being increased in proportion to the width. These improvements were applied to the smaller as well as the bigger warships, and there were vague efforts to develop three different rates of warships. The largest and most renowned ship, Tromp's first flagship, the *Aemilia* (600 tons), carried forty-six guns, had a length of thirty-nine to forty meters, and was built at Rotterdam in 1632. As a result of some alterations, she could later carry fifty-seven guns and a crew of 200 hands. The *Aemilia*, like the *Brederode* (in 1643, on the slipway), was the most powerful man-of-war the Dutch navy could send to sea during the 1640s. Such a ship could be constructed for about fl.42,000 in either an admiralty shipyard or a private one.

The problem, however, was that the admiralties could not afford to have an adequate number of ships like the *Aemilia*. Smaller ships were cheaper and more desirable for admiralties in dire financial troubles during the last stage of the war against Spain. In November 1643, the admiralty at Rotterdam had to rent out four of its frigates to a local privateering company, and as soon as the peace negotiations permitted it, admiralty ships were sold—even the *Aemilia*.

Early in 1648, Lieutenant Admiral Tromp developed a peacetime plan for the navy that centered in sixty-two of the best and newest ships: twenty-four at Amsterdam, twelve each at Rotterdam, Zeeland, and the Noorderkwartier, and two at Harlingen. The plan also included a procedure for the replacement of obsolete ships with new ones. Most admiralties disagreed with the plan, however, and no new ships were constructed in the following years. The only exception occurred in Amsterdam, where two big ships, bigger than the *Aemilia* and the *Brederode*, were built in 1650 and 1651. From this admiralty, which was incontestably going to take the lead in naval affairs, also came the suggestion for a one-third increase of the tariffs of the convooien and licenten. Once this increase was implemented, the tariffs became the source of a major augmentation in the admiralties' income from 1651 onward.

Neither Tromp nor the admiralties were now worried about a possible shortage of naval vessels. Their discussions dealt with the minimum number of ships that should be kept available in peacetime. In the event of an emergency, or if more ships were needed than expected, both Tromp and the boards of councillors were convinced that they could rely on the old custom of leasing East and West Indiamen, "Straatvaarders," and other armed merchantmen.[83] After all, had not this practice proved successful in the past? Private shipowners had always been eager to rent out the bottoms of their vessels, even at short notice. And recent experience had shown that squadrons of twenty ships could be fully fitted out and manned within two to three months.[84] The near future, however, would reveal that this old practice had become obsolete.

PART TWO

The "New" Navy, 1652–1713

By 1648, the Dutch Republic was recognized as an independent state and a leading economic and seafaring country with interests that spread over Europe, the Americas, Africa, and Asia. Its financial resources were respected and envied, its political structure considered an amazing experiment.[1] Political instability in France as well as in England, together with great rivalries among the Baltic powers, enabled the Republic to attain its preeminence in European power politics in spite of its relatively small territory, its population of under two million, and the vulnerability of its commercial interests and even of its public revenues. When the European balance of power was at stake in the last decades of the seventeenth century, Stadholder William III headed the coalition forces which halted the aggression of Louis XIV of France. The beginning of decay of the Dutch Republic during the War of the Spanish Succession at the start of the next century therefore came as a surprise.

According to Jonathan Israel, the Dutch economy reached its zenith at mid-century (1648–1672). The peace with Spain in 1648 was a watershed, after which Madrid treated the Republic as its most favored nation economically. Madrid's action had a tremendous effect on Dutch trade with Spain and in American and Mediterranean waters. The time of embargoes and raids had passed. In the West Indies, the Dutch became the principal carriers of goods. The VOC was able to expand its empire considerably in Asia. The four "rich" trades from Asia, Spain, the Levant, and Archangel—worth some fifty million guilders annually—provided Dutch industry with the raw materials for refining and manufacturing. The Leiden cloth industry reached its peak. The wars with England from 1652 to 1654 and from 1665 to 1667 had no lasting economic impact. Much more damaging was the initiation by France in 1667 of numerous protective measures aimed at ending the Dutch ascendancy over large sectors of the French economy. This was the beginning of a "guerre de commerce," later waged by other countries as well. The "rampjaar" 1672 (the year of calamity) was not fatal, and the Republic was able to survive both politically and economically. In that year, both France and England, in cooperation with two German princes, launched a massive attack on the Republic, but with no lasting result.

By the final decades of the century, however, the Dutch economy had passed its zenith. The most threatening development in this respect was the continuation of French economic warfare, resulting, for instance, in the overthrow of the Dutch commercial position in the Levant and the loss of Leiden's textile export trades. Many other trades (Baltic, Iberian, Asian, West Indian) and also whaling continued to thrive, and a great number of industries, bolstered by mercantilistic measures taken by the State, expanded: linen, sailcloth, paper, ceramics, tobacco pipes, and gin. The decline in relative and absolute terms started during the War of the Spanish Succession when Spain came under French influence, thus undermining one of the pillars of the Dutch trading system.[2]

The population of the seven United Provinces as a whole remained stable at about one and nine-tenths million. In the highly urbanized province of Holland, however, the number of inhabitants grew by thirty percent between 1620 and 1680 (from 670,000 to 880,000).[3]

As in the period from the late 1500s to 1652, the Republic was almost continuously involved in wars. The only substantial break from hostilities was from 1678 to 1688, though the skirmishes with the Barbary corsairs went on. After the conflict with Spain had ended in 1647, the political leaders at The Hague, Amsterdam, and other Dutch cities had not expected this constant involvement in further wars. They had therefore decided, almost overnight, to reduce expenditures on the navy and not to spend any more money on new ships. England rudely disturbed this complacent and unrealistic attitude, however, by going to war with the Netherlands—giving the Dutch a new and surprisingly strong opponent.

The "Old" Navy Out of Date

The establishment of the English Commonwealth in 1649 had a great and immediate impact not only on English naval administration and fleet but, by example, on those of the Dutch as well. Within a month of the execution of Charles I, the English republican leaders began to remodel the navy. Above all, the navy had to become politically reliable, but the style of command was also to be changed. One-man leadership was abolished, and three colonels were appointed "admirals and generals of the fleet." These new commanders were well equipped, and their title of "generals at sea" was created to stimulate a close liaison between the army and the navy. An interchange between service afloat and ashore was even envisaged. The officer corps was reconstructed, though the old guard was not completely dropped. Naval service became more attractive. Conditions of service were improved. Officers' salaries were increased—captains even received a fifty percent raise—as part of a new, overall wage structure, set up in 1653. Each seaman's share in prize money was enlarged. Discipline on board ship was regulated by "Laws and Ordinances Martial." Shore administration was also reorganized.

The new republican leaders of England also embarked at once on a major program of naval shipbuilding and rearmament, their first orders for new ships placed in March 1649. By the end of 1651, twenty new men-of-war had been built and a further twenty-five added by purchase or capture, almost doubling the size of the British fleet. The names of several older ships were even changed on ideological grounds: the *Royal Sovereign*, the largest ship, was renamed the *Commonwealth* but later came to be known as the *Sovereign*.[4] The great majority of ships built were men-of-war, by tradition more heavily constructed than their Dutch counterparts. And the new naval leaders discovered that most of these ships could carry far more guns than was specified in the original design. An increase of forty-two to fifty-six or sixty guns was quite common. On the eve of the first confrontation between the English and the Dutch, the navy of the Commonwealth had at its disposal a complement of about eighty-six ships. The armament of no less than fourteen ships was equal to, or far greater than, the number of guns aboard the Dutch flagship *Brederode*. And even smaller English ships were considered to have greater fighting power than Tromp's own flagship.[5]

This newly modeled English navy, already quite effective in 1649, by the end of 1651 had swept the English Royalist naval forces from the seas. By then, it had also begun to play a role in foreign policy. Naval pressure was successfully applied against Portugal, and even hostile France was not spared. English naval might was forcibly displayed—in ways including the obvious self-confidence and assertiveness in the behavior of its commanders. Oliver Cromwell and his parliamentary army colleagues were soon well aware of the potential of their new naval force, especially with regard to the Dutch Republic.

There were all manner of long-standing economic grievances between the two countries which had assumed a new intensity after 1649. The Act of Navigation in 1651 was considered a blow to Dutch commerce but was not sufficient cause for the Dutch to declare war, as England played only a minor role in Dutch commercial life. English claims to sovereignty of the seas were a much more serious bone of contention. The English insisted on the right to stop and search merchant ships and to confiscate any enemy goods found aboard. The Dutch claimed that goods were protected if on board neutral vessels. Incidents and clashes began to occur in 1650 and increased during the following year. Dutch naval and merchant ships were forced to dip their flags in salute to English men-of-war. Though political leaders in Holland in particular wished to avoid war,[6] it finally broke out in the spring of 1652.

That the English navy was stronger and much better disciplined than the Dutch became apparent in the numerous battles and clashes that took place. The battle formation of the single line ahead (the ships sailing astern of each other) was oriented to gunnery broadsides and formulated in the "Instructions for the better ordering of the fleet in fighting," issued in April 1653 by the three English admirals and generals at sea. There was nothing of this kind for the Dutch navy, which continued to use the boarding tactic as its principal method of fighting, augmented by the guns.

The Dutch preferred actions with a limited number of ships, swiftly operating from a windward position and immediately engaging their opponents by boarding. They were divided into squadrons, although in battle this tactic was important only as a means of closing with the enemy in an orderly way and of preventing their crossing each other's course. Thereafter a captain would select the best position opposite an opponent. If necessary, Dutch captains were not even obliged to wait for their flag officers. In 1652, however, the appearance at sea of immense fleets of ships made it imperative that order be kept and collisions prevented—a need which was in itself sufficient reason for an arrangement of five squadrons.

The squadrons sailed to the attack in line and then tried to attack and board with superior force. Winning the weather (windward) gauge was a prime objective, and Tromp's instructions did not go much further than that. The Dutch were not yet used to following numerous regulations in print concerning the maintenance of the line ahead during the battle. Fighting instructions with rules for all kinds of situations had to wait until the Second Anglo-Dutch War. The order of the squadrons was in fact the only topic specified, while the method of Dutch combat was still ruled by tradition.[7]

The lack of any uniformity among the types of ships in the Dutch fleet would indeed have caused great problems with regard to a more strict and continuous order in battle. The vessels' sailing capacities differed greatly, and many a master of a hired merchantman was not used to obeying sailing, let alone fighting, instructions. In 1652 the situation remained the same for the Dutch, except that now the number of ships involved was greater. With the two countries on the brink of war, the States General resolved in March of that year to expand the navy by resuming the old practice of leasing armed merchantmen. No fewer than one hundred and fifty such vessels were required. The admiralties themselves had no more than seventy-nine vessels at their disposal, most of which were old and in a bad state of repair. There were few new ships, as we have seen. The hiring policy itself was rather successful. By June, 1652, ninety-nine merchantmen were available and, for better or worse, were being transformed into fighting units; more were hired later.[8] But sheer numbers of ships were not as vital as the numbers and the weights of the guns and the quality of the captains and the sailing practices. As numerically strong as the Dutch fleet often seemed to be, it was rarely equal to that of the much more heavily armed, faster, and better trained English opponents.

The Dutch were plagued with yet more handicaps. At the start of the campaign, the prevailing westerly winds placed the Dutch in the lee-gauge (downwind of the English coast and the approaching enemy fleet). Geography further favored the English in the fact that a great deal of Dutch merchant shipping had to pass through the Channel and thus to run a long English gauntlet. Seaborne trade was vital to the Dutch economy, and Tromp's foremost responsibility was always the protection of his convoys. He realized that the destruction of the English fleet would mean security for Dutch shipping. But offensive actions—the strong preference of Dutch officers—always had to be coupled with the defense of the convoys. Thus Tromp was severely hampered, seldom free to operate as he would have liked. The Dutch emerged victorious in only a few of the many naval engagements. The war itself was an almost complete naval disaster for the Netherlands. Only political considerations and alarming English losses in the Baltic and Mediterranean trade prevented humiliating terms when peace was concluded at Westminster in February 1654.

In 1652 the Dutch navy still had a chance against the English. Major defeats like the one at Kentish Knock (October 8) were partly counterbalanced by a minor victory by De Ruyter—who had only recently entered the navy after the conclusion of a career in the merchant marine—over George Ayscue near Plymouth (August 26), and by a resounding victory at Dungeness (December 10) by Tromp over Robert Blake. Tromp's great numerical superiority in ships had been important on that occasion. Merchantmen's endeavors to use every possible safe moment for sailing ensured the continuation of fighting during the winter season. Many flag officers were criticized for their lack of success. Even Tromp was relegated to remaining ashore for a couple of weeks and replaced in command by Witte de With. A considerable group of hired merchant captains refused, or did not dare, to fight and deserted the fleet in battle. Admiral De With once sarcastically promised his captains that there could be no doubt that sufficient timber was available at home to make gallows for all those who deserved punishment.

The next year was truly disastrous as the Dutch experienced defeat after defeat—off Portland (February 28, March 1 and 2), off the Gabbard or North Foreland (June 12 and 13), and off Terheide, south of Scheveningen (August 10)—which brought merchant shipping almost to a standstill. Guesses at the number of merchant vessels and men-of-war captured by English privateers and warships range from 1,000 to 1,500. Most battles were very bloody, with huge losses in ships and lives. Tromp himself was killed off Terheide on August 10 on board the *Brederode*. Like Piet Heyn, he was buried in the Old Church of Delft. The only important setback for the English during this period took place in the Mediterranean when, on March 13, 1653, an entire English squadron was destroyed by Commodore Johan van Galen and his force as it attempted to break out of the Italian port of Leghorn.[9]

It was not too long before the authorities in The Hague and the admiralties realized that battles against a professional fleet could not be won by a haphazardly assembled naval force. Success would require the same kind of ships the enemy sent to sea—i.e., not armed merchantmen, but men-of-war built as such and armed with at least forty to sixty guns, preferably installed on two different decks. Discussions about this issue began in October 1652. Tromp suggested the construction of some ships bigger than the English vessels or at least of equal strength. The final outcome in February 1653, however, was a historic decision: the States General ordered the construction of thirty men-of-war. Two million guilders from public funds was allocated for this building project, which was to be completed in admiralty as well as in private dockyards. Tromp's suggestion, however, had not been followed: with the exception of one ship—the new flagship—all vessels would be no larger than the *Brederode* (fifty-four guns and 600 tons, or even smaller). The results of this wartime building program did not affect the course of the war, but the die had been cast. While peace negotiations were being held, a second set of thirty men-of-war was ordered in December 1653, with exactly the same specifications as had been stipulated for the first set. Once again, the pleas of the leading flag officers for ships of a larger size were in vain.

Nonetheless, the decisions made in both February and December of 1653 can rightly be called historic, even though the term must be judged in light of what the States General did next. The building project was not the first of its kind; such a program had been instituted before, but due to lack of funds, it had never been fully implemented. This one of 1653 was carried to completion, however. An innovative measure, it was also a crucial one for the future. The States General stipulated in January 1654, shortly before the peace of Westminster was concluded, that these sixty ships be considered national property. As a consequence of that stipulation, the five admiralties were not permitted to sell these vessels at the end of the war, as had been the customary practice. The ships would thus form the core of a standing navy, a permanently available fighting force.[10]

The two building programs and this fateful decision together proclaimed a new naval policy and a break with the past—when naval power had included armed merchantmen and the fitting-out of all sorts of ships and squadrons on short notice. The masters and the owners of the merchant vessels, along with the merchants themselves, would now lose an attractive source of revenue. The First Anglo-Dutch War had taught the authorities that the "old" navy was sadly out of date.

John de Witt's New Navy

It is unlikely that anyone in 1654 anticipated that the next two decades would become the most glorious and spectacular period in the history of the Dutch navy, an era full of battles, nearly all graphically portrayed in the many paintings and drawings of father and son Van der Velde. Any prediction along these lines would have appeared ridiculous in view of the 1652–1654 defeats against the English navy, the ignominious behavior of some captains, or the loss of eleven men-of-war off Texel during one stormy November night in 1653.[11] Nevertheless, the important changes in Dutch naval politics noted above had already been set in motion. In addition, the city and the admiralty of Amsterdam were increasing their influence on naval affairs, outstripping the financially weak admiralty of the Maze, pushing the economic priorities of Zeeland in Brazil and the West Indies into the background, and giving pride of place to their own commercial interests in the Baltic, the Iberian Peninsula, and the Mediterranean. At Amsterdam's suggestion, the admiralties' ordinary income had already been increased by one third.

It was primarily the efforts of Grand Pensionary John de Witt (1625–1672), however, which prepared the Dutch navy for the most splendid and illustrious episode in its history. At the age of twenty-eight, in the midst of the naval disasters during the summer of 1653, De Witt became the most important and influential civil servant in the Dutch Republic. He was born at Dordrecht, the oldest city in the province of Holland, and was the son of one of the leading provincial regents. Appointed city pensionary in 1651, he represented Dordrecht in the States of Holland and was a member of Holland's delegation in the States General. Soon involved in naval affairs, he made suggestions for the better control of the admiralties. Out of ten candidates, he was unanimously chosen as grand pensionary on July 23, 1653. The office of grand pensionary of Holland was in principle almost purely administrative and did not entitle the holder to any special authority with the navy. An appointment was for five years and could be prolonged, making the grand pensionary a rather permanent figure in a political scene composed of continuously changing groups of representatives of the different cities and provinces.

Since the days of Van Oldenbarnevelt (1586–1619), most grand pensionaries were the unofficial makers of Dutch foreign policy. They also chaired a number of influential ad hoc and, later, permanent committees in the States General and the States of Holland. But the grand pensionary appointed in 1653 was the first ever to take a personal interest in the navy, not only in his official actions but also in his correspondence, to the point of vividly describing the details of naval battles.[12]

The temporary standstill of trade and shipping and the ensuing political unrest in 1653 fully convinced John de Witt of the importance of a strong navy. But it was to him only an instrument, not an end in itself. It could help to establish peace for the Republic and safeguard his political views and system. Holland's economy was so vulnerable during naval hostilities that public unrest could easily erupt—as it did in 1653 and later, in 1665 and 1672. After the sudden death of William II of Orange in 1650, no stadholder had been appointed. The majority of the regents in most provinces naturally felt themselves competent to rule the country and to exert their own sovereign rights without sharing power with the semi-dynastical princes of Orange. In addition, the simultaneous disappearance of the admiral general had created something of a vacuum in naval administration.

John de Witt filled the vacuum as quickly as he could. Although his instructions did not specifically entitle him to do so, he began in July 1653 a regular correspondence with the three admiralties in Holland and, before long, with the others. He requested information on all kinds of practical topics like manning, provisioning, and ammunition and also pushed them to speed up the building program. The war situation demanded quick responses, and soon De Witt, gifted with a natural ability to lead, had brought most of the admiralties under his personal control. The long-standing need for coordination was now answered to some degree by a policy which aimed at centralization. In return for their loss of independence, De Witt involved the admiralties in the decision-making process; he always gave their desires a willing and understanding ear. Even more importantly, it was De Witt who prepared most of the naval resolutions for the States of

Holland—decisions which were nearly always endorsed by the States General. Consistency, coordination, and speed were introduced into Dutch naval administration. Operating in such fashion, in accordance with the policy of Amsterdam, he De Witt piloted the second building program, an Amsterdam initiative, through the political morass of the States of Holland and States General.

Not only involved in the political, financial, and administrative aspects of the navy, De Witt maintained a keen interest in the corps of flag officers and captains. The position of lieutenant admiral had become vacant with Tromp's death in the battle of Terheide. The obvious candidates were for various reasons unacceptable. The admiralties of Amsterdam and the Noorderkwartier suggested De Ruyter, who at that time was only a commodore. But De Witt took the suggestion seriously and invited the former merchant skipper from Flushing to a private dinner at his home. De Ruyter firmly rejected any offer in this direction, and De Witt—though strongly impressed by De Ruyter's vision in naval affairs—had to accept the man's decision. Nevertheless, over the years a bond of friendship grew between these two men of such different backgrounds.

There was no acceptable alternative to De Ruyter to be found among the flag officers for the lieutenant admiralship. Impressed by the performance of army officers in command of the English navy, and acting in accordance with the earlier tradition in the Republic, De Witt finally proposed as Tromp's successor the nobleman Jacob van Wassenaer-Obdam (1610–1665), whose father had occupied the same position between 1603 and 1623. Jacob was a cavalry colonel in the army, a member of the nobility of Holland, and an active participant in the States of Holland and the States General, as well as a political friend of the grand pensionary. But the choice turned out to be an unfortunate one, even though it had been unavoidable under the circumstances. De Witt immediately began a program of increasing the corps of flag officers with two new vice admirals in Holland and also three rear admirals. De Ruyter became the new vice admiral at Amsterdam.[13]

In many ways John de Witt became the leader of the Republic. A navy stronger than ever before was available to support his foreign policy. With the decision in 1654 not to sell the men-of-war, the navy was composed of two categories of ships: the fighting vessels—in 1654, no less than sixty-four of them, each armed with forty to sixty guns—and the convoy escorts, about eighty to ninety in total, smaller in size and armament. The fighting vessels were mostly laid up to be fitted out when it was deemed opportune or necessary. The escort ships were regularly deployed in those European waters where merchant vessels opted for naval protection. The Republic was therefore prepared for war and had ships that were a match for those of its most likely opponent.

The Dutch national interest, or rather the economic interests of the province of Holland, generally benefitted from a policy of peace in Europe, which De Witt pursued as long as he reasonably could. He was successful in the Baltic, using the navy as an instrument for peace and the restoration of a balance of power between Denmark and Sweden. While he ultimately failed with regard to England and France, his navy proved that it could also serve national interests at large and help to preserve national territorial and commercial integrity.

The battle fleet was expanded during the 1660s. When war with England became unavoidable, the United Provinces launched a new building program: no fewer than sixty ships of the line were built between 1664 and 1667, all larger than the existing ones. The last product of the naval dockyard at Amsterdam had measured roughly forty-eight meters in length and carried more than eighty guns. Developments in overall warship design had progressed dramatically from Tromp's *Aemilia* and *Brederode* of the 1640s to the *Dolfijn* of 1667. Developments in foreign navies followed the same pattern, however.[14]

This modern kind of navy with a standing fighting fleet and an extensive number of convoy escort vessels required a sound financial base and the permanent attention of naval administrators as well as the nation's rulers. De Witt managed to restore the balance in state finances and even to create reserve funds. He reduced the level of interest to a mere three and one-half percent and devised a new, more profitable procedure for the sale of life annuities by the state.[15] As a consequence, Holland's admiralties, and the other two as well, had sufficient funds both for shipbuilding and for equipping the ships. De Witt's regular correspondence with the admiralties ensured that he remained well informed about the state of the navy. He was, however, unable to introduce any fresh sources of income. The Republic's political leaders had never been able to put the navy's finances on a solid base, depending instead on ad hoc arrangements which provided the admiralties with the sums of money required for the battle fleet. But De Witt, and later William III, handled matters in such a way that the provinces generally transmitted their contributions on time and yet remained themselves responsible for the way their portions were collected—i.e., via provincial taxation or loans. The admiralties' own sources of income were higher than during the previous period, thanks to the flourishing state of most economic activities and the increased tariffs. The major admiralties could provide sufficient money to meet their convoying commitments.

John de Witt would never have been as successful as he was in creating a strong navy if his policy had not corresponded with Amsterdam's interests. The city had a strong influence on the admiralty, which also happened to be administered by two capable and powerful secretaries—the aforementioned father and son, David (1611–1671) and Job de Wildt (1637–1704). From 1659 until his father's death, Job acted as an under secretary. Both men operated in full accord with Amsterdam's burgomasters. Amsterdam was the driving force behind the plans for building a standing fleet of ships of the line. But such a navy required permanent accommodation for the storage of ships, provisions, guns, and adequate facilities for repair work in the dockyard. All of these needs were met during the 1650s. Shipbuilding and equipping activities, which had been located in the center of the city, were moved to the new outskirts, where ample space was available. A new dockyard with a ropeyard was constructed, along with a huge and well-designed storehouse, the so-called "'s Lands Zeemagazijn," completed in 1656. It is remarkable that the admiralty at Rotterdam, in earlier days more prestigious than Amsterdam's, did not follow this trend and refrained from introducing any innovations at Hellevoetsluis.

The De Wildts regularly went to The Hague for consultations with De Witt and with colleagues in the Haagse Besogne. They kept the grand pensionary well informed through extensive correspondence. Impetuous as he could be, De Witt only occasionally rebuked them for delays. The two secretaries were also practical-minded men. They insisted, for instance, on uniformity in armament by all admiralties. At the instigation of Amsterdam, the so-called "directieschepen" were abolished in 1656; they had performed badly in the First Anglo-Dutch War and no longer fitted into the new navy. Appropriate convoy escorts were now always at hand. A second, partly independent navy was no longer needed.[16]

How closely De Witt and the two De Wildts worked together is shown in their response to the capture of some WIC territories on the West African coast by an English naval squadron under the command of Robert Holmes in 1664. Regarding such an action as one step too far for peacetime, on August 6 the States of Holland decided to propose in the States General the prompt fitting out of an adequate naval force to counter and deter Holmes's activities. Since the Dutch expected that the awkward English ambassador at The Hague, George Downing, would be informed about this expedition and try by force to prevent its sailing, the two secretaries and De Witt devised a cunning scheme to thwart the English—a rather puzzling move, incidentally, since the grand pensionary wanted to maintain peace with England at all costs. Since Admiral De Ruyter happened to be operating with a squadron of a dozen ships in the Mediterranean, it was decided to send him orders to sail to the Guinea coast and recapture the WIC forts there. The secretaries De Wildt would send the orders "in all secrecy."

The problem, however, was keeping this decision from Downing and his friends in The Hague and Amsterdam—an almost impossible task because such orders had to be decided on in the States General, a large body with numerous delegates, amongst whom the English ambassador had his informers. For De Ruyter to launch a successful attack, it had to be utterly unexpected. The grand pensionary, David de Wildt, and some fully reliable delegates jointly worked out an ingenious scheme by which the decision was lawfully taken but the crucial delegates remained unaware of it. One of Downing's friends was in the chair on August 9, when Holland's proposal to send a squadron to West Africa was carried. On Monday, August 11, a delegate who was involved in the plot chaired the meeting. The minutes of the previous session were read, and certain proposals by a committee headed by De Witt concerning De Ruyter's squadron were presented as mere amplifications of the resolution of August 9. All was read in terms "so confused that those who might have been listening would have had difficulty making out what was being said." Those delegates who could not be relied upon were hindered in various ways—for instance, by being taken individually aside to the windows for a whispered "consultation," or out of the room on some flimsy pretext. De Witt made certain that he registered the day's resolutions in his own hand. De Wildt sent three express couriers in deepest secrecy to Spanish ports, and De Ruyter received his new instructions off Malaga on September 1. He could now start his operations on the Guinea Coast. The result of that campaign was the recapture of most of the territories taken by Holmes and the capture of the English main fortress. De Ruyter then went on to conduct operations against English shipping in the West Indies and their Newfoundland fisheries. In early October 1664, resolutions were adopted by the States General with regard to the naval force proposed on August 6.[17]

This intriguing story illustrates how an ingenious political leader, having strong influence over his colleagues, could carry important decisions quickly through the Dutch administrative machine when it was really necessary. Such a plan could not have been executed, however, if the city of Amsterdam and the majority of the members of the States of Holland had not agreed with De Witt's goals. In naval affairs, the support of the admiralty at Amsterdam was indispensable. John de Witt had put enormous energy into the navy. Already in 1659, five years after the first war against England had ended, De Ruyter, in command of a fleet destined for the Baltic, wrote to David de Wildt that never before had a better fleet been fitted out with such large, well-armed, and well-manned ships.[18]

According to the instructions he received when taking office, a grand pensionary was not allowed to interfere in nominations for any kind of position, but that restriction was ignored, and John de Witt was soon a central figure in the process of the captains' and flag officers' appointments. Letters of recommendation and nominations were often personally addressed to him. The absence of a stadholder and admiral general since 1650 made it all possible. It is quite remarkable that many a city government directly recommended one of its citizens to the grand pensionary if the usual short list of two candidates compiled by an admiralty board happened to include that particular individual.[19] De Witt's greatest mistake had been the appointment in 1653 of Obdam, who proved to be incompetent for a naval command. Obdam did not resign and even caused a sort of boycott by the admiralty at Amsterdam from 1659 until 1661, much to De Witt's displeasure. However, his death in the battle of Lowestoft in June 1665, when his flagship was blown up, solved the problem. Then, De Ruyter could at last become supreme commander of De Witt's navy. Two months passed before De Ruyter returned from the trip to West Africa and the West Indies, but this time he accepted the lieutenant admiralship with unanimous approval ashore as well as on board.

Until August 1665, the strong Dutch navy had lacked good leadership at sea. This situation was now rectified by the appointment of De Ruyter. The admiral, whose aversion to pomp and circumstance made him popular amongst the ratings, was a great support for De Witt ashore. With increasing authority and a strong insistence on maintaining his prerogatives with admiralty boards, De Ruyter helped to coordinate the naval preparations by regularly visiting the diverse admiralties. Beginning in 1665, De Witt, De Wildt, and De Ruyter formed a powerful triumvirate behind the enormous naval efforts of the United Provinces.[20]

De Witt also took a personal interest in ships and the sea. That became apparent in 1665, when a second Anglo-Dutch war had become unavoidable. He wanted to be sure that the fleet was fitted out as quickly as possible. While almost forgetting the other commitments of the grand pensionary (a deputy was appointed), he had himself together with some other members of the States General commissioned to the Texel roadstead. There he could supervise and coordinate the final efforts to fit out the squadrons of the admiralties of Amsterdam, the Noorderkwartier, and Friesland. He disliked relying on Obdam or on written reports. In order to remain in touch with the activities at The Hague, Hellevoetsluis, and Flushing, De Witt designed a practical system of signals along the coast. He also gave evidence of having navigational insight and daring when he made soundings in person in the inlets to the Texel roadstead and proved that more inlets could be used, even by the biggest ships of the line, than had previously been assumed by local pilots and mates. The use of these additional inlets with their different wind conditions gave the navy more flexibility in "coming and going" than it had formerly enjoyed. De Witt's finest hours came when he embarked on board the flagship in July 1665 as one of three States General delegates who would instruct the naval commanders in their campaign after Obdam's defeat off Lowestoft. He thoroughly enjoyed life at sea, sleeping in a special hammock designed by the great inventor Christiaan Huygens—"suspend dans le vaisseau par une grosse boule et a peu pres de la mesme facon que sont suspendues de horologes" (hung in the ship from a large ball and almost in the same manner as timekeepers are hanging)—and intended to prevent De Witt from suffering from seasickness. When De Ruyter took command, De Witt also remained on board until the end of the campaign in early November. De Witt returned to sea in late September 1666, on which occasion he was the sole representative of the States General. It was a bitter disappointment for De Witt that no battle took place under his guidance.[21]

An Era of Naval Campaigns against England and France and in the Baltic

Beginning in 1654 was an interlude of several years when Dutch shipping was not threatened by any western or northern European power, much to the shipowners' and their crews' relief. It was a new feature of life at sea, since the continuous war against Spain and the Dunkirkers had been quickly followed by the first confrontation with England. Old hands from Tromp's navy who well remembered the endless struggle with the Dunkirk privateers during the Eighty Years' War were now faced with a fundamentally different pattern of naval operations. Only the usual scheme of regular convoys to and from France, the Iberian Peninsula, Italy, and the Levant was maintained. At fixed times, a certain number of convoy escorts accompanied merchantmen to these destinations as a matter of routine, paid for out of the admiralties' ordinary income.

Peace, however, is a relative notion for a seafaring country. Not every part of the European shipping lanes was free of hostilities. Moreover, the United Provinces had become one of the leading powers whose support was ardently sought by others and whose commercial, financial, and military strength was a source of envy. England and France actively tried to diminish the Republic's power and influence. War against both countries required the commitment of all available resources, simply because great national interests—at times, even the territorial integrity of the Republic—were at stake. The menace to commercial interests in most cases required the attention of the main trading cities and the admiralties. John de Witt's navy was able to handle both of these contingencies.

The interests of Amsterdam mainly defined when and where naval power should be deployed in defense of trade and shipping. There were two areas of tension and risk: the Mediterranean and the Sound in the Baltic; the Dutch navy intervened in both areas.

One of the consistent elements of Dutch foreign policy was to act as the fulcrum in the balance of power between the Nordic states of Denmark and Sweden in order to prevent either one from controlling the Sound. When diplomacy failed, naval intervention was used, as in 1644 and 1645. It became unavoidable again in 1658, after Sweden's King Charles X, wanting the Baltic to be converted into a *mare suedicum*, had conquered much Danish territory, including the shores of the Sound. Two years earlier, a Dutch fleet of forty-two ships under Obdam, without firing a shot, had been instrumental in frustrating Charles X from occupying Danzig, the Baltic's most important trading center. Now, on November 8, 1658, the armed intervention began with a straightforward naval battle in the Sound. The Swedes were stronger in sheer numbers, but the thirty-five Dutch men-of-war managed to defeat them—at the cost, however, of heavy losses and the death of one of the Netherlands' most renowned flag officers, Vice Admiral Witte de With. The Sound was reopened for commercial shipping.

The following year, all of John de Witt's diplomatic talents would be used in an attempt to prevent an escalation of the hostilities. With France and England having allied with Sweden, the Dutch built up in Danish waters a naval force of no less than seventy-five ships, augmented by an army of 4,000 soldiers. The presence of the English naval force had made the situation complex. But the opportunity to use this force occurred during a confrontation in 1660 when the restoration of the monarchy in England resulted in the return of an English squadron to its own waters. In collaboration with Danish forces, De Ruyter succeeded in recapturing the island of Fünen, but further operations became unnecessary when Charles X suddenly died in February 1660, and peace in the Sound and Baltic was restored. Dutch commercial interests had been carefully protected as a result of the judicious use of naval forces in a most delicate political environment.[22]

The activities of Barbary corsairs both in and outside the Mediterranean were another matter of great concern to the city council and admiralty board at Amsterdam and elsewhere in Holland. The corsairs would remain a continuous problem for the Dutch Republic as well as for other seafaring nations for another century and a half. War, when officially declared by the rulers of the Barbary states of Morocco, Algiers, Tunisia, or Tripoli, became an organic part of these countries' economies; the profits they realized from the capture of enemy merchant vessels could be quite substantial. War against the Republic promised them large numbers of rich targets. Fleets of twenty Barbary warships were no exception, and they regularly operated even off the coast of Portugal. Merchantmen were taken, ships and cargoes sold, and seamen enslaved until ransom money arrived. The Twelve Years' Truce had shown, however, that retaliation by special naval squadrons could temporarily safeguard Dutch shipping. That policy had been taken up when war against England had finally ceased in 1654; at that time the Mediterranean losses were really alarming the big merchants at the Bourse at Amsterdam, involved in that trade. Sufficient convoy escorts and ships of the battle fleet were kept at hand.

Almost every year from late 1654 onwards, a squadron of ten to twenty ships of the line sailed to the Mediterranean, their arrival sometimes partly coinciding with the departure of the ordinary convoys for that area. The Mediterranean became a training ground for many flag officers and captains, who learned to sail in small units and to be constantly prepared for actions against fast and daring opponents. De Ruyter was in command of those squadrons several times. The Barbary corsairs suffered substantial losses through those Dutch operations but could not be persuaded to maintain a lasting peace with the Republic or to switch their depredations to ships of other nations. From 1657 until 1661, most Dutch squadrons also had to participate in the recently resumed war against Portugal. The Tagus River was occasionally blockaded and a good number of rich Brazilian sugar ships captured, offering attractive prize money to captains and crews of the marauding ships. On the other side, however, Portuguese privateers did considerable harm to Dutch West African and West Indian shipping. Peace was eventually established in late 1661.[23]

The Nordic intervention had resulted in a temporary reduction of the Dutch operations against the Barbary states and Portugal. And although the size and quality of the Dutch navy were so substantial that it could undertake many different actions simultaneously, war against England was soon to claim all its available means and manpower.

It was a national confrontation for the Dutch people, one in which patriotic feeling ran high. English actions of undeclared war had inflamed Dutch public opinion, first of all when it was learned that in November of 1663, King Charles II himself had agreed to the Holmes expedition to West Africa. De Witt's stroke of genius to instruct De Ruyter to undo Holmes's captures, however, remained a secret in the Republic until the last months of 1664. Meanwhile, rumors materialized as the facts that in September another English expedition had occupied New Netherland and that New Amsterdam had, as a result, been renamed New York. Privateering commissions had already been distributed for the West Indies. The final act of aggression had been Thomas Allin's attack in December on a Dutch homeward-bound convoy of Smyrna ships near Gibraltar—an attack which, however, almost completely failed. Ambassador Downing could only mention Dutch attempts to hinder English progress in West Africa and Asia as creating anti-Dutch feelings in England. The official declaration of war was not made until March 1665. But English prospects of new sweeping gains as had been made thirteen years before were not going to be fulfilled, though Charles II's navy was again equipped with more heavily armed ships than the Dutch navy.[24]

John de Witt's new navy was prepared for this second struggle with its English rival. However, to every Dutchman's disappointment, the first official battle ended in disaster. The most powerful fleet ever assembled in the Republic was soundly beaten by the English under the command of the Duke of York, off Lowestoft on June 13. Tactical mistakes by Admiral Obdam and the ensuing disorder in the command structure had contributed to this defeat. Obdam's lack of leadership ability and naval insight had long remained hidden by the fact that the very capable officer Egbert Meussen Cortenaer (ca. 1605–1665) had been his flag captain and direct adviser during the previous Baltic campaigns. Cortenaer, meanwhile promoted to lieutenant admiral, was also killed in this battle. The English were not able to exploit their victory, however, and order amongst the Dutch was quickly restored by Tromp's son Cornelis (1629–1691) and De Witt. No further battle took place between the two grand fleets, not even after De Ruyter had become supreme commander. In August alone the English, with the tacit cooperation of the Danish government, vainly attacked a part of the returning Dutch East Indian fleet that had sought shelter in the neutral harbor of Bergen.[25] The Dutch main fleet remained at sea well into the autumn, and during the winter, a strong squadron under the command of Cornelis Evertsen cruised in the North Sea.

The longest battle of the war between England and the Dutch Republic was fought from June 11 to 14, 1666—the so-called "Four Days' Battle" —an outright Dutch victory, though not a decisive one.[26] The clash began between the Downs and Dunkirk. Until the fourth day, the English were outnumbered. After the four days of line-ahead maneuvering, mutual broadside exchanges, and boarding and grappling fire ships, the English had lost three ships of the line and five fire ships; six others of their ships were carried away by the Dutch, four of which sank, and three fire vessels were burned. Thousands of seamen were dead, and many had been taken prisoner. It was one of the bloodiest battles in naval history. Seven weeks later, Admiral Monck, now the Duke of Albemarle, was able to defeat De Ruyter as heavily in the Two Days' Battle (the St. James's Day Fight), August 4 and 5. Holmes's action a fortnight later against a huge number of merchantmen at anchor off the isle of Terschelling was another blow to the Dutch during that month.[27] But, by and large, the war continued to drag on with no obvious victor emerging. The English had lost their initial appetite for the war and had discovered also that privateering was not as successful as it had once been. There were no more than 500 Dutch merchantmen and fishing boats to be captured. Dutch privateers and men-of-war, however, operated with astonishing results against the much smaller number of English commercial ships. Nearly 400 such vessels were taken, at least seventy-five of which had rich cargoes of sugar and tobacco on board. The proceeds of the auctions at Amsterdam and in Zeeland (data are unavailable on those at other places) reached well above four million guilders, providing the admiralties with substantial extra income.[28]

Late in 1666, the English decided to lay up their larger ships, an action forced on them by lack of money and inadequate naval stores. The war would be fought defensively from that moment on. The Dutch were not hampered by such problems. Grand Pensionary De Witt immediately grasped the opportunity to have his favorite plan executed: a bold attack on the coast near London. With John's brother Cornelis as the representative of the States General on board the flagship *Zeven Provinciën*, De Ruyter carried out the famous raid up the Medway in June 1667. During the action, the main body of the fleet remained out in the Thames estuary. First, a landing-party captured the magazines and storehouses at Sheerness; then the next day, a group of ships sailed upon the Medway, broke the boom across the river, and forced their way up to Chatham. Six deserted and defenseless ships of the line were burned, and to the utter humiliation of the English, Monck's flagship *Royal Charles* was towed away to Hellevoetsluis. Early in 1667, a squadron commanded by Abraham Crijnssen had captured from the English the country of Surinam in the Caribbean. The peace treaty of Breda, signed in July 1667, was highly favorable to the United Provinces, representing the bountiful harvest of John de Witt's naval and diplomatic efforts. Retention of New York had to serve as England's consolation prize.[29]

The treaty of Breda did not create a lasting peace, but the next few years were the quietest period in the Dutch navy's existence to date. No hostilities had to be faced anywhere, apart from the Mediterranean and its Barbary corsairs. Powerful squadrons under the command of good officers like Willem van der Zaen and the former captain of the marines Willem Joseph, Baron van Ghent (1627–1672) inflicted very serious losses on the Algerians, but their government could not be compelled to finalize a peace. At the instigation of Amsterdam, the finances of the admiralties were put in good order again.

Dark clouds, however, were gathering over the United Provinces. Kings Charles II and Louis XIV had resolved upon a joint Anglo-French attack on John de Witt's country, and in 1671, they gave clear signals of that intention. The core of the Dutch fleet concentrated in the North Sea was put on alert, providing De Ruyter with a fine opportunity while holding maneuvers to teach his officers what he thought was the best method of fighting a superior enemy. The fleet was in excellent condition. The ships of the 1664–1666 building program were all available; the officers' corps were well trained. Indeed, naval service had become rather popular. The flag officers had distinguished themselves in many previous operations, giving confidence not only to the fleet but to the Republic at large—a fact which has been attested by the great naval historian J. C. M. Warnsinck, who, writing in the 1930s, devoted numerous books and articles to these officers' lives and exploits.

The English method of the line of battle—composed of three squadrons, each subdivided into three "smaldelen" (divisions)—had been copied by the Dutch navy during the war of 1665–1667. Group tactics had been dropped, and each ship received its ranking order in the line. To these general ideas about the so-called "single line ahead" battle formation, De Ruyter added, though not in any written instruction, his far-reaching and innovative thoughts about concentration of forces and breaking through the enemy's line. Against a superior fleet, he considered it proper tactics not to divide his own force into three equal squadrons but to create equality with two of the enemy's squadrons and to instruct his third squadron's commander only to keep the battle simmering. If superiority could be gained in one section of the line, a breakthrough had to be tried in order to "double" the enemy and to push him into disorder.[30]

1672 was a year of disaster for the Republic. De Witt's foreign policy of peace and good relations with France and England had failed. The Republic was attacked by the armies and navies of Louis XIV and Charles II and by the prince bishops of Cologne and Münster. Dutch territory was invaded from the south and the east, and a great deal of it was soon occupied. Only the so-called "Waterline" kept the province of Holland free from occupation. In August, De Witt was murdered by a mob in The Hague, and twenty-two-year-old William III was appointed stadholder and supreme commander of the army and navy. A defeat at sea would have meant that the coasts of Zeeland and Holland were both open to invasion. In four great battles, the Anglo-French navy, commanded by the Duke of York and later by Prince Rupert, tried in vain to defeat De Ruyter's fleet. On June 6, 1672, the Dutch even surprised the allied navy in Southwold Bay, falling upon it before its line was properly formed and inflicting so much damage that the planned English crossing to the Dutch coast had to be canceled. Part of the crew on board of De Ruyter's fleet had to be shifted to the hard-pressed army defending the Waterline.

The Dutch were unable to repeat the surprise in 1673. The inferior fleet was forced onto the defensive, but De Ruyter fought a brilliant campaign with three indecisive battles, which meant that the allies failed to reach their objectives. In the two battles at Schooneveld near the isle of Walcheren (June 7 and 14), De Ruyter made splendid use of the sands off the coast to prevent the enemy from deploying its superior forces. The safe return of the East Indian fleet compelled De Ruyter to leave his "hole" on the Zeeland coast, but the Dutch were again able to resist the enemy in the battle off Kijkduin (Texel) on August 21. In close cooperation with Adriaen Banckert (1620–1684), the lieutenant admiral of Zeeland who was also gifted with great tactical insight, De Ruyter created a breakthrough during the first battle and achieved superiority over one section of the hostile line during the final engagement. When the second fight began, an unprepared enemy was forced to retreat to the English coast. The Dutch navy had given ample evidence of what Dutch courage really meant! It had developed its greatest strength during the battle of

Kijkduin: sixty ships of-the-line, fifteen frigates, armed with 4,233 guns, and manned by 17,368 sailors and 2,092 soldiers. The allies were at least one third stronger in all respects.[31]

No further fighting had taken place by the time the second Peace of Westminster was concluded in February 1674. Honors were shared evenly between England and the Republic, and Charles II gave up his alliance with Louis XIV. Outside the scope of the main naval operations some interesting activities had meanwhile taken place in the western hemisphere. Late in 1672, the Amsterdam and Zeeland admiralties had both dispatched small squadrons commanded by Jacob Binckes (?–1677) and Cornelis Evertsen the Youngest (1642–1706)—separately and unknown to each other—for either a raid against the English East Indian fleet or a looting expedition in West Indian and North American waters. By sheer coincidence, both squadrons met near Martinique early in June of 1673 and joined forces, playing havoc with English and French shipping first in the Caribbean and later in Virginia. Next, New York was reconquered, while the raid was carried on to the Newfoundland fisheries. The Dutch authorities, however, were reluctant to send reinforcements to New York, which was finally returned to the English at the Peace of Westminster. The profits from this looting and the success of privateering were much greater than in 1665–1667. No fewer than 650 English and French merchantmen were captured and sold at public auctions for well above five million guilders.[32]

After 1674, naval warfare changed completely. The Anglo-Dutch Wars were over, and the scene of naval operations moved from the North Sea to the Channel and the Mediterranean. The war against France had not ended. Far from it. During the next four decades, France and the Republic under the leadership of William III were almost constantly at loggerheads or at war. From a naval point of view, this conflict had three important consequences. First, the efficiently organized French privateering fleet, among which the Dunkirkers were quite prominent, seriously endangered Dutch merchant shipping in all European waters except the Baltic. Second, where Spain was the traditional enemy of France, it became a matter of course for The Hague and Madrid frequently to coordinate naval operations, thereby making Dutch squadrons regularly dependent on timely preparations by the Spaniards of their own ships and the availability of provisions. From 1689 onwards, England joined the Republic in this naval policy. And third, the importance of warfare on land increased, necessitating greater expenditure on the army, now under the active command of William III. The process of the navy's losing its pride of place had slowly begun.

In the first instance, however, the Dutch in 1674 concentrated their naval operations against the French Atlantic coast and Martinique in the West Indies. Two expeditions under the command of Cornelis Tromp and De Ruyter were dispatched, but both attacks failed. The French had been warned in advance. The die had been cast, and from then on, more expeditions followed. The shortage of money, the slowly increasing failure in naval coordination, and the inadequate maintenance to ships began to show their effects in the performance of Dutch squadrons. One of the victims became old De Ruyter, who in 1675 sailed to the Mediterranean with too weak a force. The French were supporting an anti-Spanish uprising on the island of Sicily. De Ruyter joined forces with a small Spanish squadron, and though considerably weaker, he managed twice to compel his French opponent Admiral Abraham Duquesne to break off the fight. In the second battle, however, near the volcano Etna, he was mortally wounded and died a week later on April 29, 1676, at the age of sixty-nine. De Ruyter had been amazed at the small size and the poor quality of the fleet he had to command. When a councillor of the admiralty at Amsterdam had dared to remark that the old tar seemed to have become scared and was losing his courage, De Ruyter had riposted: "I shall go wherever the Gentlemen of the State order me to go, even on board just one ship, but I feel sadly, that these Gentlemen are ready to lay down the honor of the State by dispatching this small force."[33] A few months later in 1676, the Dutch-Spanish fleet was severely trounced by the French and was thus pushed into undertaking only defensive operations. The war went on until peace was finally concluded at Nijmegen in August 1678. Meanwhile, more ships and other flag officers had tried to help the Spaniards.

The war against France had still more consequences for the Dutch. French economic sanctions, expensive warfare in the Southern Netherlands, fruitless operations in the Mediterranean as well as successful Dunkirk raids on Dutch merchant shipping and whaling were among the problems the Dutch had to face. Jean Bart was the most famous Dunkirk corsair, and his name was greatly feared in the circles of the underwriters of Amsterdam. Squadrons of frigates were on the alert almost continuously in the North Sea, even as far north as the Norwegian coast, and yet in several instances, they could not prevent substantial losses. Hostilities also went on in the West Indies. The exploits of Binckes and Evertsen in 1672–1674 had evidently given the Dutch a taste for more activities of this kind, and their very dispatch, separate from each other, had been a symptom of a growing lack of coordination in the naval administration. The admiralty at Amsterdam, still with sufficient financial resources, went its own way in this respect. Plans were developed for a colony on the Guyana coast, but Jacob Binckes's second mission to the West Indies in March 1676 made a greater impact. With a force of seven small men-of-war, Binckes attacked French Cayenne and Guadeloupe and occupied Tobago—although a second French attempt resulted in his surrender of Tobago in 1678.

The Baltic also became part of the scene of battle against France, though in an indirect way. Sweden had sided with France, and a coalition against Sweden had been shaped in 1675. The Habsburg empire, Brandenburg, Denmark and the Republic belonged to it. The Dutch role consisted of the dispatch of auxiliary naval forces to Denmark in 1675, 1676, and 1677 in squadrons of ten to fifteen ships. A resounding victory was gained in the battle of Oeland on June 11, 1676. Cornelis Tromp was even made supreme commander of the Danish navy for two years.[34]

The geographical scope of Dutch operations had become so wide during the preceding five years that the Grand Fleet had to be permanently split up, while the protection of commercial interests at times required more vessels than were available. If peace had not been concluded in 1678, the naval policy would have had to be readjusted soon. A substantial break in the almost continuous equipping of large naval forces was a very welcome event for the admiralties' financially, allowing them to catch up on the payment of a great many outstanding provincial subsidies. Naval operations were kept to a minimum and were restricted to a few sporadic efforts to curtail the Barbary corsairs. Only once in 1682 was a rather powerful squadron fitted out to keep a close eye on some French designs in the Baltic. On the squadron's return, a November gale played havoc among the ships off Texel, destroying eight of them.[35]

The ten years up to 1689 turned out to be the calm before a long, raging storm: the Nine Years' War of 1689–1697 and the War of the Spanish Succession of 1702–1713. The balance of power in Europe was at stake with Louis XIV's France striving for hegemony on the Continent. William III, until his death in 1702, was the leader of a strong coalition, of which England, the Habsburg empire, and the Republic formed the hard core. Though not in every detail, the pattern of naval operations was more or less the same as in the previous war against France. Year after year, diverse squadrons—gradually becoming smaller in size—were fitted out and sailed into the North Sea, the Channel, and the Mediterranean. There was, however, one great difference from the earlier wars: the Dutch navy was no longer operating independently, a circumstance that existed as a result of the Glorious Revolution of November 1688.

England's change from enemy to ally of the Dutch had some important implications for the Dutch navy. William III's strong stand against French hegemony since 1672 had caused him to try to secure English cooperation on land as well as at sea. Soon after his marriage to Mary, Charles II's niece, in November 1677, William had initiated talks about closer mutual commitment in the event of war. On a secret mission, Cornelis Evertsen the Youngest had offered detailed suggestions for a naval alliance, while already hinting that the financially weak admiralties would not be able to bear a fifty-percent share in any such alliance. Peace with France had overruled these talks. The Glorious Revolution, however, put William III in a position to realize his old ideas, having become king of England and being the unrivaled leader of the United Provinces.

The Dutch navy, in crossing from Hellevoetsluis to Torbay in November 1688, had unwittingly heralded the uncomfortable situation that William's plans would create for its naval officers. Arthur Herbert, later Earl of Torrington, had been put in command of the purely Dutch naval force which carried the Prince of Orange to England. During the summer and early autumn of 1688, an enormous number of men-of-war and merchant vessels had been concentrated at the naval base of the Rotterdam admiralty. They made quite an impressive show of force—forty-eight ships of the line and frigates, with twenty-eight smaller naval vessels, manned by 9,500 seamen, plus an expeditionary force of 15,000 men and 4,000 horses on board 300 hired merchantmen and sixty fishing boats. Some 400 ships and 25,000 men were joined in one expedition, but it had long been unclear for what purpose they were there. The admiralties had had to dig deep into their purses, and extra financial resources had been inventively arranged.[36] The bill was later presented to the English government, which, after vigorous debates in Parliament, finally paid £600,000 of the total cost of £663,752.

Herbert's command in 1688 had been given him for obvious political reasons with regard to his English colleagues, but it was continued because of the mutual distribution of power at sea. Anglo-Dutch negotiations continued for more than four months before an agreement about naval cooperation was reached in May 1689. The Dutch suggestion that the two parties should contribute naval contingents in the proportion of five English ships to three Dutch had been accepted. This was the reverse of the proportion agreed for the land forces to be commanded by William himself. These proportions meant that the Dutch navy was always in the minority in joint operations—a fact which created hard feelings among Dutch officers who could still vividly remember having defeated Anglo-French fleets in the past. England naturally claimed command of the combined fleet. The Dutch negotiators had argued that this claim would be acceptable only where the English officer was of a higher rank than his Dutch colleague. The final text of the treaty, however, created a situation in which no Dutch flag officer could ever command joint fleets, squadrons, or detachments; it was an insult in Dutch eyes, and self-evidently proper in at least some English eyes.[37]

The cooperation of the two maritime powers bore no immediate fruit. The initiative was with the French navy, which was more powerful in sheer numbers and commanded by the very capable Admiral Tourville. Preparation had to be made for the possibility of invasions in Ireland and England, forcing allied operations to be confined mainly to home waters even though the superior French navy lacked a naval base in the Channel. On July 10, 1690, Torrington's fleet of nearly sixty ships was defeated by Tourville's fleet of eighty. The allied fleet engaging the enemy, with the Dutch leading the van, were outmaneuvered by the French. A sudden calm in the wind befell the Dutch in the brunt of the battle, and only Torrington's order to anchor, thus preventing the ships' drifting away with the tide towards the French, saved most of the Dutch fleet. The ensuing allied quarrels about the cause of the Beachy Head defeat finally ended in the discharge of both the English and Dutch admirals, the latter being Cornelis Evertsen the Youngest. A small allied squadron destined for the Mediterranean had been unable to prevent the French Toulon fleet from joining Tourville off Brest; it could only protect some merchantmen. The situation did not much improve throughout 1691, though the French were less active.[38]

The potential naval and maritime powers of England and the Republic, however, were far greater than that of the French. From 1692 onwards, both countries' contribution to the allied fleet increased. On May 29, 1692, the allies, under the command of Edward Russell—the Dutch squadron was led by Philips van

Almonde (1644–1711), a disciple of De Ruyter—destroyed a major part of the French fleet off La Hogue (Barfleur). Tourville's force was exactly half the size of the allies' eighty-eight men-of-war because his union with the Toulon fleet had not yet been accomplished.

The balance had still not definitely turned in favor of the allies. In 1693 Tourville skillfully rallied his forces at the right place and time to surprise a huge allied convoy of outward-bound Smyrna ships off the Spanish Atlantic coast and captured ninety-two of them. Allied attacks on the French privateering ports of St. Malo and Dunkirk and some others were of no avail. By 1694, however, the French government was compelled to diminish its naval expenses—a circumstance which provided the other maritime powers with more opportunity to broaden their operational plans. At the instigation of William III, in 1694 a second front against France was opened in the Mediterranean. William had convinced flag officers and naval administrators of the profits to be gained by leaving the allied fleet in Cadiz instead of bringing it home during the winter months. The need for a permanent overseas naval base was beginning to be felt.

From 1695 onwards, most French naval efforts were put into the *guerre de course*, using men-of-war as well as privateering vessels. The opponent became more elusive and its exploits more daring. Blockades and bombardments of French Atlantic ports had little effect. Allied naval supremacy often failed to have much impact. The French also considered the West Indies as part of their looting grounds, but the English had not wished to include that area in the treaty of 1689 for joint operations. The continuing activities in the Mediterranean prohibited both England and the Republic from diminishing their naval strength. Far to the contrary, the Dutch admiralties in 1696, for instance, had more ships in active service than ever before: sixty-one ships of the line, thirty-three frigates, and twenty-one smaller vessels, armed with 5,026 guns and with 24,369 men on board.[39] The Peace of Rijswijk in September 1697 was a relief for everyone, and by then the Dutch admiralties were financially exhausted.

Expectations of a lasting peace were not very great, however. The problem of the Spanish succession was in the offing. France's opponents would certainly not voluntarily accept a member of Louis XIV's Bourbon family on the throne at Madrid, and, sure enough, war was to break out again in 1702. The growing tensions around the issue of the succession added to a new conflict in the Baltic which did not allow the interlude of five years of peace to be at all quiet. In 1700, an Anglo-Dutch squadron bombarded Copenhagen and the Danish fleet, helping to restore peace in that region. Under strong pressure from William III, the Dutch admiralties also resumed their construction program of 1690, and another nineteen ships of the line and three frigates left the slipways, completing an impressive building program started in 1682. By 1700, no less than 100 ships of the line and fifty frigates had been added to the battle and convoy fleet, including fifteen carrying ninety to ninety-five guns each.[40]

The reaction by merchants and shipowners to the wars against France followed the traditional pattern. Quite a number of them, not only in Zeeland but also in other ports such as Amsterdam, put their financial means into privateering. Detailed research has revealed that from Zeeland alone—though it was by far the most active region—more than 100 actual privateering vessels sailed between 1702 and 1713, with another 150 merchant vessels deployed in additional privateering activities. Their total prizes are estimated at 1,800 vessels, with proceeds of at least eighteen million guilders. This quantity of prizes compares favorably with the 1,685 captures made by privateering vessels from Dunkirk, the 1,275 by those from St. Malo, and the 1,176 by those from England.[41]

From a financial point of view, the War of the Spanish Succession was disastrous for the Republic as a whole and for the admiralties in particular. The war dragged on for more than ten years, ashore as well as at sea. The army had become the big spender, next to the navy, and the level of military expenditure finally exhausted financial resources. The 1689 conditions for Anglo-Dutch cooperation were still operational even though the five admiralties increasingly failed to fulfill their three-to-five ratio commitments. By and large, the naval operations were not unsuccessful. The command was always in English hands, with the result that the leading Dutch admirals—Van Almonde, Gerard Callenburgh, and Jan Gerrit van Wassenaer—could never operate independently. Many of the operations were supplementary to the warfare in Spain itself, often on the coast of Catalonia, a fact which implies that William III's naval strategy was adopted by his successors.

Naval operations during this war followed a typical pattern. Squadrons of frigates remained active in the North Sea, occasionally fighting or hunting groups of Dunkirk or other privateers. Some bloody fights took place in which individual captains and their crews gave evidence of ample courage. But even these episodes could not prevent victories by the privateers—in 1703, for instance, they captured, almost the entire herring fleet of the leading fishing port, Enkhuizen, rendering a blow that was never overcome. Further Dutch naval activity centered in convoy trips to the Iberian Peninsula and the Mediterranean. The main effort was always the Grand Fleet, which, wintering regularly in a Portuguese or a Spanish port, had to coordinate its program with that of the English. In general, however, agreement about the naval strategy was less strong between the two allies than during the previous war, in which William III had strongly put his mark upon the mutual exploits. The Dutch had then also appeared as the more effective partner and had in some respects taken the initiative. In this war, the English complained about Dutch reluctance to support the strategy. The Dutch had a preference for convoy rather than blockade and, after 1705, for instance, withdrew from the blockade of Dunkirk. Moreover, Dutch merchants had lost a fairly small portion of their ships to the French, while their English colleagues had suffered extensive losses. The failure of the Republic to meet its annual naval obligations reflected not only financial problems but, to a certain extent, disagreement about the aims of the campaigns as well.[42]

A few events deserve special mention. After an attack on Cadiz had failed, an Anglo-Dutch force trapped the Spanish Mexican treasure fleet and a French squadron in Vigo Bay (on the northwest coast of Spain) on October 23, 1702. Both hostile fleets were virtually annihilated. On August 4, 1704, the allies accomplished the conquest of Gibraltar, a stronghold which was eventually retained by England. The only battle of significant size in the whole war took place off Malaga on August 24 when the French fleet tried to reconquer Gibraltar. The two fleets were of almost equal strength (about fifty ships of the line in each), and no clear victor emerged. In 1708, the island of Minorca was conquered and transformed by the English into an overseas naval base, thus marking the establishment of what was to become a permanent British involvement in Mediterranean affairs. After 1708, French war efforts dwindled considerably, and after 1711, privateering activities did likewise—creating the situation that allowed the Dutch admiralties to cease most of their North Sea operations. In 1712, some display of naval power was instrumental in bringing the Barbary states to peace with the United Provinces. One of the very rare episodes in which Dutch naval forces acted independently occurred in 1709 when a detachment of eleven ships sailed into the Sound and the Baltic trying to hinder the transport of grain to France. In 1706, 1707, and 1709, two Amsterdam escort vessels were sent to the West Indies.[43]

The peace of 1713, concluded at Utrecht, was even more of a relief than that of 1697. France and the Republic were completely exhausted. Both countries were the losers—the Republic because it did not receive much compensation for all its war efforts. The tide had definitely turned against the Dutch. Most of the bills for army and navy expenditures had not yet been paid in 1712, and even enormous loans had not been sufficient to cover them. By 1713, the Republic had already in fact stepped down from the ranks of leading European powers.

Changes in the Naval Administration

In contrast with the period of the "old" navy when the admiralties often operated on their own, more coordination of naval activities and the presence of a central figure in the naval administration were features of the second half of the seventeenth century. This development was a logical consequence of the important role the Dutch had played in European politics and the existence of a strong, permanent Dutch fighting fleet. (The importance of Grand Pensionary John de Witt in this respect has already been discussed.) The greater coordination and centralization were unrelated to either the absence or the presence of a stadholder and admiral general. The Union of Utrecht of 1579 and the arrangement of the admiralties' structure of 1597 were so vague and flexible that when the conditions of the time required it, one person could temporarily appropriate more power than was normally the case. Such was indeed the requirement during this period, but this person's success depended entirely on the tacit cooperation of the vast majority of the members of the States of Holland, including the city of Amsterdam. If Holland's interest in naval affairs should wane, the fate of any idea about coordination and centralization was sealed. John de Witt was able to rely upon sufficient support in this respect, and so was William III.

William III did not take a personal interest in naval affairs, however. For him, the navy was no more than an instrument in the struggle for the preservation of the Republic's territorial integrity in the war of 1672 and later in his conflicts with France. He never went to Texel or Zeeland to inspect naval preparations as De Witt regularly had done, and, so far as is known, only once did he ever step aboard a ship of the Grand Fleet. On August 12, 1673, William addressed the council of war when De Ruyter's fleet was anchored off Scheveningen near The Hague. In November 1688, the fleet was for him personally no more than a means of transport to England, as were individual men-of-war in the following years. As a statesman, he fully recognized the fleet's value and therefore not only gave great consideration to the navy as a whole but also continued to use De Witt's choice of secretary of the admiralty at Amsterdam, namely Job de Wildt.

De Wildt held the post of secretary the rest of his life. Through his father, David, he had become familiar with all aspects of that job, on the purely naval as well as the national level. Job de Wildt was the second in a sort of dynasty at the Prinsenhof, for his son David joined him as a secretary in 1688 and succeeded him on his death in 1704. Financially, Job was quite secure; one of his business activities, which did not require much active personal involvement on his part, was grazing oxen—animals that were in high demand when East Indiamen and men-of-war had to be provisioned. In 1690, Job's daughter married Simon van Slingelandt, the later grand pensionary (1727–1736) who together with his father conducted the secretaryship of the Council of State.

Job de Wildt was soon on good terms with William III and became his confidant for naval affairs. Though not closely related to the ruling élite of Amsterdam, De Wildt had considerable influence with the admiralty board at Amsterdam and was nearly always present at The Hague when important decisions had to be prepared or taken. He was fully convinced of the importance of a strong navy and in 1675 tried to prevent De Ruyter from sailing with too weak a force to the Mediterranean. The next year, De Wildt advocated a new building program, which was finally started six years later, in 1682. He reached the peak of his influence and power in 1688 when the Glorious Revolution was planned: he was one of the central figures in all secret naval preparations. On William III's invitation, Job twice went to London between 1689 and 1690 for naval consultations. A year later, he was appointed the personal representative of the king-stadholder on all boards of admiralty, though the boards in Zeeland and at Rotterdam never really complied with this directive. De Wildt had become the central naval administrator in the Republic, the result both of his personal merit and of William III's and Amsterdam's prestige. In England, Samuel Pepys operated in more or less the same role. The Dutch naval commanders were obliged to report to De Wildt and to receive their instructions from him. He also was in frequent touch with the English ambassador at The Hague or with the Duke of Marlborough. De Wildt's death in 1704 at the age of sixty-seven—he had suffered from gout—was a heavy blow for the Dutch navy. It marked the end of a period of half a century in which both John de Witt and Job de Wildt were able to provide Dutch naval administration and naval politics with the kind of coordination and leadership that had been lacking in their basic structures. A few months before his death, De Wildt with sharp foresight stressed the urgency of drastic reforms: "Our naval affairs regress with such great steps and are bound to come to such a decay that redress will be impossible."[44]

Grand Pensionary Anthony Heinsius (1689–1720), who became the Dutch leader in European politics after William III's death in 1702, was not a commanding person and never really took the navy to heart. In his role as the grand pensionary, he allowed more than three years to pass before he invited, in 1692, the admirals at sea to report to him. During the War of the Spanish Succession, Heinsius did remain in regular touch with naval preparations and operations, but he lacked the personal motivation and the pushing power of De Wildt and De Witt. David de Wildt, moreover, hardly operated at a national level after 1704.[45] The lack of central control allowed the boards of admiralty to revert to their former freedom of action—the more so because William III had not been succeeded as stadholder, and in most provinces, there was no one holding that office, a situation which was to continue until 1747.

In principle, no change whatsoever took place in the manifold activities of the five admiralties, nor in their sources of income. The scale of activities and the level of expenditure involved, however, were much greater than in the previous period. The huge shipbuilding programs required more and better facilities for maintenance and repair and the construction of more slipways. (The improvement of the facilities at Amsterdam during the 1650s is discussed above.) Compelling reasons to extend the areas where ships could be safely harbored arose during the 1680s when there were such large increases in the numbers of ships being launched. More dredging to increase the capacity of the harbor solved the problem at Amsterdam, and in 1687, serious thoughts were given to the construction of a completely new dock area at Willemstad, south of Dordrecht. This plan never materialized, but at Flushing, the old dock area got a new sluice in 1693, enlarging it to the extent that it could handle about eighty men-of-war. Eleven years later, the facilities at Flushing were still further improved with the completion of a dry dock. Other examples of the great vitality of the naval administration until the very end of the seventeenth century are the dredging works and the construction of a new sluice at Hellevoetsluis between 1697 and 1700.[46]

The ordinary annual income of the admiralties reflected the fairly prosperous state of trade and shipping overall. From 1687 to 1690, the task of collecting half of the taxes was farmed out, and the new system insured sufficient ready money for William's plans concerning the English throne. Of much greater benefit to the admiralties, however, were the subsidies granted by the States General and paid by the seven provinces. During the whole period under discussion, subsidies were annually voted. For the years 1682 through 1701, for instance, no less than eighty-one million guilders were allocated for admiralties' spending on construction and fitting out, one-and-a-half to two times as much as their own incomes.[47]

The subsidies granted to the admiralties were badly needed by the two small institutions in the Noorderkwartier and in Friesland. Both had, within the range of their resources, contributed to the naval operations during the three Anglo-Dutch wars but had thereafter fallen back into a state of lethargy. Their ordinary income could not cover the costs of shipbuilding and the fitting out of even one more ship. And the animosity between the provinces of Friesland and Groningen prevented any construction of warships. Only intervention by William III in 1691 cleared the way for the building of four ships of the line and two frigates in the years from 1693 to 1696, vessels that were clearly needed in view of the fact that shortly before this time, the Frisians had been forced to lease yet another ship from the admiralty at Amsterdam. It is interesting to note that the Frisian rear admiral, Douwe Fije van Roorda, on the payroll from 1678 until his death, never commanded a ship. At Hoorn and Enkhuizen, Job de Wildt had been able to acquire reasonable influence upon the naval authorities and thus stimulated the construction of fourteen ships of the line—three belonging to the first rates—between 1682 and 1699. Ordinary income, temporarily higher due to the farming-out of the tax collecting, allowed the building of two frigates, which were launched in 1691.[48]

No information is available on the composition of the admiralty boards and their daily functioning during this period, other than that focusing on the board at Middelburg. The number of councillors on four of the five boards remained constant. In Zeeland, however, the absence of a stadholder—as had been the situation from 1650 to 1672 and from 1702 to 1747—had an immediate consequence, the councillors being reduced to nine. For the tenth member—a provincial nobleman—was a representative of the Prince of Orange in his capacity of "first nobleman" in Zeeland. The Prince of Orange also held the title of Marquis of Flushing and Veere and selected those cities' representatives on the admiralty board, giving the stadholder a mighty voice in admiralty and in provincial business. The six or seven councillors from Zeeland were at the same time the executives (*Gedeputeerde Staten*) in the provincial governing authority. The stadholder's friends always occupied three of these seats. This combination of admiralty and provincial ruling forestalled the opportunity for any of the Zeeland ministers to play the kind of dominant role that those at Amsterdam, for instance, had enjoyed. William III's sole representative during his stadholdership was Willem Adriaan van Nassau-Odijk (1632–1705), his second cousin, who was titled Viceroy of Zeeland. Odijk, with all his prerogatives, was a useful instrument for imposing William's naval policy upon Zeeland, a province that by tradition tried to resist Holland's domination in naval affairs. Odijk's notoriously corrupt behavior, including the sale of offices to political protégés, gave him, however, a bad reputation.[49]

The frequency of the Zeeland board meetings varied a great deal. There were regular meetings on Mondays and Saturdays and, if necessary, on Wednesdays and one other day, but very seldom were there more than four a week. In the decades before and after 1700, only about five members regularly attended the meetings. In 1705, the board agreed that a quorum of five out of nine was required for valid decisions to be taken, and that one of the five should be a non-Zeeland member. It is noteworthy that the three members from the isle of Walcheren, which harbored all the admiralty facilities, were the most regular attenders of the meetings. Odijk was often absent, preferring to stay in one of his houses at The Hague or in the province of Utrecht; he was then kept informed of the proceedings by correspondence. Lieutenant Admiral Cornelis Evertsen the Youngest, after being discharged of his command of the navy in 1690, also served as a member of the board, and until his death in 1706, he attended meetings regularly.

Unlike those in Holland, most members in Zeeland held their posts for seemingly endless terms. Very few changes took place in the overall composition of the board. David van der Nisse from Goes started in 1661 and was dismissed in 1705. The city of Veere's Johan de Mauregnault's terms extended from 1679 to his death in 1717, and Iman Cau van Dussen represented his city of

Zierikzee from 1698 to 1734. Nanning Cloeck from Amsterdam could show a good record of attendance over his twenty-two years from 1680 to 1702, when he died. A great turnover occurred in the years from 1702 to 1705 when upheavals after William III's death drove five of the seven Zeeland members into political limbo.

With regard to admiralty personnel, Cloeck and the other two non-Zeeland members had no influence whatsoever in the Abdij at Middelburg, the medieval complex which housed all the provincial institutions as well as the admiralty. All decisions were made by the Zeeland members. In two secret agreements of 1685 and 1690, they had ruled that all appointments, from the lowest to the highest ranks, would be their business only, and a scheme had been designed by which each member would have his turn to appoint officers for each of the various classes of office. In many positions, a son succeeded his father, and in this way, experience and tradition were passed down. It was no different at the other admiralties. The family De Wildt had its counterpart at Middelburg, where secretary Johan Steengracht in 1656 took over the position that had been in his family since 1627. His son Adrian in 1690 became his assistant, serving in that role until they separated into different camps during the political upheaval of 1702–1705.[50]

In Zeeland, more than at any other admiralty, the board was regularly involved in the jurisdiction over the many hundreds of prizes captured during the Nine Years' War and the War of the Spanish Succession. A strict set of rules accompanied this work. Booty was inventoried, guarded, unloaded, and finally sold at public auction in Flushing, Middelburg, Veere, and Zierikzee—all managed by admiralty personnel. The procedures of the admiralty, the various sentences of the prize court, and the occasional revision of sentences could be time-consuming. In some instances, differences were settled out of court by the parties involved. One of the offices that was most prone to fraud was that of auctioneer, a position usually occupied by a local regent. Around 1700, auctioneer Isaac Hurgronje, member of the city council of Flushing and councillor of the VOC, was accused of not having administered all his auctions and of having bought at his own auctions in the name of his minor children and his wife.[51]

Corruption and abuse of power were not, however, the monopoly of the admiralty in Zeeland—a fact which was publicly revealed in a 1689 issue of the monthly magazine *De Hollandse Mercurius*. In 1685, a court case had been started against officers of the admiralty of the Maze who controlled the application of the levy of duties. These "commiezen ter recherche" had been put into jail. Over two years had passed before the committee of investigation, appointed by the States General, had secured the relevant documents, the board at Rotterdam on several occasions having refused to hand them over. It finally turned out that not only the officers but the councillors as well were involved. A general lack of control came to light, and it was discovered that the administration of these officers had never been scrutinized. Confiscated goods had been for some reason or other returned to their owners, or were privately sold back to them. So-called "blind names" were discovered in the books, as well as names of persons who had nothing to do with the corruption. Fines had been refunded at the intercession of some councillors, and board members had appropriated for themselves remunerations higher than permitted. No oath of purgation on entering office had been taken by new appointees who had paid for their positions. Prices were also revealed: fl.6,000 for an auctioneer's position, fl.3,600 to fl.6,000 for that of a "commies ter recherche," although substitutes often did the actual labor.

Secret agreements between groups of councillors like those in Zeeland were also revealed in the *De Hollandse Mercurius*. The committee of investigation in its report twice made the observation that there was "relaxation, decay and disorder in all departments of the admiralty," but the committee remarked as well that the situation was not any different in the other admiralties. Historians must accept this observation, knowing also that it was made on the eve of a war in which the admiralties undertook activities on a scale never before known. Only the poor "commiezen ter recherche" were punished; the councillors got off scot-free.[52]

Those councillors of the larger admiralties who took their jobs seriously were kept quite busy, for in addition to being present at the regular weekly meetings, one or more of them had to supervise the activities in the dockyard, to attend the mustering and the signing off of the ships' crews, and to inspect the ships on their departure and return to the roadsteads of Texel, Hellevoetsluis, and Walcheren. At consultations in the Haagse Besogne and with the States General, each admiralty was expected to be represented by two or three councillors and its secretary, or "advocate fiscal" —one of the most influential and financially rewarding offices in the naval administration. All this business could be time-consuming, the more so when traveling was done by coach, barge, or the admiralty yacht. The ordinary meetings and discussions seldom filled the whole day, however. A councillorship was considered a major function which was not supposed to be combined with any other major government job. The representative of the city of Amsterdam, for instance, did not have another commission in his city during his councillorship. Amsterdam's representatives were always prominent former burgomasters who, after a period at the Prinsenhof, were in most cases elected for second terms as burgomasters. Cornelis Geelvinck was burgomaster in 1684, admiralty councillor from 1685 to 1687, and then in 1688 again one of the burgomasters. These officials certainly looked after their own interests and those of their relatives. While Henrick Hooft was on the board in the years from 1666 to 1668, his son Hendrick was appointed advocate fiscal. Geelvinck, who had a personal score to settle with Cornelis Tromp, withheld naval assignments from him in the admiral's later years.[53] At Harlingen, however, the councillor must have been a gentleman of leisure during most periods, due to the small scope of the Frisian administration and the few naval activities.

During the three Anglo-Dutch wars (1652–1674), the regents were in frequent and close touch with the naval affairs being handled by the admiralty boards, the Provincial States, and the States General. Naval matters in those days were closely linked to politics, and many a regent came in contact with flag officers and other seamen ashore and on board. The very territorial integrity of the Seven Provinces was at stake, and vital economic interests were threatened at various times by England, France, and the Baltic states. The new standing navy had become a powerful weapon, but it was also an expensive one. The rulers had no choice but to be involved with it. John de Witt's strong personal interest gave the navy even greater visibility. For political reasons, in 1652 he had openly expressed the view that regents could better safeguard Dutch maritime interests than a prince of Orange in his capacity as admiral general. And De Witt put his conviction into action. Immediately after having been appointed grand pensionary, he arranged that thirteen members from the States General went to Texel's roadstead to inspect the fleet that had just fought the battle off Terheide (August 10, 1653), in which Maarten Tromp had been killed. The States General was in supreme command, and the delegates were fully authorized to make any necessary decisions.[54] It became a common practice for deputations from The Hague to join admiralty councillors at Texel, Hellevoetsluis, and Flushing. Also, as noted above, some members of the States General remained on board the admiral's flagship during most of the campaigns of 1665–1667 as a consequence of De Witt's policies.

Johan Boreel—who together with De Witt and the seventy-three-year-old Rutger Huyghens served as a representative of the States General on De Ruyter's flagship *Delfland* in September 1665—described with a good sense of humor how these three respectable gentlemen had to live at sea, lodged in a cabin with two additional persons. This cabin, equipped with a bed for each man, functioned as a room for sleeping, meeting, and eating; it served also as a toilet and a storage-cupboard filled with provisions of bread, herring, cheese, wine, beer, and candles. "It is a chaos and it tosses about like an ants' nest," said Boreel. The water was stinking, the beer sour. The dinner served at midday forced them to eat groats, broiled herring, stockfish, salted meat, and other basic foods which, to Boreel's surprise, were in no way unpleasant: "it all tastes good and we suffer no bad effect from it." There was no idle time in the whole day, a fact all the more assured by the high waves which "make us work for two in soul and body." Perhaps John de Witt worked less than the others, thanks to the special hammock designed by Christiaan Huygens.[55]

Direct contact and supervision by officials was also maintained during the campaigns of 1672 and 1673, although the permanent presence of a deputation from the States General was not repeated. States General members and admiralty councillors visited the fleet frequently and took part in councils of war, not the least in 1673 when the fleet was operating mostly in Dutch coastal waters. Five times during that year, the so-called "High and Mighty Gentlemen" embarked early in the morning on De Ruyter's *Zeven Provinciën* and stayed on board the entire day.[56] In his log, De Ruyter could not even remember all their names, especially the Frisian delegate's. These gentlemen were often accompanied by admiralty councillors who visited the fleet on their own, as did a delegation from the States of Holland. Even the tactics for the expected battle at Schooneveld on June 14 were discussed a few hours before the fighting began.

The direct involvement in the navy by such officials disappeared soon after 1673, however. The danger was over, and most naval operations moved away from the North Sea. Visits to the fleet during a campaign became practically impossible. Moreover, William III extended his grip on naval affairs through Job de Wildt, who made needless and undesirable any kind of active participation by the States General. De Wildt had control of all the ropes. Around 1700, a regent's presence on board a man-of-war was no more than a reminiscence of the past, with the exception of the traditional inspection by admiralty councillors upon departure and return. William III's grip on the army was arranged in more or less the same way.[57]

There was, however, still another reason why such close contact between naval personnel and members of the ruling bodies—not to mention the intimacy of sharing living quarters with seamen on board a man-of-war for weeks on end, as Boreel's generation had done—was bound to diminish. In Holland, a process of aristocratization was well on its way by the second half of the seventeenth century and was completed by the first part of the following century. It had started in big cities like Amsterdam and Leiden and was, in a number of respects, to assume importance for the navy at large. The members of the city councils had always been chosen from among the élite citizens, but the councilmen now derived their patrician status from the fact that they were regents. Considering themselves a separate social group, they closed ranks—ranks which they filled by giving important offices to those of their own kind. The right to rule at all levels became their privilege alone. Mobility from the urban lower classes to the regent class did not entirely disappear, but it became more exceptional and happened only when there were no viable candidates for a particular office from within the regent class, or when regent families took advantage of the opportunity to acquire more capital via the marriage of their daughters to rich entrepreneurs and rentiers.[58]

Changes in mind and manners mirrored the new aristocratic perspective. The regents' life-style began to differ greatly from that of other citizens. Their houses were larger and were located along the important canals; expensive furniture and a fair number of servants were commonplace. The use of carriages became standard. During the summer season, life in the countryside—in homesteads, country houses, and small castles—was the fashion. By and large, however, there was no tendency to compete with the nobility, and overly conspicuous consumption was generally avoided. The city remained the regents' base.

As the regents became investors and rentiers, they withdrew from trade and industry. There had always been rentiers in the city councils, but their numbers now increased rapidly in the smaller as well as the bigger cities. From the middle of the seventeenth century in Leiden, for example, no regent played any direct and active role in his city's economic life. In Hoorn and smaller cities, however, some regents remained involved in the business of the VOC or invested money in local breweries as well as shipyards. In general, the regents invested their capital in stocks and bonds. Provincial bonds were highly valued as an investment. Holland in particular needed considerable sums as a result of the many expensive wars. Around 1700, half of the regents' capital was invested in provincial bonds. Investment in real estate (land) and in foreign enterprises was far less common.

The impact of these changes was noticed in the admiralty boards. No longer did the son of a sailmaker sit down at the table in the Prinsenhof, nor did there exist a councillor who had been at sea like Jacob van Neck in earlier days. Another Joost van Coulster with active involvement in shipowning became unthinkable. Though the changes did not occur overnight, they resulted in the disappearance of men with personal experience in shipping and all it entailed. Many a councillor had had a private interest in the "old" navy when merchant vessels were hired and the fleet had to be provisioned. This change in the men's backgrounds might also perhaps explain why the board at Amsterdam gave such great latitude to their minister Job de Wildt, who had been linked with the Amsterdam élite only by his marriage to a daughter of a late city councillor.

One other new trend leading to the regents' growing lack of concern with naval administration was the nature of the new kind of warfare, far-away and geographically widespread. The uncertain situation at sea did stimulate others to coordinate their interests: the merchants and shipowners had learned their lessons from the war against France. The Grand Fleets could no longer operate in the North Sea, having moved their battleground to more southerly waters. With insufficient protection organized for merchant shipping, whaling, and the fishery, the North Sea became a free hunting ground for French privateers. Strong forces of frigates were required, as well as a good system of information about dates of departure of convoys and the whereabouts of the privateers. Businessmen joined together in new, though rather loose, organizations which acted as pressure groups in government and admiralty circles. These organizations like the so-called "Directie van de Oostersche Handel en Reederijen," founded in 1689, coordinated joint sailings to and from the Baltic, the Gulf of Archangel, and the whaling grounds, and promulgated instructions for proper sailing practices in a convoy.

The admiralties, especially the one at Amsterdam, had also adapted their activities to the new circumstances. More frigates were built, and exactly half of the ships fitted out in 1696 were for convoy duties. The same trend could be noticed in the English navy. When war broke out in 1702, it was almost a matter of routine for the Directie to be consulted by the board of admiralty at Amsterdam.[59] While the concern about the naval obligations with the English allies diminished, the attention and the opportunities for convoys increased. The Directie and its sister organizations put pressure on the allocation of the convoy escorts.

BATTLE OF GIBRALTAR, APRIL 25, 1607. Fifteen years after the event, the admiralty of Amsterdam offered a huge painting (180x490 cm) of this successful battle to Prince Maurice, stadholder and admiral general. This fragment shows the *Rode Leeuw* of vice admiral L. J. Alteras of Zeeland with lots of human details.

Painting by C. Cl. van Wieringen, 1622. Collectie Vereeniging Nederlandsch Historisch Scheepvaart Museum, Rijksmuseum Nederlands Scheepvaartmuseum, Amsterdam.

BATTLE OF THE DOWNS, OCTOBER 21, 1639. To the right, M. H. Tromp's flagship, *Aemilia*; in the middle, vice admiral J. Evertsen of Zeeland—both showing the bloody flag at the poop. In the background, Spanish vessels; and to the left, the English coast.

Painting by H. van Antonissen. Collectie Vereeniging Nederlandsch Historisch Scheepvaart Museum, Rijksmuseum Nederlands Scheepvaartmuseum, Amsterdam.

PIET HEYN (1577–1629), LIEUTENANT ADMIRAL OF HOLLAND AND WESTFRIESLAND IN 1629. His previous career was with the East India Company, the mercantile marine, and the West India Company. His most daring and still well-known exploit was the capture of the Spanish treasure fleet off Cuba in 1628.

Engraving by W. Hondius after J. Dame, ca. 1624. Collectie Vereeniging Nederlandsch Historisch Scheepvaart Museum, Rijksmuseum Nederlands Scheepvaartmuseum, Amsterdam.

MAARTEN HARPERTSZOON TROMP (1598–1653), THE MOST OUTSTANDING AND BELOVED ADMIRAL IN THE PERIOD OF THE "OLD NAVY". Engraving by C. van Dalen after J. Lievens, ca. 1652–1653. Collectie Vereeniging Nederlandsch Historisch Scheepvaart Museum, Rijksmuseum Nederlands Scheepvaartmuseum, Amsterdam.

COUNCIL OF WAR ON JUNE 10, 1666, ON THE EVE OF THE FOUR DAYS' BATTLE. All flag officers and captains went on board the *Zeven Provinciën*, Admiral M. A. de Ruyter's famous flagship.

Pen drawing by W. van de Velde the Elder. Rijksmuseum, Amsterdam.

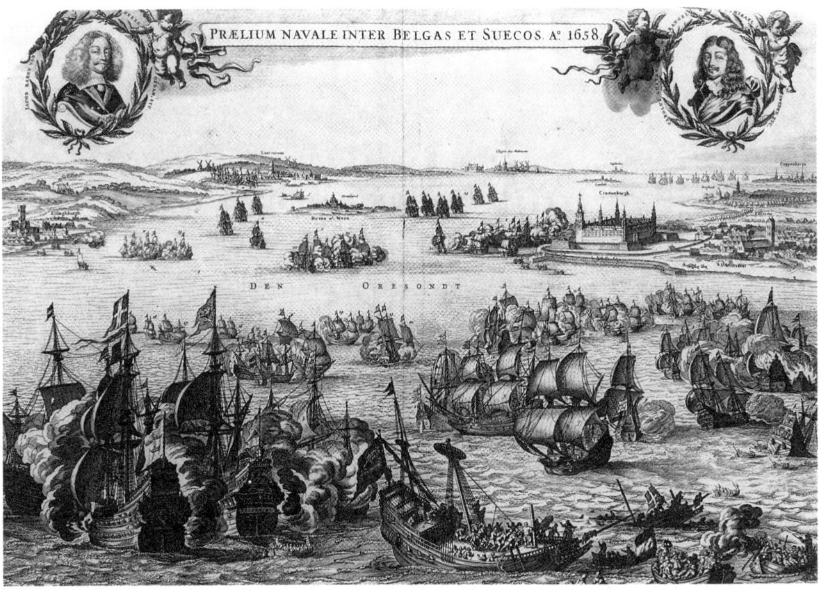

BATTLE IN THE SOUND, NOVEMBER 8, 1658. To the left, the fight between the Dutch and Swedish commanders J. van Wassenaer-Obdam and C. G. Wrangel on board the *Eendracht* and the *Victoria*. In the middle, Vice Admiral W. de With's *Brederode* in sinking position; the vice admiral himself was killed.

Engraving by C. J. Visscher. Collectie Vereeniging Nederlandsch Historisch Scheepvaart Museum, Rijksmusem Nederlands Scheepvaartmuseum, Amsterdam.

FOUR DAYS' BATTLE OF JUNE 11–14, 1666. During the last day of the longest sea battle in history, Prince Rupert's flagship *Royal James* was so badly damaged that it had to be towed away.

Painting by W. van de Velde the Younger. Collectie Vereeniging Nederlandsch Historisch Scheepvaart Museum, Rijksmuseum Nederlands Scheepvaartmuseum, Amsterdam.

MICHIEL ADRIAANSZOON DE RUYTER (1609–1676), REGARDED AS THE MOST OUTSTANDING ADMIRAL IN DUTCH NAVAL HISTORY. At first active in whaling and in the mercantile marine—his naval command in 1641 was only temporary—he joined the navy in 1652. Like P. Heyn and M. H. Tromp, he was killed in battle.

Painting by F. Bol, 1667. In the background, probably the *Zeven Provinciën*, painted by W. van de Velde the Younger. Collectie Vereeniging Nederlandsch Historisch Scheepvaart Museum, Rijksmuseum Nederlands Scheepvaartmuseum, Amsterdam.

JOHN DE WITT (1625–1672), GRAND PENSIONARY OF HOLLAND AND THE DRIVING FORCE BEHIND THE "NEW NAVY". In the background, a meeting hall at The Hague.

Engraving by L. Visscher after J. de Baan (ca. 1672). Collectie Vereeniging Nederlandsch Historisch Scheepvaart Museum, Rijksmuseum Nederlands Scheepvaartmuseum, Amsterdam.

JOHN DE WITT PILOTING THE NAVY. The grand pensionary took a keen interest in all kinds of practical naval affairs. In August 1665, he showed hesitant pilots that the Spanjaardsgat, one of the inlets of Texel, could be navigated by a naval squadron. He was on board as one of the representatives of the States General and remained at sea until November.

De Witten Wonder Spiegel (fragment), etching by R. de Hooghe. Stichting Atlas Van Stolk, Rotterdam.

BATTLE OF TEXEL, AUGUST 21, 1673. A stubborn single combat between the Dutch and English seconds-in-command C. Tromp on the *Gouden Leeuw* and E. Spragg on the *Royal Prince*. Spragg's mizzen mast had already been shot down.

Painting by W. van de Velde the Younger. Collectie Vereeniging Nederlandsch Historisch Scheepvaart Museum, Rijksmuseum Nederlands Scheepvaartmuseum, Amsterdam.

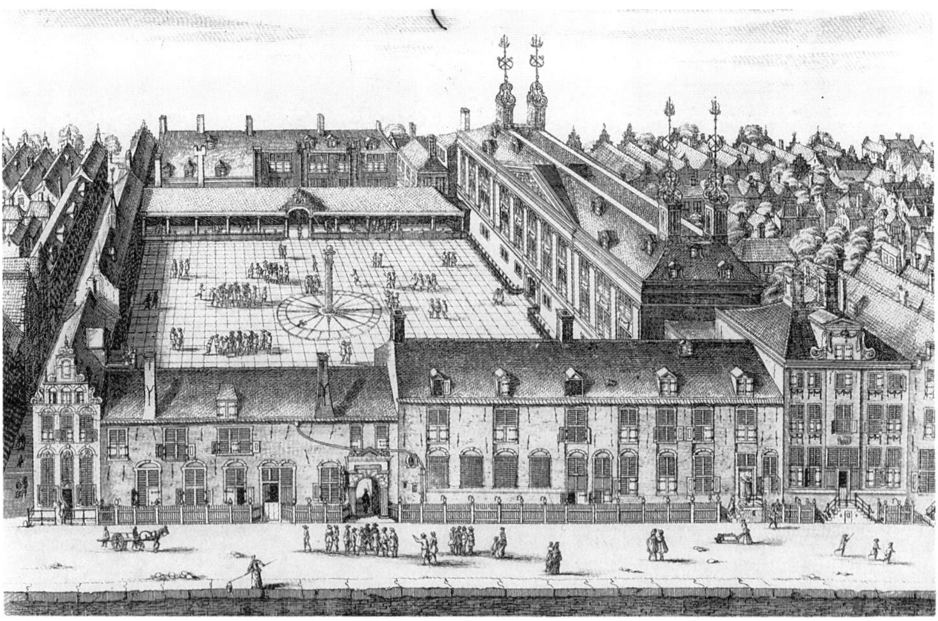

THE ADMINISTRATIVE CENTER OF THE ADMIRALTY AT AMSTERDAM, THE SO-CALLED "PRINSENHOF," LOCATED IN THE CENTER OF THE CITY. Here the councillors almost daily met.

Print in O. Dapper, *Historische beschrijving der stadt Amsterdam*, 1663. Photo by Historisch Topografische Atlas Gemeentelijke Archiefdienst, Amsterdam.

THE NAVAL DOCKYARD AND THE HUGE STOREHOUSE " 'S LANDS ZEEMAGAZIJN" AT AMSTERDAM.

Print in C. Commelin, *Beschryvinge van Amsterdam*, 1693. Photo by Historisch Topografische Atlas Gemeentelijke Archiefdienst, Amsterdam.

CORNELIS SCHRIJVER (1687–1768), NAVAL CAPTAIN AND FLAG OFFICER OF THE ADMIRALTY AT AMSTERDAM. A sharp critic of the decline of the navy in his days, he was a successful commander against the Barbary corsairs and an innovator of shipbuilding methods.

Painting by J. M. Quinkhard, 1736. Westfries Museum, auxiliary branch Huis Verloren, Hoorn.

MARIA LE PLA (1697–1784), WIFE OF CORNELIS SCHRIJVER, AND THEIR DAUGHTER MARIA PHILIPPINA (1732–1798). Pendant portraits were quite common.

Painting by J. M. Quinkhard, 1736. Westfries Museum, auxiliary branch Huis Verloren, Hoorn.

LUBBERT ADOLF TORCK (1687–1758), NOBLEMAN FROM GELDERLAND, COUNCILLOR OF THE ADMIRALTY AT AMSTERDAM FROM 1717 TO 1741 OR 1744. A strong and influential personality, he was often in conflict with the Holland members in the Council.

Painting after A. Boonen, ca. 1723. Photo by Iconografisch Bureau, The Hague.

THE NAVAL RECRUITMENT. At the start of the Fourth Anglo-Dutch War (1780–1784), the navy needed many hands. Music, drinks, and bounties were used to attract men to the recruitment offices.

Anonymous watercolor, 1781. Collectie Vereeniging Nederlandsch Historisch Scheepvaart Museum, Rijksmuseum Nederlands Scheepvaartmuseum, Amsterdam.

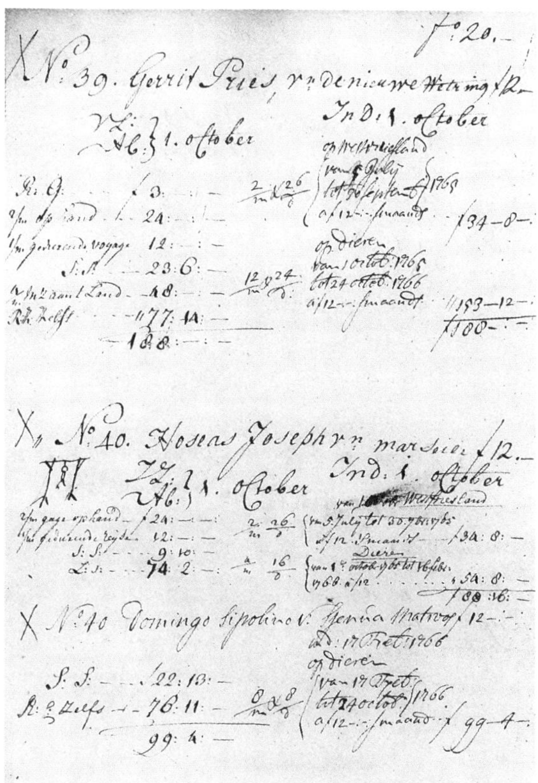
f° 20.–

X N° 39. Gerrit Pries, v: de nieuwe Wetering f 12.–

X N° 40. Hosea Joseph v: marseille f 12.–

X N° 40 Domingo Sipolino v: Genua Matroos f 12.–

PAGE FROM THE MUSTER ROLL OF THE *DIEREN* OF THE ADMIRALTY OF THE NOORDERKWARTIER, 1765–1766. No. 40, a seaman from Marseille, France, ran away on February 16, 1766, together with a colleague from Naples, Italy. He was sentenced to the gallows. The simple sketch of the gallows makes this clear.

The Hague, General State Archives, Admiralties Archives 3124.

JAN HENDRIK VAN KINSBERGEN (1735–1819), important naval officer in the last quarter of the eighteenth century; full of innovative ideas, he was the author of several naval instruction books. From 1771 to 1775, he served in the Russian navy.

Print by R. Vinkeles after H. Pothoven, 1781. Collectie Vereeniging Nederlandsch Historisch Scheepvaart Museum, Rijksmuseum Nederlands Scheepvaartmuseum, Amsterdam.

BATTLE OF THE DOGGER BANK, AUGUST 5, 1781. The Dutch and British (to the left) squadrons, both sailing in single line ahead.

Engraving by R. Muys after E. Hoogerheyden, 1784. Collectie Vereeniging Nederlandsch Historisch Scheepvaart Museum, Rijksmuseum Nederlands Scheepvaartmuseum, Amsterdam.

De Ruyter and the Other Naval Officers

It is difficult to present a consistent picture of the naval officers of the first half of the seventeenth century. The term "corps" is hardly applicable to that group as it was then. Much changed after 1650. The navy, though split up into five admiralties, now was an independent organization, with its own ships, captains, and other officers. The merchant masters and the commanders of the urban "directieschepen" disappeared during the fifties. The captains and other officers were all selected by the admiralties themselves. They began to form a corps, manifesting the elements associated with that term—officers of all ranks with the technical skills necessary for handling a ship, especially in battle. At the very least, they were now able to give the appropriate orders. It was exceptional that a landlubber or an outsider was put in direct command of a fleet or even a single ship. Obdam, both an exception and a mistake, was the last of such. Almost all the post-1650 captains had spent at least a few years in junior ranks before they received their captain's commission.

Officers were required to have some specific knowledge and experience and to adhere to the printed instructions with regard to shipboard life and fighting that had been issued after the Second Anglo-Dutch War. Young nobleman Johan Willem baron van Rechteren, for instance, recorded all he learned on board during the years from 1690 through 1697 in his "memorial," dealing with navigation, rigging, masts, ropes, signals, and so on. Most officers remained in naval service for their entire careers; the navy was not an intermediate station for a totally different occupation, or a stepping stone to higher offices. Officers began to be considered a group of professionals with common experiences from naval campaigns and convoy trips. The "new" navy held a complete monopoly of force, for the wars against England and

France had given ample evidence that only the navy could safeguard certain elements of the national interest.[60]

The establishment of a standing navy, especially after its drastic expansion in the 1660s and the commitment to fit out squadrons and whole fleets, almost continuously compelled the naval administrators to ensure that they could rely on a qualified corps of officers. Ships were larger and often manned by four to six hundred seamen and soldiers. And more ships required more captains and flag officers. The admiralties at Amsterdam and Rotterdam responded to this demand by appointing greater numbers of captains for permanent service in 1661 and 1663, who were guaranteed the so-called "extra-ordinaris" captain's promotion to an "ordinaris" (permanent) post when a vacancy occurred.

In the early 1660s, more decisions were made to enlarge the reservoir of naval officers, the admiralty at Amsterdam generally setting the example for the others. The number of flag captains on board flagships was increased to two or three, depending upon the rank of the flag officer. Officers not yet holding the rank of captain were given command of frigates and could use the title of "Commandeur." In the "old" navy, captains usually had only a single lieutenant at hand; now the number of lieutenants was doubled and tripled according to their ships' rates. The same sort of structure applied to midshipmen; four were placed on board the larger vessels, for example. Admiralty councillors by rotation had their turn to suggest candidates for officer rank. Second lieutenants were regularly recruited from the staff of petty officers. Though the admiralties of Zeeland, Noorderkwartier, and Friesland lagged behind in taking these kinds of measures, the overall size and quality of the officers' corps were greatly enhanced. Sailing and fighting experience was always quickly gained by these men.[61]

Virtually no other reforms were introduced throughout the rest of the period. In 1683, the difference in rank between ordinares and extra-ordinares captains was abolished; only the financial aspect of the two ranks remained in force. An officer's appointment did not depend on the candidate's passing any sort of exam The right connections with the naval administrators and practical experience ("sea legs") counted. No admiralty checked the navigational knowledge or any other qualifications of its officers. The admiralty of the Maze was the only admiralty to introduce an exam for its "commandeurs" and first lieutenants which was administered by the senior officers. This practice was initiated in 1698 but was not undertaken by the other admiralties.[62]

Regular employment, much practical experience, a measure of official instruction, and a hierarchy of ranks and types of commands were instrumental in the creation of an officers' corps for the "new" navy. It would, however, take until the second half of the eighteenth century for the naval administration to have any real influence upon the professional knowledge of its officers. In the meantime, the top echelons of the corps were enlarged, thereby increasing the opportunities for officers to move up the in the hierarchy of leadership. The financial rewards for flag officers and captains were often very substantial. The social background of naval officers became more homogeneous, with the process of aristocratization having made its impact.

The size of the flag officers' corps quickly adjusted to the demands of the time. The expansion resulted not only from rational arguments but also from provincial rivalry between Holland and Zeeland. During the first half of the seventeenth century, only three flag officers had permanent appointments: the lieutenant admiral and the vice admiral of Holland and West-Friesland and the vice admiral of Zeeland—the latter province having had its lieutenant admiralship unoccupied since 1627. All other flag officers were appointed for just one campaign. The Provincial States were responsible for these appointments; the States General or the admiral general could choose between only two candidates for a captain's position. In November 1653, Holland, at De Witt's instigation, increased its number of flag officers. Each admiralty from then on would have a vice admiral and a rear admiral, with one lieutenant admiral for Holland as a whole, thus creating seven positions for flag officers.

Zeeland did not follow this example, having always been eager to provide the fleet with the supreme commander. Provincial antagonism with Holland was no longer tempered by the influence of an admiral general, and Zeeland wanted to forestall a new insult over the issue of the second-in-command. After Tromp's death in August 1653, Vice Admiral Johan Evertsen was not accepted by Holland as the temporary supreme commander. On the eve of the Second Anglo-Dutch War, in December 1664, Zeeland appointed Evertsen to the vacant lieutenant admiralship position, taking for granted that its highest flag officer would now be the second man in the Grand Fleet. Six weeks passed before Holland reacted by upgrading its three vice admirals to the rank of lieutenant admiral in the three respective admiralties and immediately filled the slots of vice and rear admirals. Holland now had ten flag officers. The Provincial States of Friesland then also decided to have its own flag officers as well and, in April 1665, created its own lieutenant, vice, and rear admirals.[63] Obdam, lieutenant admiral of Holland, was in the company of fifteen other flag officers, and the Zeeland plan to have Evertsen become second-in-command failed. It was Cornelis Tromp, not Johan Evertsen, who commanded the fleet after Obdam's death in the battle of Lowestoft. Only on one occasion would a Zeeland flag officer command the Dutch fleet—in 1690, as noted above.

The sixteen flag officers' positions remained in existence, and vacancies were regularly filled. The total of about eighty captains thus had bright prospects of promotion, the more so when wars took their toll among the flag officers. The battles during the Second Anglo-Dutch War alone cost the lives of eight flag officers, while the Third War claimed five. The financial rewards of flag rank were considerable: a lieutenant admiral's monthly salary was fl.300; a vice admiral's, fl.200; and a rear admiral's, fl.100. The flag officers were also entitled to a portion of prize money distributed to captains and crews of their own admiralty. Even without an active command, an officer could depend upon basic earnings that were quite substantial. Frisian flag officers in particular enjoyed this luxury once the wars against England were over; George Johan van Weede during his lieutenant admiralship of the Noorderkwartier (1682–1697) never commanded a ship or a squadron.[64]

The Provincial States typically appointed their own citizens as flag officers—although De Ruyter, from Flushing, was one of the rare exceptions when in 1653 he became a vice admiral of Amsterdam. The officers of Holland, however, were always able to move from one of its three admiralties to the other. Promotion was earned in stages; a vice admiral, for instance, moved to a vacant lieutenant admiral's position. A rear admiral was often selected from among senior captains and commodores, though very junior promotions also occurred. In 1673, De Ruyter's son Engel was promoted rear admiral at the age of twenty-four, in spite of his father's suggesting another candidate! A few examples of flag officers' careers illustrate the system. Aert van Nes (1626–1693), commissioned a captain at Rotterdam in 1652, was promoted to rear admiral in 1662; three years later, he was advanced to the rank of vice admiral and in 1666 was upgraded to lieutenant admiral when Cornelis Tromp moved from Rotterdam to Amsterdam. Jan den Haen (1630–1676), beginning service with the admiralty at Amsterdam in 1659 as a captain, won promotion to rear admiral in 1670 and to vice admiral three years later; he was killed during the Mediterranean campaign. Gerard Callenburgh (1642–1722) became a captain at Rotterdam in 1674, won an unexpected appointment as vice admiral of the Noorderkwartier in 1689, and ended his career as the lieutenant admiral of the Maze, a position he had attained in 1709. Karel van de Putte (ca. 1640–1695) had been a captain in Zeeland since 1666; having risen to rear admiral in 1679, he was made vice admiral of Zeeland five years later.

Promotion to a higher rank was not always routine. On several occasions, William III demonstrated his grip on naval affairs by transferring a number of flag officers to other admiralties—a privilege of the Provincial States—and by passing over obvious candidates.[65] Generally it is hard to discern the reasons why persons failed to be promoted, but some have been recorded. For example, Grand Pensionary John de Witt was concerned about securing a highly qualified corps of flag officers. On June 19, 1667, the rear admiral of Amsterdam, Jan Gideonszoon Verburgh, died and was succeeded four days later by Commodore Willem van der Zaen. De Witt had received the nomination from David de Wildt on June 21. De Witt's brother Cornelis, expecting Verburgh's death, had, however, the previous week strongly recommended another candidate, their cousin Jacob van Meeuwen from Dordrecht. John, believing that Van Meeuwen lacked judgment, was not impressed by Cornelis's letter on Van Meeuwen's behalf, written on board the *Zeven Provinciën* on the Medway. Explaining his own reasoning on the matter, John said of their cousin: "excessive drinking has spoilt his brains or perhaps a former illness has done him harm." Six years later, Van Meeuwen was passed over again, this time in favor of Engel de Ruyter.[66]

Normally it was not a problem to find good candidates for the flag officers' ranks. The almost endless wars, with their naval campaigns and often enormous fleets, provided numerous captains with tactical and practical experience. Apart from a few who held honorary positions, all of the flag officers could show a more or less impressive list of commands. Some officers built up such reputations that distinguished families vied with each other to send their sons to serve under these officers as midshipmen. Particularly in the 1660s, even youngsters from foreign navies were finding their way into the service of Dutch captains and flag officers. From France came Jean Bart and the Count De Guiche, while future Danish admirals Cort Adeler and Niels Juel and the nobleman Rosencrans received their tactical instruction in the Dutch navy.[67] A position on board De Ruyter's ship was highly sought after. The instruction and discussions must have been held in the Dutch language which, in the maritime affairs of those days, was often the international *lingua franca*.

Knowledge of other languages among Dutch officers was undoubtedly rather sparse. By and large, they picked up only a few basic terms in foreign ports. During the Eighty Years' War, however, quite a few officers had spent time in Spanish jails and so became familiar with that language. Vice Admiral Isaac Sweers as a youngster had worked from 1638 till 1646 at Seville and later in Brazil and learned both Spanish and Portuguese. French had not yet become the fashionable mode of conversation in the upper classes. Some curious situations in the effort to communicate must have existed in the common Anglo-Dutch councils of war that were introduced in 1689. A few English officers were familiar with, if not fluent in, Dutch—Henry Killigrew, for one. De Ruyter knew some English. In 1690, Rear Admiral Gillis Schey and captains Abraham Taelman and Rudolf Swaan, who knew no English, were given the help of an interpreter when they were witnesses against the Earl of Torrington in a council of war after the defeat off Beachy Head. Admiral Edward Russell in 1692 had an English and a Dutch secretary, the Dutchman also acting as an interpreter.[68] There is not much evidence that Dutch officers' knowledge of English increased very quickly through the combined naval operations of the seventeenth century. Indeed, during the eighteenth century, it was still remarkable if an officer was familiar with that language. There is no reference to any proficiency in French.

Although the flag officers earned higher salaries and received some special remunerations, they too were very much interested in the financial rewards to be gained by the ships' provisioning system. In the context of the "old" navy, the manner in which men-of-war were provisioned and the finances were arranged has been explained above; that system was continued until 1808. After some fluctuations, the daily allowance was fixed at seven stuivers per seaman and soldier, and nine stuivers per officer (twenty stuivers = one guilder), while the food rations prescribed were not altered. The naval authorities tried to reduce the daily allowance on a number of occasions—for instance, in 1656 and in 1669—and each time, flag officers and captains were successful in jointly lodging written objections against such a decision, complaining that the margin of profit would then be so small that a fair monthly salary would be more preferable. On the eve of the Second Anglo-Dutch War, the admiralties promised to give priority to the "kostpenningen," or provisioning pennies, in order to strengthen the officers' credit with their suppliers.[69] This promise was not kept in later wars.

A captain's—and even more so, a flag officer's—position in the "new" navy was financially attractive. The size and scope of naval operations guaranteed almost permanent employment, and the construction of ever larger ships with more people to feed offered higher earnings. The margin of profit from each daily allowance varied between one third and one fifth. Large sums were involved—for example, the spectacular earnings of De Ruyter. This admiral's personal records reveal how much he spent on victuals and beverages for his men and how big were the portions of food and drink he actually distributed to them. The bookkeeping is in his own handwriting. In 1672, for instance, the *Zeven Provinciën* had a complement of 550 men and was in active service for twenty-five weeks. De Ruyter's margin of profit was about one third, which implies that he made at least fl.10,000 out of his provisioning pennies during that campaign.

An ordinary captain also made good money from his command. Captain Eland du Bois (1642–1676), a younger son of a Schiedam burgomaster, made three short convoy trips with a light frigate over a period of eight months between 1669 and 1670, which he soon followed by a sixteen-month voyage to the Mediterranean on a small ship of the line. The peacetime complements were eighty and 170 hands respectively. In the three years after April 1669, Du Bois received provisioning pennies in the total amount of fl.36,400, the last of which was paid on July 25, 1672. His net profit must have been about fl.10,000.[70]

From the time of the First Anglo-Dutch War, the money involved in the provisioning system was increased almost annually. And this fact was reflected in the social position of the average captain ashore. Obdam's former flag captain Cortenaer, in 1659 promoted to vice admiral, had been only briefly profiting from the provisioning pennies when in 1660 he bought a house worth fl.11,500 on the Nieuwe Haven at Rotterdam. He was of rather common descent, his father having been a soldier. Cortenaer's colleagues benefitted to a similar degree. Captains Jacob Cleydijck and Marinus de Clercq also moved to the Nieuwe Haven during the early sixties. De Clercq had in addition bought a small plot of land and a summer house outside the town gate. Others of their colleagues invested in shares in ships and government bonds or loaned money to private persons, and all of them possessed a number of gold and silver articles, jewelry, and paintings. Several had pendant portraits made of their weddings. The ownership of etchings and some paintings was very common in Dutch middle class and higher households. The inventories of naval officers' households, passed before a notary at their deaths, provide such information. Apparently, ready money was always in the house—at De Clercq's, fl.680; at De Vries's, fl.4,663 (in nine bags). A similar situation was revealed at Harlingen after the Frisian Lieutenant Admiral Tjerk Hiddes de Vries had been killed in the Two Days' Battle of August 1666. Also found after many such officers' deaths were traces of the provisioning of their ships. Stockfish, peas, salted meat, or ship's biscuit were stored in lofts or in private warehouses or perhaps were registered as still being on board their ships. The same applied for all sorts of casks and other packing materials.[71]

Illustrative of the importance of the provisioning pennies with regard to the captain's and flag officers' annual income is the fact that in 1674 the municipal government of Rotterdam seemed to have used its local naval officers' earnings from these pennies as a yardstick when imposing a sort of income tax. Three flag officers and two captains were assessed on the highest scale, two other captains on a lower scale. Ten captains were not assessed because their 1673 income fell just below the assessment limit of 2,000 guilders.[72]

One of the captains in the top scale was Jan van Brakel. Born in 1638, he had distinguished himself as a young captain on the Medway in 1667 and thereafter had been rewarded with the command of large men-of-war. In 1673, while in charge of the *Voorzichtigheid* with 442 men, he was assessed for taxes on an income of fl.6,570. Van Brakel lived in the harbor district of Rotterdam on the Scheepsmakershaven, where he had bought a house in 1672 upon his marriage, and was eventually promoted to rear admiral. When he was killed in 1690 off Beachy Head, his property was valued at about fl.45,000. His widow, who remained in the house, must have had some business acumen, for she bought more property in the harbor district, participated in private trade to Batavia, and had a coach house installed nearby for two black mares and two calashes. At her death in 1700, her daughter was at boarding school in Utrecht. Jan van Brakel and his wife had also taken a great interest in paintings. The inventory mentions the rather extraordinarily high number of seventy-six paintings and three drawings, among which were several seascapes, still lifes, and scenes of daily life by Van der Velde, Steen, Van der Neer, Saftleven, and others. There were also portraits of family members and of four admirals under whom Van Brakel had served: De Ruyter, Cornelis Tromp, Cortenaer, and Jan Corneliszoon Meppel. It was not uncommon for naval officers to own portraits of colleagues; Cornelis Tromp and De Ruyter, for instance, also had quite a number of them in their houses.[73]

Provisioning their ships with victuals and beverages offered captains and flag officers a good additional income but also required much of their personal attention. De Ruyter's records listed all the names of the suppliers whom he had to contact before his ship could sail. While Eland du Bois was already on board his ship, his wife Maria in Schiedam, where her father was a burgomaster, had to take action on her husband's requests to send barley, vegetables, and extra pewter plates and napkins; she was also responsible for a hen coop and empty casks that were returned from the ship. She had a cousin who was a brewer and looked after the beer and its transport. Du Bois managed to buy his bread at nearby Hellevoetsluis at a local bakery. In 1674, Maria du Bois learned at the Prinsenhof that prompt payment of the "kostpenningen" could not be expected; extra provisions had to be forwarded to her husband's and other ships on the French and Spanish coast.[74] Captains occasionally faced complaints about the quantities and the quality of their provisioning. Hendrik Jansz. de Munninck's crew were in a constant state of unrest when they were based in the roadstead of Danzig in September 1656. They had too little to eat, the meat was rotting, the beer was distributed only three times per day (instead of being continuously accessible), and water was not available. De Munninck was fined fl.300 by the council-of-war.[75] At the end of the century, officers began to entrust special agents ("solliciteurs") with the provisioning of their ships.

Apart from the normal profit from the "kostpenningen," captains and flag officers had a few other opportunities to garner extra earnings. So-called "freight money" was quite common in this regard. Merchants regularly wanted safe transport of their bullion, especially the large quantities en route from Cadiz and Lisbon to Amsterdam but also that on other routes. Men-of-war were allowed to provide such safe transport, with the admiralties receiving one percent of the transported value. The commander of the vessel was entitled to a quarter of this freight money. Often, many hundreds of thousands of guilders were carried by one or more men-of-war.

War provided the only opportunity to win prize money. The Dutch captured many hostile merchant vessels and war ships and were often able to retake their own ships that had been captured by the enemy. The richer the prize, the higher the distribution of prize money, but the total amount shared by all on board was rarely more than a few thousand guilders.[76] Flag officers benefitted most from these prizes because they received a comparatively high share of money paid out by their admiralty. Special placards were displayed announcing the tariffs per kind of hostile man-of-war captured or burned. These premiums were more substantial rewards, offered by the States General. Commanders of fireships were rewarded separately for their dangerous efforts. Van Brakel and his men received fl.12,000 in honor of their achievement on the Medway in 1667. Captain Jan Krook of the Noorderkwartier and his crew were awarded fl.6,000 for their timely towing of an English fireship out of the Dutch line of battle during the battle off Kijkduin in 1673.[77]

Not permitted, though often done, was the transport of private goods. Strict rules were in place to prevent this practice but were regularly evaded, even with the connivance of admiralty councillors. In 1671, Du Bois was instructed by one of his councillors to buy three carpets at Smyrna, for which he could draw a bill of exchange on the admiralty's cash at Rotterdam. Like most of his colleagues, Du Bois was not averse to buying luxury goods in Italian and other Mediterranean ports. He spent a total of fl.2,500 on tobacco, silver cutlery, silk stockings, tablecloths, floor tiles, and other items. Such practices were mentioned only in private correspondence or in cases where a commander was prosecuted for some other reason, as occurred with Cornelis Tromp in 1659. During his whole career, Tromp's relations with the naval authorities were problematic, and in 1659 he was sued for not having obeyed their orders. It turned out that on several occasions he had privately arranged the transport of bullion, storing the bags and coffers of gold and silver in his cabin under the bed. Tromp had to repay the admiralty at Amsterdam the 4,200 guilders he had pocketed in this way. It was also proved that he had bought 1,200 to 1,300 pairs of silk stockings at Messina, most of which he had later traded in Spanish ports. Commodities such as floor tiles, olive oil, wines, and Parmesean cheese were all part of Tromp's commercial ventures, for which he was fined an additional 4,000 guilders.[78]

Due to the often unknown opportunities for naval captains and flag officers to earn some extra money to supplement their ordinary monthly wages and the "kostpenningen," it is difficult to give a reliable picture of their overall financial state during the second half of the seventeenth century. The admiralty's administrative records are not a sufficient source of information; one must also study private papers. The claim that most officers were well-to-do citizens has been substantiated above and will be further illustrated below. Although private naval archives virtually do not exist, those of De Ruyter reveal his sources of income and expenditures. His wealth was so extraordinary that he cannot be considered representative of the officer cadre at large.

When De Ruyter was appointed commodore of the admiralty of Zeeland in 1652, he had just retired from merchant shipping. It is not known how much wealth he had accumulated up until that time, except that he had recently bought a comfortable house at Flushing. From 1652 onwards, he commanded squadrons and grand fleets for seventeen terms and was on board a man-of-war more than thirteen years in all. Between 1652 and 1667, he was away from home for about 130 months out of 204. His biographer P. J. Blok has estimated De Ruyter's estate in 1676 at fl.350,000. When he was ashore in 1670 at Amsterdam—living in the large house on the Prins Hendrikkade he had bought in 1661 at a price of fl.28,000—the admiral himself calculated his annual income from interest at fl.10,000, suggesting a principal of fl.250,000 (the rate of interest was four percent). To this sum could be added earnings from diverse sources which would have totaled about fl.7,000 in 1670. His profits from the provisioning pennies up till 1670 had been about fl.70,000, and those from prize money at least fl.35,000. These were his major sources of income. Most of his money was solidly invested in life annuities for his children and in bonds and some East India company shares. Well known for his modest style of living, De Ruyter could easily have expanded his properties during the ensuing years—while commanding such huge ships as the *Zeven Provinciën* and receiving his ordinary wages and diverse other remunerations—to the amount estimated by Blok. A dowry of 12,000 guilders to a daughter would not have been a problem for him.

In an inventory drawn up after De Ruyter's death off Etna, a box whose contents were thirty-eight bonds, seven annuities, and several acknowledgements of debt by private persons is described—a sum amounting to a bit less than fl.300,000. In his account at the Amsterdam Bank of Exchange was fl.16,720, while stored in fifty-two bags in his house was a total of fl.32,500. An extensive collection of precious foreign coins was registered in the inventory, plus a number of jewels and gold and silver objects, often gifts from foreign princes, as De Ruyter's parrot had been. Taking the value of the house itself into account, it is obvious that the admiral's fortune was not far below 400,000 guilders, earned in a way which cannot be criticized by either seventeenth-or twentieth-century standards.[79]

The officers' corps was a varied group of characters and types, often at loggerheads with each other. Misconduct in battle did occur occasionally, but examples of outright incompetence were rare indeed. Personal disagreements were set aside in the national interest, as for example was the quarrel between De Ruyter and Cornelis Tromp in 1673. De Ruyter was above any criticism. The title of "Bestevaer" had been passed on to him. Nevertheless, at times he could be rude to colleagues, even to his second-in-command Aert van Nes.[80] At home in his later years, De Ruyter was regularly visited by distinguished foreigners. His ships' logs still betray his Zeeland dialect and his great religiosity. De Ruyter's death came as a great shock to the people, making his funeral in the Nieuwekerk at Amsterdam an impressive event.

Cornelis Tromp was an entirely different person. He was said to have watched John and Cornelis de Witt's murder by the mob at The Hague in August 1672 without showing any disapproval. As a fighter at sea, he was surpassed by none. In the first battle of Schooneveld (June 7, 1673), he had to change his ship four times. On the English side, only Edward Spragge could be compared with him. The day after the battle, Tromp wrote to his sister: "I have entered into the dance and thank God I am still in good health. I have enjoyed myself like kings."[81]

Eland du Bois, writing about the same battle in a letter to his wife, paid attention to those who had been killed, among whom was the husband of the woman on the Vismarkt at Schiedam. Du Bois's letters to his wife, Maria, all beginning with "Wijffje lief" (Dear Little Wife), are remarkably and disarmingly frank and tender. Written between 1669 and 1674, they reveal his concern for his wife, her pregnancies, and their small children. His sense of humor is apparent when he tells her that he had had all his hair cut off in an attempt to make thicker hair grow in its place—he was then only thirty-two years old—and meanwhile was wearing a small woollen cap. Several letters are very outspoken in his desire to make love with his wife. After having been ill for several months, he died of kidney failure in December 1676.[82]

The complete difference between Du Bois and Tromp had nothing to do with their social background. Tromp had also been well educated. His father had sent him to France to learn some French. Through his stepmother and brothers-in-law, he regularly mixed in the worlds of city and state magistrates, especially after his marriage to an Amsterdam regent's widow in 1667. From then on, Tromp lived either on the Herengracht, one of the most fashionable canals of Amsterdam, or in his magnificent country house at Graveland, designed in the shape of a man-of-war.[83]

Some officers were notorious for their ill-tempered behavior. In 1667, Jan van Brakel came to blows with a lieutenant of the marines on board his ship over a trivial matter. De Ruyter once lodged a complaint with the admiralty at Rotterdam after having been treated improperly by Van Brakel in the street. Nevertheless, Van Brakel was later promoted to rear admiral of the Maze.[84] Captain Cornelis van der Hoeven had slowly climbed the officers' ladder to command the *Oranje* (fifty guns) in 1690, when he got involved in troubles with his senior officer on board. Just returned from having drinks with a colleague and now dressed in his night clothes, he was disturbed by his lieutenant, who had a few questions to ask him. Van der Hoeven got furious, and the two men began to fight. Hearing the shouting, some petty officers rushed to the captain's cabin and saw Van der Hoeven sitting on top of his lieutenant, pounding on him. The two fighters were separated from each other, but a few minutes later, Van der Hoeven, still in his night clothes, came out of his cabin, sword in hand, to look for his opponent. When he discovered the lieutenant, Van der Hoeven swung at him but missed and broke his sword in a doorpost. Van der Hoeven then dug the rest of his sword into the body of the lieutenant, who soon succumbed. What happened further is not known. A clerk briefly mentioned the incident in a ship's log.[85]

Dutch officers took a great dislike to the way in which the allied English admiral Torrington lived aboard his flagship in 1690: captains attended him during his rising and dressing; he often drank to excess, and kept several prostitutes aboard. To the Dutch officers, such ostentatious behavior was simply unbecoming. However, Dutch officers as a whole were by no means saints themselves. When, in 1653, Captain Anthonius van Salingen died while drunk in the bed of a prostitute at Leghorn, Italy, it was officially reported that he "passed away in the Lord." The English opponents knew better and provided their superiors with more explicit information. Engel de Ruyter, in command of a small force to the Levant and cruising in the Cyclades archipelago in 1675, remarked with some chagrin that it was hard to make love with the women of the island of Kea for the simple reason that they were wrapped in hundreds of yards of underwear.[86]

The process of selecting candidates for the post of captain and the higher ranks is difficult to discern. Ability and good connections both counted. Seniority was also a factor but seldom one of prime importance. Many young captains were appointed. The board of an admiralty nominated two candidates, the final choice being made by the States General or the admiral general. William III strongly championed some favorites, and John de Witt was frequently approached by regents to support their local candidate. It is obvious that those cities represented in an admiralty board had certain claims on a captain's position. For some positions, it was explicitly stated that the candidates had to come from, for instance, Enkhuizen or Medemblik. Those councillors who did not participate in an internal board agreement governing appointments complained about their lack of success in promoting their own favorites. The representative of the province of Utrecht at Amsterdam in 1670 finally got a captainship for his provincial nobleman Adam van Brederode, despite the "*manquement* [lack] of friends." In 1667, De Ruyter was not reluctant to recommend his brother-in-law Jan van Gelder and his "sole" son Engel in private letters to the grand pensionary. Secretary Job de Wildt also strongly pushed for his own relatives.[87]

No doubt lieutenants and "commandeurs" who came from the right cities or provinces had better prospects of advancement than equally capable colleagues from other parts of the country. A study of the records of those who were nominated demonstrates that all the candidates had been at sea for many years and had much fighting experience, some of course more than others. Hardly any landlubber was nominated. Diverse candidates had served previously with the East India Company or the merchant marine. Masters of merchant vessels and privateers considered a captain's position a promotion—those who made such a rise in 1665, for instance, being David Vlugh from Enkhuizen, Jan Krook from Alkmaar, and Nicolaas Naaldhout from Veere. Along with seafaring relatives Cornelis de Liefde had a profitable but unspecified market business at Rotterdam. In the case of Maarten de Boer of Enkhuizen, De Boer's father, Jacob, a late rear admiral, was respectfully mentioned by his supporters.[88]

A high proportion of captains and flag officers were closely associated with the regent class, through either their fathers or brothers, or other relatives. Quite a few burgomasters put in a good word for their sons. But these "fashionable" naval officers could also show formidable naval records. And sons of regents in the navy were nothing new. In addition to the two aforementioned Teding van Berkhouts, there were two other officers by that name who commanded naval vessels during the 1670s through the 1690s. The impressive list of such families includes the Sweers, Van Meeuwen, Du Bois, Van Almonde, and Callenburgh; officers such as Joost Verschuur, Willem Schepers,[89] Willem van Ewijk, Philips de Munninck, Philips van der Goes, Gerard and Paulus van der Dussen, Maurits Sels, Jacob Teengs, and Cornelis van Vlooswijk also belong to this category. To this list should be added the increasing number of sons from the nobility in Holland, Friesland, Gelderland, and the remaining provinces—notably, Hans Willem baron van Aylva, Frederik Willem graaf van Bronkhorst-Stirum, Johan Willem baron van Rechteren, and Jan Gerrit baron van Wassenaer. Several members of naval officers' families were incorporated into the group of regents' families—in Zeeland, for example, the Evertsens, Banckerts, and Le Sages. During the 1690s, nine sons of noblemen and regents were among eighteen new captains at Amsterdam.

Generally the admiralties gave most of the officers, from the lower to the higher ranks, ample opportunities for active service and thus for a naval income of commensurate size. The international situation as well as the necessity of permanent protection for convoys provided these opportunities, yet sufficient employment for all of the numerous flag officers did not exist. Several stayed ashore for many years—some, due to age. There were also a few officers who operated on two fronts, in the navy and in local government. In 1665, Tjerk Hiddes de Vries combined his membership of Harlingen's city council with the lieutenant admiralship of Friesland. Gerard Callenburgh was named to the council of Vlaardingen in 1679 and was many times a burgomaster of that fishing village before being appointed a flag officer. Jacob Teengs the Younger, a captain from 1696, became a member of the council of Edam in 1701. Twelve years later, he resigned his captaincy in order to represent his city on the board of his own admiralty.[90]

The changes in minds and manners and the aristocratization of the corps particularly affected the composition of the group of flag officers in the 1680s. It was the same case with all admiralties, but it represented a new trend only insofar as the fact that virtually no common seaman or merchant skipper could now expect to be promoted to the higher ranks. Another Cortenaer and De Ruyter became unlikely. By and large, the current assembly of flag officers had a homogeneous social background, and all could still show a record of active naval service from their youths.

Those officers of the "new" navy who fought in the battles of the three Anglo-Dutch wars traditionally received the bulk of attention from contemporaries and later generations. In order to have a more balanced view of the period as a whole and to do justice to the process of "verdeftiging" (developing aristocratic manners), one must consider the lives of a few representative officers from the second part of this period. First, there was Philips van Almonde (1644–1711) of Brielle, whose father, Pieter, had been a member of the local city council from 1623, a burgomaster, and an active citizen on a provincial level as well. Philips's mother was a sister of Captain Jacob Cleydijck, who had the boy as midshipman on his ships from 1661. It had been arranged that Philips succeed to his uncle Jacob's position after his death, which occurred in 1665. Philips also moved into Cleydijck's house in Rotterdam. Year after year, Philips commanded ships and learned naval tactics from De Ruyter. In October 1673, Philips was promoted to the rear admiralship of the Maze and, in 1684, to the vice admiralship at Amsterdam. He became one of the naval confidants of William III and helped to prepare the trip to Torbay of 1688.

Van Almonde proved to be the right person to command the Dutch naval force in the combined Anglo-Dutch fleets from 1691. The next year he was promoted to lieutenant admiral at Amsterdam, and the same rank at Rotterdam—the highest position by tradition—was bestowed on him in 1708. He was gifted with the right talents to function productively with his English colleagues. In a certain sense, Van Almonde played the same role at sea that Job de Wildt did ashore. He never married. His naval earnings must have been high, for he was able to invest in several vessels, to buy a shipyard and a warehouse in Rotterdam, and, after the peace of Rijswijk in 1697, to pay 32,000 guilders for the country house "Haaswijk" at Oegstgeest, near Leiden, where he lived until his death.[91]

The last direct scion in the Evertsen dynasty was Geleyn Evertsen (1655–1721), the son of Cornelis the Elder and the younger brother of Cornelis the Youngest. Like his father had done with his uncle Johan in earlier days, he followed his brother in rising through the naval ranks. He was two levels below Cornelis when Cornelis became a rear admiral of Zeeland in 1685. Geleyn received his captain's commission in 1679. He took part in most of the naval campaigns in the Nine Years' War and in the beginning of the War of the Spanish Succession. From 1704 on, he stayed ashore like many other flag officers—including Van Almonde, from 1706—in order to avoid having to serve under an English officer of lower rank. Geleyn Evertsen had become a vice admiral in 1695, and in 1707, he succeeded his brother to the lieutenant admiralship. Geleyn married twice but had no children. His first wife was the daughter of the provincial treasurer, his second belonged to the most influential regent family, the De Citters of Middelburg. At his death, Geleyn bequeathed his wife Johanna a house at Middelburg, the homestead "Zeerust," and some land, jewels, bonds, and East India Company shares, all together valued at 200,000 guilders.[92]

Both Jan Gerrit baron van Wassenaer (1672–1723) and Philips Schrijver (1649–1711) received commissions as ordinary captains at Amsterdam in 1690. Jan Gerrit, only eighteen years old at the time, already had eight years of naval experience. Philips Schrijver was forty-one and had been an extraordinary captain since 1685. Jan Gerrit belonged to the well-known Van Wassenaer family of the nobility of Holland, though he was not directly related to Obdam. Philips Schrijver, whose father had held the office of postmaster at Amsterdam, married the daughter of naval captain Cornelis Tijloos in 1684; they had five children. Jan Gerrit married the daughter of another nobleman of Holland in 1707, when he was thirty-five—about the same age Schrijver had been when he was wed. Here the similarities ended, however, for the baron Van Wassenaer enjoyed much more support in his career than Schrijver did.

Van Wassenaer's career began in 1690 as Van Almonde's flag captain, with his own commands following soon and regularly. His knowledge of English made him especially useful. In 1700, he was made rear admiral, and in 1703, vice admiral at Amsterdam. With regard to this second promotion, Job de Wildt remarked that Van Wassenaer would not have any problem in getting the nomination "thanks to the influence of his friends."[93] Van Wassenaer thereafter became the leading flag officer of the Dutch navy in the final phase of the War of the Spanish Succession. In 1709, he was appointed lieutenant admiral of the Noorderkwartier. One of the consequences of this promotion was a reshuffling of flag officers at Amsterdam and a vacancy for a rear admiral.

Philips Schrijver distinguished himself for valor in major battles and other encounters with French men-of-war and privateers—after 1697, being regularly accompanied by his second son, Cornelis, who was born in 1687. In 1707, Philips was the commodore of the squadron protecting the return fleet of the VOC. It was for Schrijver the third opportunity to be promoted, but again he was passed over, this time in favor of nobleman Cornelis van Aerssen van Sommelsdijk. Philips gave up and, in 1710, asked to retire. The following year he died, according to his son Cornelis, "out of deep chagrin." That same year, Van Wassenaer returned to Amsterdam to become lieutenant admiral of his old admiralty. Cornelis Schrijver, who had recently acquired more seagoing and fighting experience on board the flagships of Van Wassenaer and Van Aerssen, was in 1711 appointed ordinary captain, probably out of respect for his father.

Unlike Van Wassenaer, Philips Schrijver had relied on the navy as his main source of income. Schrijver had invested in bonds and in a merchant vessel, and in 1701, had bought a house on the Herengracht. It took his five children five years to divide the inheritance because of the simple fact that the admiralty was not able to pay the "kostpenningen" past the year 1709. At long last, the total value of Philips Schrijver's properties was confirmed at more than 200,000 guilders.[94] The problems of the admiralty at Amsterdam with which the Schrijver family happened to be confronted in 1711 would affect not only that family itself but all captains and flag officers in the Dutch Republic. It was one of the signals that the navy had struck foul weather.

Well-manned Ships

Problems such as those experienced by the Schrijver family seldom occurred with the common seaman of the Dutch Navy, who had little opportunity to accumulate wealth. It was a world of great differences between the officers on the one hand, especially between captains and flag officers, and the rest of the crew on the other. Even the Frisian rear admiral Hendrick Bruynsveld with an estimated capital of only 40,000 guilders in 1672 belonged to the twenty richest citizens of Harlingen.[95] In social as well as financial matters, there was little dividing the city élite and the navy, since most officers were members of that élite or were closely associated with it. The division between classes existed mainly on board ship and was quite obvious—even in the location of berths, with all officers lodged on the quarterdeck, and the rest of the crew mostly in the forecastle.

The common seaman did not earn much money while on active duty in the navy, and always less than his counterpart in the merchant marine. In peacetime, his services were not in great demand. The monthly wage paid to an able seaman by the admiralty of Zeeland in 1669, for instance, was twelve guilders; a first mate was paid thirty guilders. During a war, the wage level rose significantly, for example, from twelve to fifteen guilders for an able seaman. It was a matter of supply and demand, and if there were a shortage of seamen, naval authorities responded to that need by increasing the wages. John de Witt was strongly against such a quick response, preferring a stable level of wages as "an iron law" that offered no hope of an increase. "Otherwise," he said, "the state is at the discretion of Jan Hagel [the riff-raff]." His thoughts, uttered in 1665, were generally accepted—a fact that prevented a repetition of the crisis in 1653 when seamen had successfully demanded eighteen guilders per month.[96]

During most wars of the period 1652–1713, the able seaman's wage fluctuated between twelve and fifteen guilders. In the years 1672 and 1673, however, so many men were needed in the navy as well as in the army that unorthodox measures were required to assure that the fleet would be adequately manned. Coastal fishermen were offered freedom from the poll tax if they joined the navy, and the wages were much higher than before. In 1673, an able seaman aboard Cornelis Tromp's *Gouden Leeuw* earned seventeen guilders, each first and second mate thirty-six.[97]

Merchant seamen and fishermen were never physically compelled to enlist—i.e., impressed—in the navy, but in wartime the authorities cleverly created circumstances in which such men were made more willing to consider naval service. In the spring, at the start of the fighting season, an embargo was often imposed on shipping; the merchant and whaling fleets, some of the fishing boats, and the privateers were simply not allowed to sail and employ the available seamen. The East Indiamen were the sole exception to this ruling. Later, in the autumn, the embargo was temporarily lifted. Seamen needing to earn a living thus had to respond to the tuck of the drum from the naval captains and their recruiting officers. Occasionally the naval authorities stimulated shipowners to help recruit men for the navy. In 1659 the whaling industry feared an embargo, for De Ruyter's Baltic fleet was in dire need of hands. In return for permission to sail, the whaling shipowners offered to recruit 1,200 seamen for the navy at fifteen guilders per month. They kept their word, and within two weeks, in May the said number of seamen were able to join the fleet already waiting for them in the roadstead. This group of men was comprised mostly of "corn-and bag-porters": former seamen unemployed because of the embargo and attracted by an enlistment bounty from the shipowners. This system of recruitment for the navy by the shipowners, also applied in later times, was called "the delivery of the third or fifth man," meaning that for each three or five men recruited by shipowners, one man was offered to the navy.[98]

In time of peace, captains seldom faced any problems when attempting to recruit the required numbers of seamen, and even during the wars, it was always unlikely that at the men-of-war scheduled to sail at the last minute would have to remain in port for lack of manpower. The embargo measures, higher wages, and some occasional bounties were effective in getting the fleet sufficiently manned. Such procedures meant that the wars were fought by crews who largely had no permanent bond with the navy, although the frequency of naval campaigns would suggest otherwise. At the end of the fighting season, all hands were paid off (discharged), and most found work with their previous employers or others in the merchant, whaling, and fishing trades. But during the interim, the navy was able to enjoy the service of trained seamen.

The navy's claim upon the labor market in time of war was high, as can be seen by the few figures already cited. Taking into account the battle fleet and convoys, some 20,000 to 24,000 men were in the naval service during both the Third Anglo-Dutch War and the Nine Years' War. Fewer numbers were required during the War of the Spanish Succession, the total dwindling from about 17,000 men at the start to some 14,000 at the cessation of the conflict. In order for these figures to appear in the proper perspective, we must realize that during the 1690s, for instance, the East India Company annually needed a fresh supply of 4,000 to 4,500 men for their outward-bound ships. The whaling and merchant fleets, which were badly hit by embargoes and other measures, required in periods of peace about 9,000 and 20,000 seamen respectively.[99]

Now and then, the naval and state authorities discussed the possibility of forming some kind of naval reserve. Their utter dependence upon commercial shipping to provide men was not to everybody's liking. In 1659, one proposal was made to have a corps of 6,000 seamen in permanent service who would each receive a retaining fee in time of peace and be immediately available if war broke out. To this proposal was added an earlier suggestion to quarter a few regiments of marines in the port cities, but these ideas were only partially implemented.

Ordinary soldiers were usually on board men-of-war, and although they belonged to army regiments, they were not commanded by their own officers, and among the seamen were often regarded as second-class. In December 1665, the States of Holland endorsed De Witt's proposal for a regiment of 4,000 "zeesoldaten" (marines) consisting of twenty companies to be recruited from people with seagoing experience. An army colonel, Van Ghent, was put in command of the regiment; soon incorporated into the naval officers' corps, he was promoted to flag officer. The corps met the expectations of the time, but the other provinces did not follow the example of Holland. As a consequence, the ordinary soldiers from the army continued to be used as well as the marines. In the English navy, the same need for a standing body of servicemen had led to the founding of a corps of marines in

1664. The regiment of Holland, however, was dissolved after the peace of 1674 and was sorely missed during subsequent naval campaigns. At the instigation of William III, various plans were discussed during the 1680s to establish a new permanent corps of seamen and marines of up to as many as 9,000 men. At long last, in 1698, a new corps of 3,000 marines, divided into one regiment of Zeeland and two of Holland, was created. Up until 1709, this corps took part in many operations in the Mediterranean. A standing corps of ordinary seamen was not set up and never considered seriously.[100]

It is well known that the Dutch labor market consisted not only of Dutchmen but also of endless numbers of foreigners. The market reacted, of course, to upward and downward economic trends and to the conditions of peace and war abroad as well as in the United Provinces. As a consequence, the proportion and the origins of foreigners aboard all Dutch vessels fluctuated a great deal. Little is known about the composition of the crews in the Dutch navy during the seventeenth century. A few random bits of information from the administration of the Zeeland admiralty, however, exist concerning two small frigates for the year 1669, and the first-rate *Zeelandia* (ninety guns) for the year 1694, and the *Oranjezaal* for the year 1709. There was a rather disproportionately low number of petty officers on board the *Zeelandia*. This ship and the *Oranjezaal* both had soldiers on board as well, but these men are not included in the tallies on Table 3 (below).

Naval crews were still a mixture of nationalities. The majority of petty officers and seamen were Dutch; their high proportion on board the two frigates in 1669 is very striking. The Zeeland captains were always able to recruit rather high numbers of petty officers from their own province, and, as before, Flushing was the major recruiting ground. In 1669, Captain Adriaan de Haze enticed six citizens of his native city of Veere to join him, thus completing his crew of fifty-five men. Recruits from the Southern Netherlands and the British Isles figure far less than they did in the 1600 sample, but the proportion of Germans and Scandinavians was slowly increasing. Generally speaking, recruits were more varied in geographical origin, coming from Smyrna, Venice, Batavia, Angola, New England, and even the Philippines. Seamen from France, the enemy in 1694 and 1709, were also used on board Dutch ships—though only on a few of these vessels, mostly from seaports like St. Malo. When several ships at one time had to be fitted out, Zeeland captains had to rely upon the recruiting officers operating outside the province, mainly in Holland. Admiral

Table 3
Geographical Origins of Petty Officers and Men aboard Zeeland Men-of-War in 1669, 1694, and 1709

	1669			*1694*			*1709*		
	petty officers	*seamen*	*%*	*petty officers*	*seamen*	*%*	*petty officers*	*seamen*	*%*
Flushing	16	34	42	7	37	7	12	16	18
rest of Zeeland	12	9	18	9	48	10	9	21	19
Holland	4	5	8	12	186	36	7	16	14
rest of Netherlands	1	7	7	2	52	10	2	4	4
Southern Netherlands	—	5	4	2	50	10	—	3	2
British Isles	1	1	2	—	17	3	—	6	4
Germany	1	2	2	1	40	7	4	16	12
Scandinavia/ Baltic	1	7	7	4	49	10	—	22	14
rest	5	3	7	—	28	5	—	20	12
unknown, but foreign	1	3	3	—	10	2	—	2	1
total	42	76	100	37	518	100	34	126	100

SOURCES: Middelburg, State Archives in Zeeland, Rekenkamer Archives 703, payrolls of the *Vlissingen* and the *Vissersherder*; Rekenkamer Archives 1336 a–d, payroll of the *Zeelandia* (P. M. van der Padt kindly gave me this reference); and Rekenkamer Archives 750, payroll of the *Oranjezaal*.

Geleyn Evertsen was lucky that his recruiting officer managed to find ninety-eight men in the southeastern part of Holland and twenty-four in Rotterdam who were willing to join him on the *Zeelandia*.

Another example is the crew of the Amsterdam man-of-war *Gouden Leeuw* in 1673 under the command of Cornelis Tromp. Of the 374 seamen registered on the payroll, about twenty-five percent (ninety-one, by actual count) were foreigners, completely in line with twenty-six percent in the 1669 figure for Zeeland. Naval service in those days was more popular than it was to be later on. Of the forty-nine petty officers recorded, however, no fewer than twenty-one came from abroad. It is again noteworthy that four petty officers, for instance—coming from places like Plymouth, Dover, and Brittany—were fighting their compatriots in the three great battles of 1673. Tromp's flag captain was the Irishman Thomas Tobiaszoon, who also had his son Jan Thomas registered as an ordinary seaman together with Tromp's nephew Maarten.[101]

When abroad, a captain could fill vacancies in his crew list in different ways. For one, he could try to find foreign and Dutch seamen in overseas ports. The fleet, anchored near the Sound in the summer of 1656, sent a galliot to Norway in hopes of enlisting some Norwegians. It was known that the Danish conscription of subject Norwegians for the navy was very unpopular; many youngsters regularly entered service on Dutch ships to avoid conscription in their own country.[102] With the master's consent, some seamen could also be recruited from Dutch merchantmen. Most seamen did not like to be transferred from one warship to another, not knowing what type the new captain would be. Their engagement was with their captain, not with the admiralty. The most notorious instance of a successful effort by seamen to refuse to accept another commander occurred in 1652, when the crew of the *Brederode* threatened to fire the guns in defiance of authority if Vice Admiral De With dared to come aboard![103]

At the moment of enlistment, crew members received a one or two months' salary in advance; the rest was paid at the end of the particular voyage on which they were embarking. The captain and his clerk were supposed to be present when the men were signed off and paid. During the voyage, captains were not permitted to give their men any money, except under special circumstances—for example, when a Mediterranean trip lasted much longer than had been envisaged. In the bitterly cold winter of 1658–1659 on board the ships off Copenhagen, all men received one month's pay. It is difficult to discover how many of the seamen collected their money themselves at the Prinsenhof. One is inclined to assume that quite a few sailors contracted with various persons involved in such business to act on their behalf. In 1676, ten seamen and two petty officers of the *Delft* jointly mandated one Pieter van Doorne at Rotterdam to collect their earnings.[104] It is also likely that the admiralties issued advance notes to seamen's relatives, often women, who cashed these notes later. This would explain how women like Marietje Vos, Judith Beekman, and Marietje Coesveld cashed the earnings of a great number of crewmen from the *Gouden Leeuw* in 1673. Many seamen collected their wages themselves or had it done by their wives. In this respect, it is worth noting that there are several examples of seamen who got married just before their ships sailed. A navy chaplain celebrated the weddings on board in the roadstead, usually on Sundays.[105]

Naval service was by no means a gold mine for the common seaman. The able seaman of the *Gouden Leeuw* in 1673 who had an extraordinary high wage of seventeen guilders at the end of a six months campaign cashed an average of between forty to sixty guilders, not including the enlistment bonus. Several small amounts were deducted: the fee for the use of the hammock, incidental fines, and expenses to the surgeon. All crew members were assured that they would get their money shortly after returning to port. At each admiralty, the payment of wages had priority above the provisioning pennies. The boards of the admiralties stuck to that policy as long as they could. At the end of the War of the Spanish Succession, however, the Zeeland admiralty was in such dire need of money that some of the crews could not be paid off. The 1709 crew of the *Oranjezaal* , for instance (referred to in Table 3), equipped in 1709, had to wait until 1720 before receiving the money owed to them.[106] By this time, it was mainly the holders of advance notes and other tickets, having bought them far below their par values, who claimed the pay. The Amsterdam admiralty still had sufficient funds to honor its debts, however, and did not resort to the policy of Zeeland.

Prize money and premiums were rare but were always settled some time after a voyage. Prize money allocated to crews may appear to have been sizable, for the records of the auctioneer at Amsterdam reveal that over the years from 1661 to 1676, no less than fl.394,657 was distributed to those on board the men-of-war which had captured prizes. In practice, however, the common seamen received little. In December 1667, four months after the successful raid in the Caribbean under the command of Crijnssen, a crew member could cash the first installment of his prize money in the amount of three-and-a-half months' wages—which, for an able seaman, was forty-two guilders. A second installment in the same amount was not paid until March 1670. Many sailors must have left in the meantime, not knowing what money they were still entitled to. The lieutenant admiral, Banckert, at that time would not have worried about this delay, however, since receiving his allowance of 756 guilders from the 1667 prize money was just one of his prerogatives.[107]

At recruitment, the preference was to find the right mixture of well-trained seamen and novices, but there are no records of complaints about the quality of naval personnel. Only experience at sea transformed a man into a seaman, and the rating of "able seaman" was the highest that could be earned by the lower-deck hands, amongst whom were ordinary and junior seamen and boys. No certificate of any kind had to be produced by a crew member when signing on. The only regulation—a rule introduced by the admiralty at Amsterdam in 1672 and, fifteen years later, also issued in Zeeland—stipulated that no second or third mate was to be appointed unless he could give evidence that he had been sailing for some years in that capacity, or that he had passed an examination. Both admiralties designated a special examiner to test the knowledge and experience of the candidates.[108] Apart from surgeons, no other petty officers were tested.

In the case of pay, the navy followed the general trend ashore, where wages had not been increased since the middle of the seventeenth century, at least in time of peace. The great jump from eight guilders in the 1620s, to twelve for an able seaman had by the 1650s been made. Anything above this was pure war-profit for seagoing personnel. A comparison of wage levels ashore with those of the navy is, of course, rather tricky. A laborer ashore was paid by the day, with lower earnings in the winter. A seaman had a monthly wage with no difference between seasons but was dismissed when his ship returned to port, and he remained unemployed until he found another "hire." It is generally assumed that during the mid-seventeenth century, laborers could work an average 275 days per year, namely twenty-three days per month. But with what kind of laborer is a seaman to be compared? One is inclined to put petty officers and able seamen on a level with skilled day laborers. A carpenter or mason, for instance, earned twenty-six guilders per month (twenty-two to twenty-four stuivers per day), a hodman (the mason's assistant) about nineteen guilders (seventeen stuivers). [109] Most petty officers' wages varied between these two amounts; some were higher, others a bit lower. The able seaman earned far less than the urban hodman.

Two observations have to be made before conclusions can be drawn. First, the daily wages quoted above were earned in the province of Holland in the cities Alkmaar and Leiden. For farm and agricultural laborers in Holland, the daily wages ranged from fifteen to twenty stuivers, while pay for similar labor in the cities like Arnhem and Groningen in the eastern and northern part of the United Provinces was much lower (twelve to sixteen stuivers). A comparison with these figures shows the navy as an attractive employer—a fact that was even more true for foreigners. The wage level abroad was in general much lower than in the Dutch Republic. In inland Germany, for instance, one could earn only half or one third of the wages paid by the navy.[110] Second, a seafaring job always included board and lodging, the significance of which is very difficult to express in terms of money. The value of free board, however, can be roughly estimated at about four stuivers a day, taking into account the captain's margin of profit on the provisioning pennies. Monthly free board would have meant an extra income of five to six guilders. Nothing can be said about the value to be placed on lodging.

One conclusion is obvious. An able seaman in naval service was no better off than a hodman at Leiden or Alkmaar. The earnings in a petty officer's position were more or less comparable to those of an urban carpenter and mason, or possibly even higher. For people from the countryside in Holland and from other parts of the Republic, naval service could be financially attractive. The merchant marine easily rivaled the navy, however , for masters of merchant vessels always paid higher wages than it did. Taking all of this into consideration, and including the then-existing embargo, it is no surprise that in 1694, Evertsen's recruiting officer was able to enlist ninety-eight men from some of Holland's small villages and towns who were willing to join the navy at a wartime wage of fifteen guilders. Indeed, almost any Frisian resident-servant who enjoyed room and board plus an annual wage of thirty to fifty guilders on a farm might have been tempted to join a vessel of the admiralty at Harlingen and become a young "hooploper," or ordinary seaman.[111]

Each man on board was assured that he would get three meals per day. The portions and the sorts of food, however, were officially prescribed, and the variations were not great. Breakfast, the "vroegkost," always consisted of groats, while the meals served at noon and early in the evening provided a bit less in the way of monotony. On Sundays and Thursdays, the midday meal was bacon or other meat—one pound per person, bones included—and yellow peas. In the evening, only peas were served. All other days, stock fish and green peas might be served twice. Once a week, the steward, under the strict supervision of an officer, distributed to each man five pounds of ship's biscuits, one pound of cheese, and a half-pound of butter. Beer could be drunk freely. This was the basic menu of food and beverage at sea. While in a roadstead, or on a short trip at sea, seamen were able to consume some fresh foods, chiefly bread and vegetables like carrots and cabbage. Herring seems to have been largely unavailable to them. During the latter part of a trip, captains usually tried to buy a few oxen or sheep in order to put fresh meat on one or two menus. [112] Otherwise, the ordinary crewman had to wait for a stroke of luck when, for instance, some fish might be caught on a quiet day, or when a few doves could be grabbed from their roosts on the main yard.[113] Delicacies were reserved for those who were entitled to eat in the cabin: officers and visitors. Official provisioning lists refer to ham, brandy, Spanish and French wines, sugar, diverse herbs, and oil.[114] De Ruyter and his table companions even enjoyed fresh eggs on board. The hens were bought by the admiral's wife, Anna van Gelder, herself.

In addition to free board and lodging, the navy's terms of employment provided crewmen with a limited degree of free medical care. In 1667, the Admiralty at Amsterdam stipulated that everyone was to receive free treatment by the surgeon and his mate(s) for common diseases and accidents resulting from work on board or from enemy action. For all other treatments—those necessitated by "Mars and Venus," as it were—the surgeon could charge the patient, although this stipulation was probably short-lived. In general, that is to say, only the injuries a crewman sustained and the illness he contracted while serving on board were treated free of charge. The captain himself was responsible for the recruitment of his medical staff. Beginning in the First Anglo-Dutch War, medical doctors appointed by the admiralties verified the contents of the surgeon's chest and his skills. Grand fleets were regularly accompanied by a doctor and a surgeon general who acted as a kind of supervisor over the ships' surgeons and who advised the council-of-war of what to do in the event of a high number of wounded or a contagious disease such as the spotted fever, which raged through the Grand Fleet in 1673. Wounded and contagious patients were often sent ashore to local hospitals. In 1645, the States General decided that those who lost their eyesight or the use of their arms and legs would receive a sum of money, a payment which was nearly doubled in 1664. The loss of both eyes or arms was compensated with 1,500 guilders, the loss of both legs with 700 guilders. The right hand's value was estimated at 350 guilders, the left's at fifty guilders less.[115]

Statistics about mortality on board naval vessels as a result of diseases, accidents, and hostilities are not available, and an average death rate is not of much value. The extremes are often more telling, as are incidental data. From a medical point of view, the 1658–1659 campaigns in the Danish waters were a disaster. On board Obdam's flagship, the *Eendracht*, during the five months following the battle of the Sound on November 8, seven petty officers, fifty-five seamen, and twenty-five soldiers out of a complement of 325 men died—most of them due to a lack of proper clothes and to "fevers." At the opposite extreme is a situation that existed in 1667. On August 22, the captains of eleven men-of-war, with crews totaling some 3,600 men, reported to Lieutenant Admiral Aert van Nes a maximum of forty-seven people, while three captains actually did not list anyone—and this at a time when their ships had been at sea for more than three months. Similarly, during the winter of 1694–1695, the squadron stationed at Cadiz faced no health problems despite the fact that the Spanish authorities largely prohibited shore leave.[116]

The normal risks of life at sea and accidents on board always took their toll, however. A stroke of lightning killed three men on a ship in the Baltic on July 23, 1656, while 156 men out of a crew of 300 were drowned when their ship, the *Ridderschap*, was struck by a gale and sank off the coast of Portugal on March 28, 1690. Surgeon Nicolaus de Graaf mentions in his diary in 1660 that three seamen were killed and ten badly wounded aboard ship when the tie of the foreyard broke and the men fell upon the anchors and the guns. On July 7, 1656, the longboat of the *Zuiderhuis* was suddenly run down by another man-of-war, causing the drowning of at least sixteen men. In another case a seaman died when he fell from the beakhead, the toilet on the forecastle.[117]

Battles also took their toll of lives, though often not as many as one might think. Nor did all ships bear the brunt of the battles. On board Aert van Nes's *Eendracht* in 1672, twenty-six men were killed, forty were severely wounded, and twenty-four were wounded slightly; the next year, the totals were twenty-four, thirty, and thirty-six respectively. Van Nes's *Eendracht* crews of about 400 had by then fought four major battles. Jan Krook's *Hollandse Tuin* was damaged beyond repair during the St. James's Day Fight in 1666, which claimed seven dead and forty wounded out of a crew of 256 men. Engel de Ruyter's *Waasdorp* lost only one man out of the 268 on board during the first battle of Schooneveld on June 7, 1673; ten were wounded. During the battle of Beachy Head in 1690, the Dutch squadron in the allied fleet suffered most from the French attacks. The four worst-hit vessels had 136 men killed and 272 wounded out of a total of 1,525. But for many a captain, battles ended without a single fatality.[118] Hence the odds on a safe return from a naval voyage could never be predicted. In time of war, the risks were obviously higher.

The more men killed or wounded or seriously ill, of course, the more the possibilities for others to be promoted. Little is known about ratings' and petty officers' careers, though Cornelis Tromp's muster roll of 1673 gives us some insight. With only three men killed and five wounded during the entire campaign, as many as thirteen advancements took place. Demotion and illness, however, created vacancies as well. Two able seamen were advanced to second and third mates. Two downgraded quartermasters were succeeded by common seamen, no doubt a fairly common occurrence.

Life on board was in principle well-organized. Articles of War, which were issued for the maintenance of order on naval vessels, regulated most aspects of shipboard life. The 1629 Articles of War were revised at the instigation of John de Witt in 1665 and went virtually unaltered thereafter.[119] Everybody was supposed to know all regulations, which were read out several times during every cruise. Those breaking the rules were usually fined. Corporal punishment was applied in the form of flogging (one or two hundred lashes), ducking from the main yardarm, and keel-hauling. These punishments were recorded in the ship's log, and the administering of them was watched by the whole crew. Desertion and double enlisting were corporal-punishment offenses. The severity of the punishment or the level of the fine was often related to the time and the circumstances in which the offense had been committed. A seaman and a soldier who had been fighting ("plockhaeren") were condemned to beat the rock-hard stockfish in order to make it softer for soaking and cooking—a sentence imposed by the Frisian Lieutenant Admiral Auke Stellingwerf in 1665. Death sentences were rarely given, not even in cases of the "acts of Sodom."[120]

Daily life on board was a matter of routine and subjected the men to a strict time schedule. It is to be supposed that some ritual or ceremonial songs were used at certain times: morning arousal, surgeon's inspection, meals, etc. Trumpets and drums were used for orders and signals. An elementary form of ritual singing (shantying) also probably existed.[121] Occasions for festivities were greatly prized. William III's birthday in November, for instance, was observed with volleys of the guns and nightly illuminations by lanterns in the rigging. The securing of peace was another gala event, as the celebration, for instance, on June 6, 1660, when Denmark and Sweden ended their war in which the Republic had been so heavily involved. The letter with the news about the treaty of Breda was affixed to the cabin of surgeon Nicolaus de Graaf's captain and caused much rejoicing at the end of August 1667. The ship's approaching certain landmarks also broke the daily routine—indeed, when sailors passed the headland Col in the Kattegat at the entrance of the Sound or the Berlingas on the coast of Portugal for the first time in their lives, they underwent an initiation rite, with extra drinks provided.[122]

Other opportunities for diversion occurred when the summer weather was nice and still and, the sails being clewed up, the crew could take a swim, or when the mail—official letters as well as private correspondence for crew members—was delivered from home. The opportunity for sending letters to loved ones was specially announced. Those who could not write or read made use of the clerk's or a colleague's skills to assist them.[123]

Most captains and flag officers preferred to have a chaplain on board, yet there was not always a sufficient number of such men to perform in that role—even though young chaplains were made available for naval service immediately on completion of their preparatory study. At times, local congregations lent their clergymen out to flag officers. Weather permitting, a sermon was preached on board chaplained ships every Sunday morning, and was often attended by officers from other ships. De Ruyter, for example, was very much impressed by Obdam's navy chaplain in 1656 and regularly attended his sermons. The Lord's Supper was occasionally held, and the official days of prayer and thanksgiving were observed. Ministers also gave comfort to the sick and held confirmation classes. Yet some clergymen complained about the unruly and wicked crowd on board.[124] If no official clergyman had been enlisted on a ship, a so-called "visitor of the sick" (ziekentrooster) took charge of ministering to the crew's spiritual needs.

One conclusion cannot be sufficiently stressed in light of all this: the "new" navy was indeed well-manned. The supply of seamen on the labor market and the regulations during wartime were such that all available and required men-of-war could always sail and could be commanded by qualified and motivated officers. The protection of economic interests and the political situation in Europe constantly compelled the Dutch ruling class to make sure it had a strong navy. The province of Holland, represented by John de Witt and later by the city and admiralty of Amsterdam, was fully convinced of the need to coordinate all naval activities. Supported by its economic strength, Holland was able to put enough money at the navy's disposal. The war situation around 1700, however, was to force the Dutch navy to go to the brink of its capabilities for the next twenty years. With only a brief interruption from 1697 to 1702, a comprehensive war had to be fought, at sea and on land. This demanded too much from Holland and the rest of the Republic. Even Holland could no longer provide the necessary financial means. This was not an abrupt but a gradual process.

In 1704, secretary Job de Wildt began to notice serious symptoms of decay in Dutch naval affairs. His death in the same year and that of William III two years earlier deprived the United Provinces of the two driving forces behind the Dutch navy. But such leaders also had become unnecessary inasmuch as the Anglo-Dutch alliance had shifted in a direction that no longer completely suited Dutch interests and had become too burdensome for Dutch resources. The interests of the Netherlands—and in particular, those of the province of Holland—were better served by reliable convoys than by warfare in the Mediterranean. Moreover, the French navy had switched over to the *guerre de course*. The obvious exhaustion of Louis XIV's France diminished the risk of an attack upon the Republic's territorial integrity. One of the effects of this process was a change in the role and the position of the navy and the admiralties as such. Their importance would be different from now on, and extra financial means would no longer be put at their disposal. This shift was to have a lasting effect on the standing navy.

PART THREE

A Second-Rate Navy, 1714–1795

The War of the Spanish Succession is generally considered a turning point in the history of the United Provinces as a major power in Europe. The Dutch were forced to fight an expensive war on several fronts, both on shore and at sea. Public finances had already been exhausted several years before the Peace of Utrecht was concluded in 1713. In July 1709, for instance, the admiralty at Amsterdam had pleaded with the grand pensionary at The Hague for financial assistance. Unless some cash could be provided immediately, the admiralty would come to a standstill.[1] The Republic had been living beyond its means for too long. Its ally Great Britain (so to be called after the union with Scotland in 1707) and its opponents had taken note of this situation, and although the peace was concluded on Dutch territory, the Dutch were not strong enough to play much of a role in the final treaty negotiations.

It was obvious that the Republic would never regain its former place among the leading powers of Europe. Britain, France, Prussia, Russia, and the Habsburg Empire were able to develop their much vaster resources, and their much larger populations began to tell. The number of inhabitants in the Republic had hardly grown since the mid-seventeenth-century peak of one and nine-tenths million, and not until the end of the eighteenth century would it exceed two million. Restoration of the depleted public finances of Holland required several decades, while the budgets of some other provinces never achieved a balance between income and expenditure. Ultimately, it was not the stagnant economy that led to financial recovery, but a nearly uninterrupted peace, introduced by the Treaty of Utrecht in 1713, which permitted huge and lasting reductions in army and navy expenditures. It was a peace which at the same time forestalled the likelihood of any willingness by the rulers to invest public money in military affairs without urgent cause. Thus Holland and the other provinces could long afford to avoid resolving their differences about the priority of the navy or the army in the budget of the States General and about the level of public spending on the armed forces.

Two important elements prevented the Dutch Republic from totally stepping down to the status of a small European power after 1713. First, the financial role of the Amsterdam merchants and bankers was essential to the many foreign princes whose internal and external policies relied on the big loans provided by the monied élite of Amsterdam. Second, the East India Company continued its extensive activities well into the eighteenth century before being surpassed by its English namesake. A decline in most other economic fields occurred in both relative and absolute terms after the War of the Spanish Succession. French influence upon Spain greatly weakened this major pillar of the Dutch trading system. Mercantilism in the Nordic countries likewise provided more competition with Dutch trade. Most Dutch industries declined in this period, as did the herring fishery and the whaling trade.

The turning of the tide did not, of course, happen overnight, but by 1740 the decline was obvious to most observers. The Caribbean trade, for example, was one of the few trades which remained in full swing and required convoy escorts. By and large, however, the Dutch Republic had become a passive storehouse, mainly for colonial products. It still owned one of the largest merchant fleets, but no longer participated actively in most of the luxury trades, or in the transportation of bulk goods.[2]

Efforts to change the fiscal regime with regard to import and export, even to introduce some kind of a free port system, were of little avail, actually resulting in a lower income for the admiralties. One tendency of the stagnating Dutch economy which must be stressed is that overseas shipping was increasingly being concentrated in Amsterdam and, on a smaller scale, in Rotterdam. Whereas the day-to-day running of an admiralty should have been financed from the economic activities in its own district, this process of concentration rendered the other admiralties of Zeeland, the Noorderkwartier, and Friesland ineffective and redundant. Nevertheless, these same admiralties protracted their separate existences along with other outdated components of the federal structure. Soon after 1795, however, the five admiralties were amalgamated into one central governing body at The Hague, while the naval dockyards and related facilities were maintained in the same places where they had always been.

Convoys and the Containment of the Barbary Corsairs

During the previous period, the Dutch had unmistakably been one of the three leading sea powers. In spite of the fact that ever since the Third Anglo-Dutch War the Republic had had fewer ships of the line than either England or France, it had nevertheless consistently followed the upward swing in the overall size of those countries' navies. Dutch men-of-war too became larger and carried more guns. In fact, from about 1690 onward, only ships with fifty and more guns were regarded as ships of the line. Table 4 illustrates the state of the Dutch navy around 1700 and at the end of the War of the Spanish Succession. These figures are evidence enough of the absolute and relative decline after that time. The downward trend continued until about 1780, much longer than it did for the British or French navy, while Spain and Russia emerged as new leading naval powers. The British navy continued to be larger than that of any other nation, but even in comparison with Spain's and Russia's, the Dutch navy could hardly have been called second-rate. From the 1740s onward, however, the Dutch navy was no longer a significant factor in European politics, its operations dealing mostly with convoys and skirmishes with Barbary Coast privateers.

Around 1713, it seemed as if the Dutch admiralties would have the opportunity to restore the balance in their budgets. Hardly any naval force had been fitted out for the Mediterranean in a year, while none had operated in the North Sea. Little attention had been paid to the struggles in the Nordic War. No ship was sent to sea in 1713, and only a few convoy vessels would be needed the following year. The debts, however, were too high to make quick recovery of the admiralties finances likely. Most provincial subsidies had not been received, and the receivers general of the admiralties had been unable to borrow sufficient cash on

Table 4
Ships of the Line in the Leading Navies

	Dutch	*British*	*French*	*Russian*	*Spanish*	*Total*
1700	86	115	118	—	26	345
1715	73	124	60	17	6	280
1730	44	111	37	23	27	242
1745	34	110	47	22	32	245
1760	25	107	50	19	52	253
1775	11	108	75	17	60	271
1790	34	137	90	75	74	410

SOURCE: G. Modelski and W. R. Thompson, *Seapower in Global Politics, 1494–1993* (London, 1988), 68–70.

the money market—the last resort for them, but the admiralties' credit was too poor. Even Holland was unable to give assistance. An enormous number of bills were left unpaid, mostly those from captains and suppliers. Amsterdam had six and a half million guilders owing, Rotterdam three and three-tenths million.

Hopes of speedily cashing overdue subsidies and a very restrictive policy on building and fitting out ships were supposed to be the main elements in a policy to put the finances back on a solid basis. But these measures worked only partially. The subsidies did not come in because the general public finances of the seven provinces were also in great disarray. Shipbuilding could easily be stopped altogether. Shortly after the Peace of Utrecht, the fleet of the five admiralties consisted of a total force of seventy-seven ships of the line and twenty-six frigates—although, at an average age of fifteen years, many of these ships were rather antiquated.[3] External factors determined what number of ships should be fitted out to protect national interests, and the Nordic War soon made it impossible for the Dutch to remain totally passive in international naval affairs.

By 1714 the balance had turned against the Swedes as Peter the Great of Russia had conquered the Baltic countries. Sweden responded by blockading important trading centers and issuing letters of marque. Anglo-Dutch Baltic shipping was faced with increasing risks. A British proposal in 1714 for a joint naval force to protect neutral shipping was refused by the Dutch. When it was repeated the following year, the Dutch accepted it, but their naval commander, Lucas de Veth, received very strict orders to abstain from any kind of hostility.[4] Under no circumstances did the Dutch government want to be dragged into the conflict by King George's other interests as elector of Hanover. Dutch rear admiral De Veth commanded a force of twelve ships, British Vice Admiral John Norris twenty—the relative sizes of the fleets determined by the three-to-five ratio established in 1689. The carefully formulated Dutch instructions also curtailed Norris's operations, for on his own he would have been too weak for actions against the Swedish navy. Another Dutch force of six ships sailed in 1716 under the command of Captain Hendrik Grave.

In 1717, Britain hardened its policy against Sweden, making things particularly difficult for the Dutch. The city of Amsterdam in particular worried about the consequences. Dutch Baltic shipping was therefore ordered to a halt. In 1718 it was again decided to return to the fruitful policy of sending a squadron. Rear Admiral Jacob van Koperen commanded eleven ships and operated successfully with Norris's twelve British vessels. Although the Great Northern War lasted until 1721, no more Dutch forces were sent to the Baltic. The Republic did not follow the swing of British foreign policy, which now sided with Sweden against Russia.

Special subsidies were required to fit out the three relatively small squadrons of 1715, 1716, and 1718. Only the three admiralties in the province of Holland contributed to the squadrons, the admiralty at Amsterdam providing no fewer than two-thirds of the ships. The operations of the squadrons were in the main successful, a fact that led merchants and shipowners to attach great importance to this kind of protection. Each time, two to three hundred merchant vessels sailed in convoy; the British commander had to protect only one hundred fewer British merchantmen than the Dutch—an illustration of the difference between the Dutch and the British commercial risks at stake in the Baltic. The Directie van de Oostersche Handel en Reederijen, which had been actively involved in this naval policy, and its sister organizations for trade and shipping to Norway and North Russia (Archangel) also lobbied successfully for naval escort. A few frigates fitted out at Amsterdam sailed annually (from 1715 to 1719) on the respective routes. But by 1719, the dangers of the Nordic War had passed. Naval captains had meanwhile noticed that some of their ships were too old and too slow for the task at hand. Indeed, the ships were in such a bad state of repair that most of the merchant vessels in the convoys were sailing far ahead of their escorts to their destinations.[5]

These services were about the most the admiralties could perform during this Baltic war. Only two other traditional tasks were carried out: the annual protection of the homeward-bound East

India fleet in the Channel and the North Sea by four large frigates or small ships of the line, and the autumn convoy to the Iberian Peninsula and on into the Mediterranean. The transportation of precious metals and jewels was one of the reasons for the need of escort ships. The activities of the admiralties of Zeeland and the Noorderkwartier were soon restricted to fitting out only one convoy vessel for the East India Company, creating a situation that allowed the states on the Barbary Coast to grasp new opportunities for easy pickings. Morocco and Algiers declared war in 1715 and 1716 respectively, but six years passed before the States General decided upon a common approach to these wars. Occasional efforts by some Amsterdam convoy vessels had been of no avail, and forty merchant ships were captured within a period of five years. All the admiralties (except the Frisian, now devoid of any men-of-war) were urged to take their share of responsibility in the special squadrons against the Barbary privateers; money from special funds was provided for the purpose.

The Dutch soon discovered that even their new men-of-war were too slow to capture Algerian vessels. In 1721, some flag officers urged the construction of frigates, especially designed for fast sailing. The *Wageningen*, launched in 1723, was one of the few results of this appeal. Under the command of Cornelis Schrijver, this speedy vessel managed to capture one Algerian ship and set fire to another in 1724, after fifteen merchantmen had disappeared and two squadrons had failed to bring the Algerians to terms. Schrijver's success impressed the Algerians sufficiently to enable a new naval force, commanded by Vice Admiral Van Aerssen, to secure peace in 1726. The appropriate observance of the terms of any peace treaty with the rulers on the Barbary Coast was always a touchy business. But Schrijver's reputation was put to good use: in three consecutive years (1729, 1730, and 1731), the Amsterdam captain sailed to Algiers—each time with three different ships, in order to create an impression of naval strength—and so fully redefined the treaty terms that the peace lasted until 1755. In addition, Schrijver's negotiations resulted in the release of some 256 men who had been captured from their ships and held as slaves—one of them since 1690.

The Algerians were dangerous opponents, operating in a very large area that stretched from the Channel to the Azores and the Mediterranean and using many heavily armed ships, twenty-four in 1724 alone. The Moroccan privateers, from ports like Salé, Larache, Tangier, and Tetuan, owned smaller vessels and were active in the more restricted area between the Canary Islands and

Cape St. Vincent in Portugal. Merchantmen, armed according to the regulations of the States General, did not have to fear much from the Moroccans, who took only a few smaller vessels. The operations of the Moroccans were nevertheless a nuisance, and the admiralty at Amsterdam, sometimes supported by its counterpart at Rotterdam, consistently tried to chase their ships and blockade their ports. The effects of these tactics were never decisive, and peace was not concluded until 1752.

Peace treaties with the rulers of the Barbary Coast invariably consisted of the same kinds of stipulations. The ruler always promised not to issue privateering commissions, and the Dutch Republic (or some other European state) would take it upon itself to organize the retrieval of its citizens and to forward annually several well-defined quantities of shipbuilding materials, guns, and bilge-water pumps, plus luxury goods, as tributes in exchange for the peace. In return, local Berber chieftains sometimes offered one or two lions or horses. If these animals survived their transportation, they were dispersed among the members of the States General by lottery. It was a continuing story during the eighteenth century, with varying intervals of peace and war. The Dutch Republic was in this respect in the same position as the other European countries, although the size of its merchant fleet and its relatively weak navy made it an attractive target for the Barbary corsairs.[6]

For many naval captains and crews, the problems with the Barbary Coast offered one of the few chances for active service. In a certain sense, that coast became a training ground for the Dutch navy. Apart from the fixed convoy trips, the operations against these states were the sole naval commitments over many years, for the Republic was not involved in any European war until 1747.

The financial situation of the admiralty at Amsterdam and, to a certain degree, the one at Rotterdam had improved since the province of Holland had intervened in 1723 to convert the rate of interest on most debts from four to three percent. Holland reimbursed the loans taken out in the final years of the War of the Spanish Succession, while it also guaranteed the interest on a new loan. This complex set of measures made it possible for the admiralty at Amsterdam to pay its last debts in 1725, Rotterdam some years later. Unfortunately, Holland was unable to find a fitting solution to the debts and other financial problems of the Noorderkwartier. That admiralty was beyond recovery, as were those in Zeeland and Friesland.

The financial recovery at Amsterdam and Rotterdam had also been aided by the fact that the costs of most naval operations, including those against the Barbary Coast, had been covered by a special fund—the so-called "Fonds van het verhoogde last-en veilgeld," introduced in 1696 and built up from the yields of an extra levy on incoming and outgoing shipping and goods. Not much is known about this fund, but from 1713 onward, it was always called on to finance special expeditions or to help the admiralties themselves. Over the years from 1715 to 1749, Amsterdam drew four and three-tenths million guilders from this fund.[7]

By 1737 the financial situation at Amsterdam had improved sufficiently for a new enterprise to be undertaken—convoy service to the West Indies. The inhabitants of the Dutch islands there and the masters of all manner of ships had a long-standing tradition of trading illicitly with the Spanish mainland and other territories. In the 1720s, Spanish colonial authorities had introduced measures against this practice that proved more effective than previous ones. Several smaller craft, as well as oceangoing ships belonging to shipowners in the Netherlands, were overpowered and confiscated. The last victim of Spanish vigilance was the *Amerika*, captured in August 1736 on its regular voyage from Amsterdam to Curaçao and brought to Havana by a Spanish man-of-war.

Amsterdam merchants asked for protection, whereupon the directors of the West India Company sent a request to the States General for naval escorts. Within a few days, the States General urged the admiralty at Amsterdam to send two men-of-war to the West Indies. Captain Schrijver, preparing his ship for an expedition to the Moroccan coast, was ordered to set sail for Curaçao. This was in April 1737, and the measure turned out to be the first of a new annual convoy service. Prior to this regular service—in which, generally, only two ships participated—there had been but a few occasions during the War of the Spanish Succession when an escort was provided. Small ships of the line and large frigates were mainly employed in this part of the world. In 1748, convoy service was also introduced for shipping to and from Surinam. This extension of naval activities was mostly Amsterdam's concern, although the admiralty at Rotterdam also participated in it intermittently. These activities reflected the growing importance of the West Indies and Surinam to the Dutch economy.[8]

There had been no major conflicts in Europe since the Peace of Utrecht (1713) and the end of the Great Northern War (1721). The

United Provinces remained a loyal ally to Britain, and on the few occasions of international tension—in 1729, for example—small squadrons had been fitted out to join the British navy. The 1740s, however, were by no means quiet years. In the first place, the Republic felt strong enough to protect its interests by fitting out extra convoy escorts. In 1741 two ships of the line prevented the Danes from attacking Dutch codfishermen operating in Icelandic territorial waters. A new conflict in the Baltic between Sweden and Russia (1741–1743) foreshadowed greater risks for neutral shipping. In 1742, as well as 1743, naval squadrons of nine and seven frigates respectively sailed to the Baltic, but to little avail. Because neutral merchant ships were not attacked, few Dutch merchantmen joined the convoys. It was the last time the Dutch navy sailed into the Baltic to protect commercial interests during wartime, ending a long tradition of Dutch intervention in Baltic affairs.

The fitting out of these extra squadrons had pushed the admiralties to the limits of their financial capabilities, yet even more serious conflicts had erupted. The War of Jenkins's Ear between Britain and Spain was fought mainly in the western hemisphere, but all leading European powers soon became involved in the War of the Austrian Succession (1740–1748). The Republic tried to remain neutral, protecting its interests as much as possible and appreciating the fact that the long peace had indeed insured the financial recovery of the two main admiralties. Yet this recovery had been made at the sacrifice of practical experience for personnel and of proper maintenance to ships, as well as of adequate new ship construction. Still worse, disorder and corruption had permeated the Dutch naval administration on a vaster scale than ever before.

The realization that the Republic was an enfeebled naval power came fast when, in 1744, Britain asked for Dutch naval support on the basis of their long-standing treaties. The call for a squadron of twenty ships for use against France proved an impossible request for a navy in which the only active admiralty was accustomed to fitting out no more than five to nine ships per year. Besides, the size of the fleet had dwindled from 103 ships in 1714 to sixty-four in 1743. Most of the larger ships of over fifty-four guns had been employed only rarely. And the appointed commander, Lieutenant Admiral Grave, was seventy-three-years-old and had last been at sea in 1728. Many months passed before his force was assembled at Spithead, near Portsmouth. Even then, the Dutch were not of much use to the British navy. Hundreds of seamen became sick, and there was a shortage of all kinds of things on board. The ships themselves leaked. In order to fulfill other commitments—the protection of merchant shipping, whaling, and fishing in the North Sea against French privateers—the States General decided to withdraw ships from Grave's squadron, causing the British Board of Admiralty to express "surprise" at the Dutch departure at a critical moment. Operations against Morocco also had to be canceled for a time.

French armies finally invaded the Republic in April 1747, occupying the southern part of Zeeland and forcing the navy to undertake a new task, the defense of the estuaries in Zeeland and Holland. Small craft had to be hired, manned, and armed. Assistance from British naval forces was very much welcome. A line of defense, composed of all manner of vessels, was organized, but luckily its strength was not tested by the French. The sole offensive naval operations against France consisted of two small, ill-equipped squadrons from Amsterdam—four ships in 1747 and five in 1748, commanded by Lieutenant Admiral Schrijver—which acted against French shipping in conjunction with the British forces. Fortunately, the war did not last long. Within a year, a general peace was concluded at Aix-la-Chapelle, putting an end to the War of the Austrian Succession.

The Dutch Republic had been brutally awakened from a long sleep. Only shortly before the peace of April 1748, the States General, the new stadholder and admiral general William IV, and the main admiralties exerted some control over their defenses on shore and at sea. All usable naval vessels were fitted out and employed for convoy service. The lack of seamen was solved by an increase in bounty and the compulsory delivery of the so-called "fifth man" by the shipowners in the whaling trade. But these measures were of little avail. By the end of 1748, the situation had returned to its former level. What had become the traditional program of small activities was resumed.

Within a few years' time, the financial administration at Amsterdam as well as Rotterdam was restored to good order. By 1751 all bills, the provisioning pennies included, had been paid. Money had been borrowed on the money market and via life annuities. Payment of interest and life annuities claimed eight percent of the Amsterdam expenditure, forty percent at Rotterdam. The finances of the other admiralties, however, were beyond recovery. Zeeland, for instance, had a debt of almost three million guilders; old bills went unsettled, and only new unavoidable expenses were paid from the admiralty's regular income. The province of Holland was also of little financial help to the navy, for its own budget had been totally exhausted. Nevertheless, the admiralties at Amsterdam and Rotterdam managed to keep their administrations running, to build annually one or more frigates or small ships of the line, and to fit out convoy vessels. Amsterdam's annual income from ordinary sources of revenue fluctuated between 1.6 and 1.8 million guilders, and Rotterdam's 0.5 and 0.6 million guilders. Money from the above mentioned fund made possible the outfitting of more squadrons for use against the states on the Barbary coast. Provincial subsidies for the construction and maintenance of a Grand Fleet were never provided. The days of John de Witt and Job de Wildt were a distant memory.[9]

During the three decades following 1748, naval operations were routine affairs. The regular convoy services were provided to the merchant marine, and those to the West Indies and Surinam were continued. Relations with the states on the Barbary coast remained fluid. There, a great many squadrons, each commanded by a flag officer, either showed the Dutch flag and brought the annual tribute or chased the corsairs and attempted to blockade their ports. Peace with Morocco was established in 1752, soon after a rather shameful incident occurred: the Amsterdam frigate *Huis ten Bosch* had been driven ashore on the Moroccan coast during a storm in 1751, its crew of 109 men and Captain Hendrik van Steenis taken as prisoners of war. Algiers made war from 1755 to 1759, and Morocco, again, from 1774 to 1777. In the intermediate years, many naval officers tried to convince local North African rulers of the value of peace with the Republic and offered extra gifts. In the West Indies, an event of a different character took place in 1763: three frigates gave support when effort was needed to suppress an uprising of slaves in Berbice (west of Surinam).[10]

In international politics, the United Provinces had ceased to be a major force. It remained a neutral nation. Because its own internal politics eliminated the option of supporting Britain—and attractive commercial profits were expected from neutrality—it did not participate in the Seven Years' War (1756–1763). But the neutral flag did not protect Dutch cargo, for Britain, following the Rule of the War of 1756, claimed the right to search Dutch merchant vessels in order to curtail Dutch efforts to transport French colonial products. Britain also wanted to enforce its own interpretation of the meaning of the word "contraband." Dutch merchants and shipowners cried for more naval protection, and extra convoy escorts were indeed fitted out—the result being confrontations between Dutch convoys and British squadrons seeking to inspect the convoy vessels. One of the officers involved in such a confrontation was Captain Johan Evertsen, the last male offspring of the famous family from Flushing. How times had changed is illustrated by the fact that this particular Evertsen was on the payroll of Rotterdam, the admiralty of Zeeland now unable to offer its officers a future. The tensions with Britain increased rapidly until, in 1759, a series of decisions of the British High Court of Admiralty gave guidance to Dutch merchants regarding what cargoes would be left undisturbed by the British navy. From then on, only a few more incidents occurred.[11]

A serious confrontation with Britain became unavoidable during the War of the American Independence (1776–1783), however. The Dutch business world was again eager to profit from neutrality, especially when France allied itself with the American revolutionaries, who relied heavily upon trade and shipping with the West Indies. In the beginning, it seemed as if Anglo-Dutch relations would develop in the same way they had during the Seven Years' War, but growing Dutch frustration over high-handed British actions during 1779–1780 led to an outcry for more convoy escorts to protect cargoes against British search and seizure measures.[12] The Dutch still owned one of Europe's main carrying fleets, ranking third after Britain and France, and were masters in forging shipping documents and using false papers. The British government cared more about the disadvantages of letting the generally undisturbed Dutch commercial practices continue than about the risks from incurring another enemy. Thus, in December 1780, Britain declared war against the United Provinces, the so-called "Fourth Anglo-Dutch War" (1780–1784). The alliance of 1689 had at long last collapsed.

It soon became clear that the British decision had been correct, with well-informed individuals in the Republic fully aware of the weakness of the Dutch navy. No more than a paltry twenty ships of the line and forty frigates were available—their average age, about seventeen years. On paper, the officers' corps was in full force, but many officers from the lowest to the highest ranks had seen little active service. The recruitment of greater numbers of petty officers and ratings proved to be very difficult. The senior flag officer, Lieutenant Admiral Andries Hartsinck, lacked initiative and hesitated to take risks. One of the few senior officers who showed any concern about improving the navy and was eager to leave the Texel roadstead and face a hostile attack was Jan Hendrik van Kinsbergen, but he was only a junior flag officer—one who soon became a confidant of Stadholder William V.[13] Worse for the Dutch efforts was the split among the members of the ruling bodies in The Hague and elsewhere in the Republic. The stadholder, an uninspiring man, could not cement these differences and became the scapegoat for all that went wrong during the war. He was even suspected of opposing cooperation with the French and of harboring secret sympathies for the enemy.

After the surprise attack by Admiral Sir George Rodney on the Dutch Caribbean island of St. Eustatius in February 1781, the new opponent did not require much special attention from the British navy. St. Eustatius had been the prime British objective because of its large-scale illicit trading with the American insurgents. Curaçao was left undisturbed. Only with French support did the Dutch manage to prevent the Cape of Good Hope—that crucial port of call and base for shipping to and from Asia—from falling into British hands. Dutch merchant shipping came to a standstill for some time, but shipowners and masters soon grasped the usual opportunities to let their ships sail under neutral flags—those either of Denmark, of various German cities, or of the Habsburg emperor as the ruler of the Southern Netherlands.[14]

Apart from a few incidental actions by individual men-of-war, almost nothing noteworthy occurred at sea. In those few actions, captains like Pieter Melvill and Gerard Oorthuys displayed much bravery. The sole event of great importance, at least for the Dutch, took place on August 5, 1781: the so-called "Battle of the Dogger Bank." The Directie voor de Oostersche Handel en Reederijen, the organization of Amsterdam merchants and shipowners, had urgently requested a convoy for the Baltic, and a squadron of six ships of the line and six frigates was put to sea under the command of Rear Admiral Johan Arnold Zoutman. When the squadron crossed the path of a British convoy, a fierce battle developed. The two forces were roughly equal in numbers, but the British had more and heavier guns than the Dutch. Although the battle ended without a clear decision, the Dutch celebrated it as a victory. Their officers were treated like heroes, and morale was boosted for a while. It soon became clear, however, that the battle would have no impact on the overall naval situation.

The Dutch fleet did not dare to leave its safe roadstead again. Plans to join forces with the French at Brest did not mature. Public enthusiasm for the navy melted away; numerous pamphlets blamed naval officers and the supreme commander, William V, for their inaction. Commissions investigated the causes of the lack of success, but their reports only aggravated the internal tensions in Holland and the other provinces. An armistice with Britain in

1783, established in the wake of the Anglo-French peace, came as a relief. The formal peace treaty of Paris, signed in May 1784, mentioned only the Dutch concessions to the British in Asia.[15]

Two matters confronting the Dutch as a result of the war against Britain are of interest: an expansion of the navy and the defense of the Asian territories. First, the conflict stimulated a program of shipbuilding, the first for the Dutch since the 1690s. The existing number of ships of the line in particular had been deemed insufficient, and extra funds to remedy the situation had been placed at the admiralties' disposal. At first, the Republic tried to buy vessels in Denmark and Sweden, but to no avail. Turning then to the option of building their own ships, the Dutch discovered that the capacity of their naval dockyards was too small to accommodate the amount of construction deemed necessary, and offers from private yards had to be accepted. By and large, the effort to expand the fleet was a success: during the late 1780s, the Dutch navy was able to deploy some thirty-four ships of the line (see Table 4).[16] Many of the new ships did, however, suffer from leakage and other defects, due to the green timber used in their construction and to the great haste of the building process itself. The consequence was a number of disasters at sea.

The second matter concerned the dispatch of naval squadrons to Asian waters. The East India Company's own naval power had been weakened by the lack of vessels to such a degree that the directors of the Company made their first request ever for naval support. After 1783, a rather large number of Dutch warships were therefore sailing to Asia. The first squadron, commanded by Captain Jacob Pieter van Braam, made a great impression in the East when it intervened successfully in conflicts between the Company and local rulers in Malaya. Van Braam's five ships of the line were much larger than any East Indiaman. Spread over the period from 1783 to 1795, no fewer than twenty-five Dutch warships operated in Asian waters.[17]

The peace with Britain did not signal a period of total calm for the Dutch. The transportation of the first Dutch envoy to the new United States in late 1783 was the occasion of the first Dutch naval appearance in North American waters since the seventeenth century. In 1784, relations with the Austrian emperor rapidly deteriorated, and a small naval force was concentrated on the Scheldt in order to blockade the port of Antwerp, in the Southern Netherlands. By the end of 1785, the problems with Austria were solved through some Dutch concessions and French mediation. Two years later, internal Dutch political troubles culminated in the organization of a line of defense, which included small naval craft, against the stadholder's party and a Prussian army en route to restore William V to his old power in The Hague. The political split between those for and those against the stadholder also permeated the naval officer corps.

Further away, the Barbary corsairs continued to cause damage to Dutch shipping, but the admiralties were able to fit out more squadrons than in the previous decades. The construction program had made more ships available, and as a result of Van Kinsbergen's suggestions for reform, squadrons were also fitted out to train officers and other crew members. Dutch conflicts with Tripoli and Morocco were kept under control, and another war launched with Algiers in 1792 was ended in March 1794 by the intervention of a strong force under the command of Melvill.[18]

Dark clouds had meanwhile been gathering over the United Provinces. In 1791 a huge fire in the enormous 's Lands Zeemagazijn (storehouse) at Amsterdam destroyed a large part of that building, as well as the naval supplies of the foremost admiralty. This fire was like a symbolic warning of worse things to come for the five admiralties and the Republic at large. The French revolutionary armies soon began their triumphal march through Europe, coincided by the French declaration of war against Stadholder William V. The first effort to invade the Netherlands in 1793 was stopped by combined Dutch navy and army forces in front of the great rivers and the estuaries, a line of defense organized under the direction of Van Kinsbergen and supported by the operations of the Austrian army, which endangered French supply lines.[19] A second effort followed the next year. Aided by a severe frost, the French invasion succeeded in December 1794 and January 1795. William V fled to London, bringing an end to Dutch independence. The Republic of the Seven United Provinces was transformed into the Batavian Republic by France. The five admiralties were dissolved.

Favoritism and Innovation

The student of eighteenth-century Dutch history will be familiar with the fact of corruption and other malpractices in governing and administrative bodies at all levels. The admiralties were no exception. While one will remember that these elements were nothing new—diverse examples from the seventeenth century have been given in the previous chapters of this study—the overall situation in the eighteenth century was significantly different. In the preceding period, such cases had been well publicized, exposure that helped make an immediate repetition of those malpractices rather unlikely. And certainly the naval part of the admiralty administration was then under regular pressure to operate as efficiently and smoothly as possible. But such pressure disappeared after the War of the Spanish Succession. Urgent naval matters very rarely arose anymore. A naval dockyard or the pay office never had to work under the pressure of great equipping or building programs. Indeed, the word "speed" seems not to have existed in an eighteenth-century admiralty's vocabulary. Operating within this newly relaxed atmosphere, most people were disinclined to expose malpractices, and those who did received little attention.

The operation of the admiralty at Amsterdam during the first half of the eighteenth century has been studied in some detail. The composition of the board of that most important admiralty remained as it had been during the seventeenth century. Half of the twelve councillors represented the nobility of Holland and five cities in that province; the other half came from the remaining provinces. A decision required the vote of at least one of the non-Holland councillors. The Holland members of the board operated as a bloc, and the other members were never able to mount a credible opposition. This made the position of most non-Holland councillors rather superfluous, apart from the one or two needed for their vote. These were usually the representatives of the province of Utrecht, Zeeland, or Gelderland. The others rarely attended the meetings. Most members from Friesland, Groningen, and Overijssel traveled to Amsterdam only the week they were officially installed in office and the week they took their leave. They automatically received the annual remunerations—from 2,000 to 2,500 guilders—no matter how little energy and time they had spent in office. Their terms were very short, lasting no longer than one or two years. Little can be said about the colorless representatives of Zeeland.

During the first half of the eighteenth century, two non-Holland councillors did gain some influence on the board, or at least their influence continued as long as they were tolerated by their colleagues from Holland. Vincent Maximiliaan Baron van Lockhorst represented Utrecht from 1710 until his death in 1740. He was a frequent attender of the board meetings and a member of several commissions; a couple of times, he combined his councillorship with the directorship of the Amsterdam chamber of the East India Company. His second marriage was to a young widow and the only heiress of a wealthy Amsterdam merchant. Lockhorst lived in immensely rich style, both in Amsterdam and on his manorial estate in the province of Utrecht. He was buried in Amsterdam in the Westerkerk. Lockhorst did not distinguish himself through his initiative, but through his constant presence and cordial relations with his colleagues from Holland.

The other influential member was Lubbert Adolf Torck van Rosendael from Gelderland, also from the landed nobility. He was a member of the board from 1717 to 1741. Torck, one of the most prominent figures in his own province, combined his activities on the admiralty board with leadership roles at home that caused him to be absent from Amsterdam for long periods of time. Torck was not greatly appreciated by his colleagues, being haughty and imperious, and was not necessarily accepted as a permanent fixture or esteemed by regents from Holland, who were themselves also filled with self-conceit. His position, however, was secure, for he had good relations with the ruling bodies at The Hague. Furthermore, financial troubles were unknown to him, the more so since he had married in 1722 the only daughter and grandchild of two former governor generals of the East India Company. Torck was intelligent and capable, and he took a real interest in naval affairs. Naval officers who wanted to introduce some reforms in the navy—Cornelis Schrijver especially—found him agreeable to their suggestions. It could thus happen that at

Torck's instigation, a major reform in naval shipbuilding was introduced by the board.[20]

Torck's terms of office were in several instances prolonged. Not uncommon occurrences, such extensions were the privilege of any city or province entitled to nominate a candidate for an admiralty board. In 1741, however, Torck's colleagues on the board were provided with an opportunity to prevent a further prolongation of Torck's membership. As a result of certain decisions in Gelderland, Torck was appointed member of the Council of State at The Hague, and he made it clear that he intended to carry on his activities at Amsterdam simultaneously. The Holland members of the admiralty board had no difficulty in convincing their political allies in the States of Holland that such a combination of two offices, both obviously quite time-consuming, should be declared unlawful. The States General decided otherwise, however. Four provinces made no objection against the combination of offices by Torck, though Holland and Friesland were against it; Zeeland abstained from a vote.

On May 24, 1741, Torck walked from his admiralty residence to the nearby Prinsenhof to attend the usual meeting of the board, taking with him the resolution of the States General, the admiralty board's superior. He knew the sentiments against him amongst his Holland colleagues, but he could not foresee the ensuing events. Two of them warned him he might as well go home; they did not want to meet him. Torck refused to leave, and when the Zeeland member suggested continuing routine business, the Holland members left the building. During the next two days, Torck sat alone in the meeting room, accompanied by his Zeeland colleague for a time. One might hope that the room was cheered up with "sweet-smelling" flowers, as was customarily done at the Rotterdam admiralty at the price of fifteen guilders per year.[21] Meanwhile, the other members met in one of their private residences. Admiralty personnel were forbidden to take orders from Torck, who at last gave up the fight and departed for The Hague and the Council of State.

Long deliberations in the States General and the seven Provincial States followed. No final decision was taken. Torck refused to give up his seat on the Amsterdam board, an act which implied that his chair was unoccupied until his term ended in 1744. Gelderland then nominated another man. The admiralty was unwilling to pay Torck's remunerations for 1741–1744, but in 1747, it had to submit to a decision of the States General and finally gave Torck the amount of 7,000 guilders. As a sort of gesture towards Holland, the States General also stipulated that combining the offices in question would be illegal in the future. Victory, then, rested with the Holland members—although their position concerning this overly influential outsider did receive its share of criticism. Torck, remarked the representative of Utrecht in 1741, had been "excluded from the board because of objections against his person"; he was a man feared because he "noticed too much and looked too much at the Holland members' cards."[22]

Torck had indeed intruded too regularly into the domination of the administration by the Holland members. For were not the admiralties of Holland, as well as Zeeland and Friesland, provincial institutions in practice though subject to the States General in principle? The dichotomy between principle and practice had existed in the admiralty of Zeeland from the very beginning. With regard to the four other admiralties, this dichotomy had never been so evident and so publicly demonstrated as in 1741. The presence of leading personalities like John de Witt, William III, and Job de Wildt had maintained the idea of central control. The eighteenth century enjoyed no person with similar stature and authority, neither a stadholder nor a grand pensionary. The province of Holland itself had supported the process of the "provincialization" of the admiralties—for instance in 1723, when it provided the three boards on its own territory with the financial means to solve their budgetary problems but abstained from helping the others. The problems of other admiralties were clearly not Holland's concern.

Internal agreements, or contracts, between a group of board members now dominated the whole course of business in the naval administration. Such agreements were kept secret, but some of them—for example, a Frisian agreement of 1699; one made in Rotterdam in 1720, with several subsequent additions; and another made in Noorderkwartier in 1729—were later revealed. Those agreements had each stipulated the particular member of the group who would nominate a candidate to fill a certain vacancy in one of the eight classes subdividing admiralty personnel. The Rotterdam contract also mentioned that the members of the group had to organize their attendance at board meetings according "to the urgency of the agenda"—the purpose being to prevent non-members from ever holding a majority. It was also arranged who would sit on the different committees. The Rotterdam contract was kept locked in a cupboard in the Prinsenhof, for which each member of the group possessed a special key.

The so-called "provincials" at Amsterdam were, from 1725, excluded from making trips to The Hague for consultations in the

Haagse Besogne and so on. Lockhorst, Torck, and, to a lesser extent, the Zeeland representative were able to gain appointments to the committees. In 1723, Torck was appointed a member of the important committee for the dockyard and storehouses. A Utrecht member, however, made a complaint in 1744 because his colleagues from Holland considered him "too inexperienced" for certain tasks. Torck's successor asked the Holland members in humble terms to favor him with the right to nominate a candidate for an admiralty office in his own province. The request was refused. The restoration of the stadholdership in 1747 partially curtailed the privileges and the independence of the admiralty boards, but as soon as circumstances permitted, these advantages were restored. One stark example of that process may be sufficient. A fortnight after the death in 1759 of Princess Anna—the widow of William IV who had ruled as the so-called "Governess" on behalf of her minor son William V—the group members at Amsterdam decided to offer Anna's privileges with regard to nominations for offices in Utrecht and Gelderland to their colleagues from both provinces. A year later, however, this offer was rescinded on the basis of the argument that the Holland members also had friends and relatives in Utrecht and Gelderland who would like to be favored with an office. Rotterdam handled the matter likewise, and the contract in question was still in force in 1786.[23]

Complaints from a man in the dockyard administration at Amsterdam shed light on the practical life of an organization which employed more than 1,500 men. In 1761, one L. W. Kramp lodged a complaint with the board that the surveyor of the dockyard, "equipagemeester" Willem Sautijn, was guilty of embezzlement and mismanagement. Sautijn was accused of using admiralty personnel and materials for private purposes and of appointing to positions for which they were unqualified the future husbands of women with whom he had had affairs. He was said to rule the dockyard jointly with five other persons, creating a gang who conducted a veritable reign of terror. Vacant positions were kept open, while the salaries were pocketed by the members of the gang, amongst whom were the under-equipagemeester, the master shipwright, and a councillor. Sautijn knew about all the internal board agreements, for he had been a councillor himself until 1759. He had represented the city of Leiden, where he had been a member of the municipal council. He was said to have been very poor when he came to Amsterdam in 1758. Four years later, however, he was able to buy a distinguished house along one of the Amsterdam canals at the price of fl.35,000.

The councillor involved in the gang was Bertram Philipp Sigmond Albert, graaf van Gronsfeld-Diepenbroick, who represented the nobility of Holland on the Amsterdam board in 1761 and 1762. Gronsfeld, a former protégéof the stadholder, was a notorious man now accused of using timber from the dockyard, transported by dockyard vessels, in his china factory in nearby Muiden. This very man was appointed chairman of an investigation committee which took almost three years to publicize its results. Gronsfeld had meanwhile resigned from the board, and another member of the committee had died. Kramp was finally told that he had not substantiated his accusations and that he had better ask Sautijn to accept his apology. Kramp, refusing to do this, was dismissed. Sautijn remained surveyor until 1780, and was succeeded by naval officer William May, the son of one of his gang members.

This affair confirmed what Cornelis Schrijver, a severe critic of malpractices, once remarked: "the dirty hands wash themselves, without ever getting clean."[24] The regents had nothing to fear—unless they took seriously such threats as, for example, were uttered by the unruly and dissatisfied wives of Rotterdam seamen who had complained about corruption on board certain ships. The "me Lords'" heads would be devoured from their bodies, vowed the women, and the Prinsenhof would be set on fire if the councillors took no action.[25]

An important difference between the naval administration of the eighteenth century and that of the previous period is the dominant role now played by one of the so-called "ministers," the advocate fiscal, who together with the secretary and the collector general formed the central core of the administration. His and their appointments were for life, not restricted to a term. Cities in which an admiralty was seated had been successful in ensuring that in practice only their own citizens were appointed by the States General to these positions. These offices, and that of the advocate fiscal now in particular, had always carried a great deal of influence and were much sought after for their financial rewards—consisting not only the usual remunerations but also of a fixed proportion of all financial transactions by the admiralty. The conviction that "the wider the conscience of the office's owner, the wider the profits" was the guiding philosophy of the contemporary office of advocate fiscal.

At Harlingen in 1748, five citizens were assessed as having property valued in excess of fl.100,000: the collector general's was put at fl.200,000 (the top), and the advocate fiscal's at fl.110,000. And that in a small Frisian city in which the ordinary income of the admiralty was no more than fl.30,000 per year.[26] Jacob Boreel Jansz. was the advocate fiscal at Amsterdam between 1737 and 1778. His relatives received an inheritance of one and a quarter million guilders. The remunerations of the secretary of the Maze are known in detail. His annual salary was fl.900, his allowance for housing and a private clerk was an additional fl.900, and for peat and candles, he received another fl.105. For his inspection of certain officials, he was rewarded with fl.414. Gifts of spices, herring, and other fish, plus free stationery that he received, were valued at fl.800. The total amount averaged fl.3,000 per year. Not included in this total is the secretary's share of each sum paid to admiralty suppliers, which varied between one-half and three percent. He was, moreover, entitled to three-tenths percent of the provisioning pennies. Because of the wider range of admiralty activities, the Amsterdam secretary was able to earn annually about fl.8,000 in all. His counterpart in Rotterdam received about fl.4,000.[27]

The working hours in the secretary's office started at 8:30 A.M. when the board would meet and on other days at 9:00 A.M. There was a break from 11:30 A.M. till 3:00 P.M. and the day's work ended at 5:30 P.M. In the Prinsenhof at Amsterdam, about eighty administrators and other personnel worked. The collection of duties outside Amsterdam and the inspection thereof required about fifty men. The number of people employed in the dockyard, the Zeemagazijn, and the rope-walk fluctuated according to naval activities. Before the war against Britain broke out, over 1,600 men were on the payroll for the year 1780. The following year, this number increased to more than 2,000. An admiralty and a chamber of the East India Company both represented the most important employers in the cities where they were established, and each had an economic impact that was even more impressive when seafaring personnel were also taken into account. The sorts of employees varied from shipwrights, porters, clerks, compass makers, and messengers to the caretaker of the cats in the Zeemagazijn.[28]

During the seventeenth century, the secretaries had been the leading figures in the naval administration. For some unknown reason, this situation changed during the first decades of the eighteenth century. One of the main activities of a secretary had always been to coordinate the contacts with and around the fleet. That activity had put him in frequent touch with The Hague and the sister organizations and placed him on a national level. David and Job de Wildt are the obvious examples in this respect. Such activities were, however, no longer much required after the War of the Spanish Succession. Lengthy discussions about reforms in the fiscal policies of the admiralties around 1725 and 1751 provided the advocates fiscal with the opportunity to play a more prominent and central role than the secretaries. Additional factors must have contributed, however, to waning status of the position of secretary.[29] For some fairly obscure reason as well, the advocate fiscal was now called "councillor and advocate fiscal"; considered a member of the board, he was thus qualified to sit on committees. In 1737, Boreel switched from the office of the secretary, held since 1734, to that of the advocate fiscal.

During the second half of the eighteenth century, the advocates fiscal became so prominent in the naval administration that they were, as a matter of course, the only persons to be consulted by Stadholder William V on many critical topics, including those which had in the past been the prerogative of a secretary. The best known personalities in the naval administration during the 1780s, for instance, were Joan Cornelis van der Hoop and Dirk Rudolf Wijckerheld Bisdom, advocates fiscal at Amsterdam and Rotterdam. They were more powerful than any other member of their boards. The diminished significance of the admiralties in public life—perhaps in conjunction with the upgrading of the position of the advocate fiscal—caused the councillorship itself to be devalued. Cities like Amsterdam, Leiden, and Haarlem no longer delegated their foremost regents to the admiralty. Second-rate regents (those on the "donkey bench") and regents of junior status went to the Prinsenhof and remained there for just one term or less. Prolongation of terms was no longer common.[30]

Occasionally, suggestions were made to reorganize and decentralize the admiralties, but these invariably came to nothing. Simon van Slingelandt, secretary of the Council of State and later grand pensionary, in 1719 proposed that in addition to the five admiralties, a central body be established at The Hague with permanent members who would coordinate the execution of the different tasks of the admiralties—which he believed were too independent from each other and too often subjected to the whims of the provinces in which they were located. Van Slingelandt's plans were rejected by the States of Holland and their three admiralties, whose councillors fought any subordination of their power. In 1727 and 1729, the States General was unsuccessful in its effort to curtail such obvious excesses as appointing children and the substitutes of substitutes to office. The admiralties remained a loose system of organizations whose representatives occasionally met as a group at The Hague in the Haagse Besogne but lacked any real commitment or intention to join forces and to cooperate with one another. That situation was expected to change, however, when a stadholder was again installed.

In 1747, William IV became stadholder of all seven provinces, and people like Schrijver expected from him great improvements in the naval administration. He made a promising start in 1749, demonstrating an active interest in naval affairs by appointing Gerard Aernout Hasselaer, a leading Amsterdam burgomaster, as his personal representative and the chairman of the board of the three admiralties in Holland. In Zeeland, William acted in much the same manner. Keenly aware of the political turmoil at Amsterdam and elsewhere, he became convinced that some of the city regents and councillors needed to be removed and replaced by new men. Though Hasselaer in his earlier capacity as director of the East India Company had encouraged innovations in the art of navigation, he turned out to be an unfortunate choice for the navy. Who could have supposed an Amsterdam burgomaster would be loyally obeyed at Rotterdam? Moreover, Hasselaer had coarse manners and proved to be politically unreliable for the stadholder and his political friends, for he remained loyal to the traditional anti-stadholder party in Holland. William IV died suddenly in 1751, and the political vacuum could not be completely filled either by Governess Anna or, later, by William V.[31]

No plans for a reorganization, like founding a Council for Trade and the Navy, were officially discussed, although the desirability of more centralization was not denied. It was always understood that reforms in this direction would have repercussions on the federal structure of the United Provinces itself, yet a more fundamental problem was the absence of someone to take the initiative. Stadholder William IV was not the sort of person to produce innovative ideas himself. Nor did the grand pensionaries often display any more than a cursory interest in naval affairs. And there were periods in which the major political leaders at The Hague did not enjoy the best of working relationships with one another. But perhaps the overriding reason for the sluggishness in naval reform in the eighteenth century is simply that the decision-making process of the different governing bodies in the Republic now worked more slowly than it had in the previous century. The States of Holland, for example, made it a habit to refer nearly every issue to a committee, and in many cases, not even a report about the issue ever reached the States. Moreover, while William V did consult the Amsterdam advocate fiscal about general commercial and naval topics, he ignored the other admiralties altogether.[32] In spite of all these obstacles, however, a few small changes were introduced into naval administration, and some practical innovations in naval operations were spurred by the war against Britain.

In 1781, Van Kinsbergen was appointed adjutant-general to William V. He represented the stadholder in carrying out typical naval commitments—visiting, for instance, the wounded seamen after the battle of Dogger Bank. Van Kinsbergen and two adjutants-general appointed later were clearly considered to be part of the court circles of the stadholder and to be competent to act as his naval advisers. Alas, however, these appointments were not sufficient to ensure a more smoothly run navy, or to silence the critics of the stadholder's naval conduct.

In 1782, a so-called "Secret Council for Naval Affairs," later designated the Department for the Navy, was created. Its first members—the advocates fiscal at Amsterdam and Rotterdam, Van der Hoop and Wijckerheld Bisdom; and three flag officers, Johan Arnold Zoutman, Pieter Hendrik Reynst, and Van Kinsbergen—were instructed to remain as much as possible at The Hague, where they would review all documents and letters concerning the navy. They were supposed to give their advice, both on the matters that were put before them and on the issues raised by the members themselves. The operation of this Council came as a great improvement over former procedures. It made a number of sound suggestions and took several of the initiatives that were stimulated by the two advocates fiscal. The peace with Britain and the subsequent political turmoil ultimately lessened the importance of the Council, but it continued to function until 1795—its existence never having made the idea of centralization of the admiralties redundant.[33]

At the instigation of the Rotterdam advocate fiscal Pieter Paulus—and later, of grand pensionary Laurens Pieter van de Spiegel—new plans were developed for a thorough revision of the admiralties' structure. In 1789 the establishment of a central Admiralty Council was proposed. This council would be seated at The Hague and composed of sixteen members. Holland would have four representatives. The five admiralties would be abolished. The Council would have a fixed annual budget. Vested interests, however, made such profound changes unacceptable for the three maritime provinces that had their own admiralties. Holland, especially, feared losing its control over the navy and the collection of the duties. In 1792, only the annual budget was introduced; the principal reforms had to wait until 1795, when the new regime took over—with Pieter Paulus as a prominent figure.[34]

The typical eighteenth-century examples of corruption and mismanagement as well as the lack of imagination and the will to reform should not obscure a number of improvements which were introduced during this period. These improvements concerned ship construction, the training of naval officers, and the building of new port facilities.

Several captains and flag officers had been impressed by the fact that British men-of-war sailed faster and maneuvered more easily than their own vessels. This fact had been brought home to them during the War of the Spanish Succession. Van Wassenaer, Van Aerssen, and Schrijver suggested the introduction of better designs into Dutch shipbuilding. The frigate *Wageningen* was an initial if inadequate effort in that direction in 1723, and mounting questions concerning both the ability and the honesty of master shipwright Gerbrand Slegt at Amsterdam forced his resignation in 1726. Councillor Torck, in close cooperation with Captain Schrijver, succeeded in persuading the board to employ an English master shipwright and to send Schrijver to England to try to engage one or more shipwrights "as secretly as possible." He found three shipwrights at the Portsmouth naval dockyard willing to go to Amsterdam, but their recruitment was discovered and prevented by the dockyard authorities.

In 1727, however, the plan to hire English shipwrights succeeded. One of the three shipwrights originally sought, Charles Bentham, deserted from Portsmouth and was appointed assistant to the master shipwright at Amsterdam. Thomas Davis became the head of the shipbuilding department, having previously worked at Naples and along the Danube. John May from Chatham came over from Toulon to become second assistant. Eight young Dutch shipwrights were apprenticed to the three Englishmen to learn English shipbuilding methods. Torck and the naval officers involved could be well pleased with themselves. Davis remained at Amsterdam until 1735 and was succeeded by Bentham. On Bentham's death in 1758, May took over; though becoming embroiled in the controversy surrounding equipagemeester Willem Sautijn, May continued to work there until 1779. English shipwrights thereby directed Dutch shipbuilding at what was unquestionably the largest and most important naval dockyard in the Netherlands for more than half a century.

Davis and his assistants introduced a number of changes in the design and construction of Dutch warships. The ships they proposed were larger, with increased proportion between length and width. And because lighter materials were to be used in their construction, the new ships would weigh less and thus, it was hoped, sail faster. The interior design was also to be changed, though only slightly. Each new vessel was now first drawn on paper, and these drawings were preserved for later consultation. The first of Davis's actual products were observed with great interest in the Netherlands as well as in Britain. When, in 1729, a British and a Dutch squadron that had been joined together were awaiting further instructions, ample time was available for the seamen to conduct a comparison of their respective ships. Van Aersen and his colleague Charles Wager therefore arranged a race between the *Provincie van Utrecht*, under the command of Schrijver, and the *Monmouth*, one of the fastest British vessels. Bets were laid on the outcome, but under the varying weather conditions of those four days in July, each of the ships alternatively sailed faster than the other, and no decision was possible!

Most captains were favorably impressed by their "English-built" ships. In skirmishes with the corsairs from the Barbary Coast, these vessels now regularly enjoyed superior speed. Bentham was especially successful in building well-designed frigates and light ships of the line. The Amsterdam chamber of the East India Company borrowed his methods for its own dockyard, the biggest in the country. The master shipwrights of the other admiralties, however, remained very critical of these foreign innovations, possibly because the Amsterdam ships had a greater draught—a feature considered dangerous in their own shallow waterways between their dockyards and the open sea. The antagonism displayed by these shipwrights was such that the introduction of one uniform ship design for all five admiralties was made impossible. Even some pressure from William IV's side failed in 1747. Nevertheless, quite a few of the new English methods of shipbuilding were imperceptibly introduced at other admiralty dockyards and at the VOC dockyard at Amsterdam.[35]

The founding of schools for nautical instruction was another innovation of this period. In 1748, such a school—the "Zeemanscollege"—was initiated at Amsterdam by the admiralty, the East India Company, and the municipality of that city itself. Young naval officers were required to take courses in mathematics and in the art of navigation before they could be eligible for promotion. The admiralty at Rotterdam borrowed the Amsterdam example for its own officers a few years later.[36]

In the meantime, however, little interest was being taken in the maintenance of the various ports of the admiralties. Some of these facilities—those at Amsterdam, for instance—were silting up, while others were subsiding. In 1744, the gates of the sea-locks at Flushing could not be opened. Repair work on them was started in 1750 and completed three years later, but soon, neglect struck again. The revival of naval activities during the Fourth Anglo-Dutch War also directed attention toward the condition of the port facilities. In 1783, an official committee—composed of two advocates fiscal, two naval officers (Reynst and Van Kinsbergen), and two hydraulic engineers—was charged with the inspection of these facilities. The dock at Flushing was thoroughly inspected, and large repairs advised. Collecting the necessary funds took some time, but in 1794, William III's dock was at long last in perfect order again—and soon to prove very helpful to the French in their wars against Britain. In addition, some buildings in the dockyards of the admiralties of the Noorderkwartier and Friesland were restored and enlarged. The ship construction program of the 1780s, however, suddenly brought before the public eye mistakes by the board at Harlingen. Two seventy-four-gun ships of the line built in the dockyard in 1786 turned out to be too large to pass under the local bridges. After lengthy discussions, it was decided to break up both vessels. They had been intended as a gift for King Louis XVI of France.[37]

In addition to this work at the existing facilities, a completely new naval base, later known as Den Helder, was built. Outward- and homeward-bound vessels from the admiralties at Amsterdam, Hoorn, and Enkhuizen had always dropped their anchors in the Texel roadstead, although the route between this roadstead and the three ports was difficult to navigate because of the many sands and shallows and the dependence on a variety of wind directions. Maintenance and repair facilities did not exist at Den Helder and storms and currents caused this most northerly tip of Holland to cave in. Investigations by a number of committees concerning the possibility of building new marine works there in the 1770s resulted in the creation of an area east of Den Helder (the Nieuwe Diep) in which a large number of naval as well as merchant vessels could safely winter or wait for more favorable weather before continuing their voyages. The year 1792 saw the start of construction on a diked place in the Nieuwe Diep with a lock which would also provide careening facilities and storehouses. These works were completed over the next twenty years.[38]

Little Work, But More Education for the Naval Officer

Several naval officers were actively involved in the discussions about the Nieuwe Diep and other port facilities, and some of these men, like William May, formulated alternative plans. The role played by naval officers in these proceedings shows that their skills had become wider and more varied than those of their counterparts a century before. A number of developments which had taken place with regard to educating and selecting naval officers made this increased participation in naval affairs a matter of course.

Far-reaching reforms in the education of naval officers had begun to be introduced in the late 1740s. A junior naval officer had to pass certain exams before being eligible for promotion, a regulation instituted at Amsterdam in 1749 and at Rotterdam soon afterwards. The Zeeland admiralty introduced examination requirements in 1761, while the admiralties of the Noorderkwartier and Friesland waited until the 1780s to do so. The navigational knowledge of each lieutenant and commander was tested by an official examiner—at Amsterdam, by the famous Cornelis Douwes. Lieutenants were required to procure good maps, protractors, dividers, and textbooks on the art of navigation. Captains, as well as their officers and mates, were required to keep a log containing specific types of information. Inspection of these registers by examiners later became common. In 1787, a more detailed regulation outlining the data to be included in a captain's log was issued at Amsterdam. Naval officers were obliged to apply certain new methods in their navigation and to use specific instruments, although the five admiralties did not coordinate their initiatives in this respect.

Amsterdam and Rotterdam took the lead where innovations were concerned, a fact which implies that at least three quarters of the entire corps of Dutch naval officers were affected by every new measure instituted. It became difficult for officers to avoid acquiring a solid knowledge of mathematics and the modern methods of determining latitude, longitude, and compass variation. They were no longer free to use their own navigational techniques. Yet many officers took so great an interest in the required subjects that they actually became quite learned—several of them, in fact, so erudite that they accepted membership in various scientific societies. Among these men were Van Kinsbergen, Melvill, William May, Zoutman, Lodewijk graaf van Bylandt and his nephew Frederik Sigismund graaf van Bylandt, Jacob Andreas van den Velden, and Johan Splinter Stavorinus.[39]

The new naval officer was in principle completely *au fait* when calculations had to be made for the naval basin at Den Helder or when the first nautical almanac was published in 1788. Frederik Sigismund graaf van Bylandt and Jan Olphert Vaillant bought chronometers themselves and tested their usefulness on board their ships. Both of the officers, and Lodewijk graaf van Bylandt and Melvill as well, tried new compasses and reported the results to their admiralties. These officers were also interested in foreign maps of the waters in which they were operating—maps they often discovered to be more accurate and up-to-date than those made by the Dutch. The process of forming of a well-educated naval officers' corps was completed around 1800, when the centralized structure of the naval administration imposed uniform regulations and standards throughout the navy. In 1808, for instance, young officers had to submit themselves to centralized week-long written and oral exams at Amsterdam.[40]

Officers like Lodewijk graaf van Bylandt, Van Kinsbergen, and Vaillant did not merely develop their own knowledge and practical experience, but wrote instruction books for their young colleagues. In 1767, Van Bylandt published a two-volume book on naval tactics and the signaling system called *Zee-tactick of grondregulen der krijgskunde ter zee (Naval Tactics or the Principles of the Art of Warfare at Sea)*. It was the first Dutch publication on the topic, and was based on a French book from 1763 by Bigot de Morogues. More than 750 copies were printed, and many interested naval officers acquired the first edition. The young officer who had helped Van Bylandt with his book, Van Kinsbergen, soon made himself known as a prolific author on related subjects. In 1767, Van Kinsbergen published a handbook for junior officers, *Korte instructiën betreffende de zeedienst (Concise Instructions for the Naval Service)*, which vastly expanded a basic instruction book written by Commander Martinus Lambrechts in 1731. Van Kinsbergen gave much attention to the organization of shipboard life and to the need for frequent practical exercises for seamen and soldiers. Discipline had to be maintained under all circumstances, he felt.

Van Kinsbergen continued his writing activities during the early 1780s, publishing works on artillery, the formation of a corps of naval cadets, and the signaling system. Three of his books were well read and widely used. In 1780, his *De scheepsdienst (Service on Board Ship)* appeared, a continuation and extension of his earlier book on this topic. It was replaced two years later by his *De algemeene scheepsdienst zowel op een fregat als op een schip van linie (The Ordinary Service on Board a Frigate as well as a Ship of the Line)*. A book used till 1795, its principles remained valid well into the nineteenth century. It contained the text of all relevant standing naval orders and instructions; described in detail the task of the commander, the maneuvers of a ship, the rigging, the artillery, and the different exercises for handling the hand weapons and for preparing a seafight; and made suggestions on how officers should handle the enlisted men themselves as well as matters relating to discipline, hygiene, and victualing. The general use of *De algemeene scheepsdienst* promoted uniformity in all kinds of shipboard practices. *Het zeemanshandboek (Manual for the Naval Seaman)*, published by Van Kinsbergen in 1781– 1782, had the same effect. Written for junior officers in particular, it included many schemes to be used as models for reports to the admiralty on a great variety of topics. This book also was a success, and separately preprinted forms soon became available and were regularly used. Van Kinsbergen's 1782 trilogy was completed with the publication of *Grondbeginselen der zeetacticq (Principles of Naval Tactics)*, which replaced Van Bylandt's 1767 book and introduced an innovative criticism of the universal belief in the strict application of line-ahead tactics in battle. It was translated into Russian but was otherwise ignored abroad.[41] Vaillant also published on the art of navigation in 1784 and 1786.

Despite the improvements in the education of naval officers that were made during the second half of the eighteenth century, exams and books did not automatically transform the whole corps into one efficient and fully qualified team. The new system of discipline and instruction meant only that well-meaning and interested officers now had a framework within which they could develop their skills and knowledge. The introduction of new regulations did not, of course, guarantee that officers would follow them at all times. Enforcement and interpretation of the rules were in the hands of the admiralty councillors, and abuse of power prevailed until the end of the old regime. One example may be sufficient. Although a long-standing rule had stipulated that midshipmen be at least fifteen years of age, in 1780 five-year-old Salomon Dedel received a certificate appointing him midshipman of the Amsterdam admiralty at a monthly wage of ten guilders. Young Dedel's father was a naval captain and belonged to the ruling class at Amsterdam; he was a brother-in-law of advocate fiscal Van der Hoop. Henrik Hooft, frequently burgomaster of Amsterdam, had signed the commission in his capacity as an admiralty councillor.[42]

The overall quality of the officers' corps—during the last quarter of the eighteenth century, in particular —was higher than ever before. The roots and the basis of this improved corps, however, lay in the earlier period. A number of very capable and devoted officers had strongly supported the reforms that ultimately were introduced around 1750, and these officers had transferred their knowledge and enthusiasm to younger ones like Lodewijk graaf van Bylandt and Van Kinsbergen. Alas, however, few of such men were able to see their efforts come to fruition, for during the period in which they lived, little change took place.

The fate of lower-ranking officers, the lieutenants and commanders, was not particularly favorable at the time of the Peace of Utrecht in 1713. They received payment only when they were in active service on a ship; their monthly salaries remained at thirty and sixty guilders respectively. When ashore, these officers received nothing. And the navy provided them virtually no other remunerations. A share of captured prizes, for example, was unlikely. If appointments to active duty followed in rapid succession, an officer was assured a fair annual income; however, any lengthy delay between assignments meant financial difficulties if he was without independent means. Large numbers of lieutenants and commanders had been employed during the previous wars, but after 1713, there was simply not enough work for them. In 1713 and 1714, at least five commanders and ten lieutenants asked the board at Amsterdam for leave to transfer with retention of rank into the service either of foreign navies or of the East or West India Company. Many Dutch officers found places in the fleets of Russia, Venice, and, in particular, Portugal—although some of these men did return later. The situation at the Amsterdam and Rotterdam admiralties was gradually restored to normal, and after 1719, new appointments were being made once again. But the reserve of lower-ranking officers remained so large in peacetime that every year, the East India Company was able to attract a few of them to serve on its ships.

For older commanders and lieutenants who were in financial need, there was the possibility of an honorable pensioning off, in which case they would receive twenty or twenty-five guilders monthly from the admiralty for life. They were paid out of the so-called "restantboek," or remainder book, of unclaimed pay and miscellaneous monies. In 1740, for instance, eight commanders and ten lieutenants were pensioned at Amsterdam; in 1746, four and eight respectively. Young lower-ranking officers not on active service and without adequate financial means were likewise supported to help tide them over until their next appointment to a ship. Plans to set up fixed positions for commanders and lieutenants with yearly salaries of 300 and 264 guilders were never put into effect.[43]

Half of the captains—the group with the least seniority—were also paid only when they were actually serving at sea. Their salary was thirty guilders a month. The other half of the captains, as well as flag officers, received this sum when not on active duty. After the War of the Spanish Succession, the greatest concern of these officers was the provisioning pennies. The admiralties were so heavily in debt that, at least for Amsterdam, it was not until 1725 that the officers could count on regular payments. For captains and flag officers of means, this situation was no burden, but for those who depended on the pennies, it was disastrous. Creditors besieged them and threatened legal action. Some of these captains refused new commands, having lost their credit from suppliers of victuals and drink. Others sought temporary relief and protection in places such as Vianen and Culemborg which granted asylum.[44] This unhappy circumstance, however, was never repeated.

The limited employment generally available to captains in these years caused them to join together to petition the States General in 1727 for an increase in salaries. This petition gave rise to long discussions. The Amsterdam admiralty approved it and recommended for junior captains forty-five guilders per month and for senior captains seventy-five when not on active service. On active service, the captains would receive the old rate of thirty guilders per month. The States General, however, made no decision. In 1730 the captains renewed their petition, but with the same result. Seven years later, they made yet another attempt. The stumbling block then was apparently the refusal of two inland provinces and Zeeland to make any pronouncement on salary increases. There was no change, either at that time or later in the century. No kind of "half-pay" regulation, such as had existed in the British navy since 1694 for temporarily unemployed or superannuated captains, was ever introduced.[45]

The main source of income for a captain or flag officer remained the provisioning system. It was not changed and was only seldom questioned. Once the problems of the War of the Spanish Succession were solved, the provisioning pennies were usually paid soon after the end of a voyage. The infrequency of commands, however, meant less income for these officers. The admiralty at Amsterdam had thirty-two captains in service; the admiralties at Rotterdam and Hoorn/Enkhuizen, thirteen each; the admiralty at Middelburg, nine; the admiralty at Harlingen, four. These numbers had been fixed and were not lowered, despite suggestions that they should be. Few ships were fitted out, and an assignment rate of one command per five years was not unusual. Admiralties began to put two captains on board each ship, one in command and enjoying the "kostpenningen," and the other—the "second captain"—making a monthly salary of 100 guilders, the traditional amount earned by flag captains.

The commands were awarded by the councillors, so the favorite of any councillor whose turn it was to nominate a candidate had the best chance. Among those who benefitted from this system was Salomon Dedel (1736–1800), the son of a merchant and former member of the Amsterdam city council. First appointed captain in 1759 at the age of twenty-two, Dedel continued, almost without interruption, to be awarded commands throughout his naval career. He had five different ships between 1761 and 1772, another one in 1776, and four between 1780 and 1782. His ship of the line *Holland* sank shortly after the battle of Dogger Bank. Most of the commands were of long duration, the shortest being eighteen months. The provisioning pennies involved in his first five commands, for instance, amounted to fl.192,000 gross. In 1772, Dedel married Sara Maria van de Poll, daughter of an Amsterdam merchant and widow of a member of the Clifford banking family.[46]

Matthijs Sloot (ca. 1719–1779)—who came from a family of lesser means than Dedel's—lacked influential friends on the board. A native of the small city of Hattem in Gelderland, Sloot was about thirty-seven when he was first appointed captain in 1756. Made a second captain in 1758, he had to wait until 1761 for his own command again; it was followed by two other commands in the years 1765 and 1772. After returning from his last trip to Morocco in 1774, Sloot enrolled together with his son at the University of Leiden. But he did not completely retire from the naval service, for he received another command in 1778. In his twenty-three years as a captain, he had grossed no more than 150,000 guilders from provisioning pennies. Such a low income could not have troubled Sloot to any great extent, however, for in 1749 he had married a wealthy widow with seven children.[47]

Reliable data on the profit margins are hard to come by. The cost of victuals and beer could vary greatly with the season and the political and economic situation. A recently discovered note in the administrative records for 1783 at the Amsterdam admiralty provides an insight into the proportion of the "kostpenningen" that a captain might regularly count as profit.[48] In that year, warships were sent to support the East India Company in Asia. The provisions for these voyages were furnished by the Company, and as compensation for loss of income, a captain received two and a half stuivers per man per day, paid him by the admiralty at the end of the voyage. This particular arrangement was evidently the norm and thus suggests that on an average, the captain of a frigate with 200 men aboard could make 750 guilders a month from the "kostpenningen."

A financial attraction of a different nature was the money a captain received for entering his son on his roll as an able seaman. The seaman's pay went straight to the captain, since his son was not actually on board. It was a universal practice. Captain Jan Louis van Hardenbroek, for example, had his one-year-old son entered on the ship's roll and continued to do the same with his succeeding children. Another example, also from the 1720s, was Captain Joost Vijgh van Isendoorn, who registered his son, then serving in the army, as a seaman. Captain Sloot probably broke all records in this respect, however, by having his twenty-eight-year-old son enrolled as an able seaman in 1778. This son had completed his law study at the University of Leiden and had settled into practicing law in Gelderland.[49]

In naval logistics, agents—the so-called "solliciteurs"—began early in the eighteenth century to take over the actual business of supplying the ships. Their names appeared regularly in the admiralty minutes, and while every captain had a solliciteur, these provisioning agents usually acted on behalf of several captains at the same time, thereby establishing some measure of uniformity and centralized buying. Solliciteurs often simultaneously held minor offices in the Prinsenhof or in the dockyard. How well a solliciteur looked after his captain can be seen from the inventory of the Rotterdam captain Daniël Pichot's cabin and galley: a random sample from the 250 different articles includes a complete set of eating utensils with different silver knives and forks for fruit preserves and desserts, curtains for the captain's window and his bed, a desk, and a variety of sweets and other delicacies like raisins, almonds, oranges, hams, and candied figs, plus eggs and hens with the appropriate fodder.[50]

The process of "verdeftiging" and the general aristocratization of the naval officers' corps had been completed during the seventeenth century, and no changes along these lines occurred during the greater part of the eighteenth. Of 112 captains and flag officers who served the Amsterdam admiralty in the four decades following the War of the Spanish Succession (thirty-five of whom were old hands appointed before 1713), it is possible to ascertain the father's profession in eighty-eight cases. If the officers are classified according to social background, it becomes clear that the majority of them came from the upper classes. Moreover, those of their fathers who engaged in business or commerce carried on their activities very largely in Amsterdam, where they were related to members of the ruling élite. The same holds for half of the fathers who were high officials, ministers of religion and lawyers. Among the fathers who were army officers, two were members of the noble family of Van Wassenaer. It thus appears that at least fifty officers came from the top social rung in the town or region of their birth. Fourteen of them were from the higher or lesser nobility, while twenty-two had fathers who were members of the local élite or were burgomasters. No more than five were of obviously middle-class origin. To complete the picture, it may be added that for half of the officers whose fathers' professions cannot be ascertained, there are indications that they were at least of "good" families. Naval officers were in most cases second or younger sons in a family, but in naval families they were most often the eldest. Many families might have brothers, brothers-in-law, or cousins serving at the same time, as captains, commanders, or lieutenants (see Table 5).

The number of regents' sons from the province of Holland to become naval officers increased after 1713, and after 1708, not a single merchant master's son became a captain in the navy at Amsterdam. With regard to the geographical origins of the 112 officers—all of which are known—no less than eighty came from Holland, and thirty-seven of these from the city of Amsterdam it-

Table 5
Professions of Fathers of Captains and Flag Officers in the Service of the Amsterdam Admiralty, 1690–1751

	1690–1712	*1713–1751*	*1690–1751*	*Total %*
1. Ruler (at national, regional, or city level)	7	26	33	37.6
2. High official in government or judiciary	3	7	10	11.4
3. Clergyman or attorney	4	2	6	6.8
4. Merchant sea-captain	2	—	2	2.2
5. Naval officer	5	14	19	21.6
6. Army officer	1	3	4	4.5
7. Businessman, or in commerce	4	5	9	10.2
8. Tradesman		5	5	5.7
Total	26	62	88	100

Note: category 2 includes such positions as pensionary, councillor in the court of Holland, and "equipagemeester" (head of the admiralty dockyard); category 7, banker, merchant, and manufacturer; category 8, bookseller, shopkeeper, and innkeeper.

Sources: J. R. Bruijn, *De admiraliteit van Amsterdam in rustige jaren 1713–1751* (Amsterdam, 1970), 105, 2nd "Dutch Men-of-War: Those on Board c. 1700–1750," in *Acta Historiae Neerlandicae: Studies on the History of the Netherlands* 7 (The Hague, 1974), 88–121, esp. 98.

self. Almost a quarter (twenty-six) of the captains and flag officers were born in other provinces, the proportion from Zeeland and Friesland being very small. The same was true for lieutenants and commanders. The noblemen and regents in Gelderland and Utrecht did, however, seek employment in the navy for their younger sons. It is a myth that the sons of noblemen served only in the army, but it was undoubtedly important for these fathers to have the right naval contacts to assure their male offspring good careers.

There were also a few foreign-born officers in the Dutch navy, although the practice had never been a common one. The Irishman Thomas Thobiaszoon commanded Cornelis Tromp's flagship in 1673, as we have seen. Nevertheless, only six Scandinavians and Germans were mentioned in the seventy-seven shortlists of the two candidates for a captain's commission offered to the States General and William IV by the board at Amsterdam in the period from 1713 to 1751. Three of these six were finally appointed captains, one in 1744 and two in 1750; their most recent predecessor dated from 1698. Only one non-Dutchman was recommended as a second choice by the board at Rotterdam over the years from 1706 to 1752.[51] Nor do we meet with many foreigners in the lower officer ranks. One wonders what might have crossed the mind of the German captain Jacob van Stöcken when he presided over a court-martial on board his ship in 1756: the issue was the impertinent behavior of Lieutenant H. B. L. graaf van Bylandt, who had recently served in the British navy together with Dedel and who insisted on being addressed as "Count."[52]

Another foreigner, Nicolaas de Beer from Holstein, Denmark, appointed captain in 1750, had a remarkable career. Born in 1706, he probably served on merchant vessels before he became a midshipman at Amsterdam in 1732. He must have been in favor with someone, perhaps a merchant and shipowner there. Later, he was a protégé of advocate fiscal Boreel, who helped him to obtain permission to serve the East India Company in 1746. Meanwhile, promoted commander in 1741, De Beer was put in command of an East Indiaman from the Amsterdam chamber. Boreel provided him with fl.2,000 for some private transactions in tea. Boreel looked after De Beer's interests and arranged a captain's commission for him in 1750, although De Beer was still in Asia and he was a Lutheran and not a member of the Reformed Church. He did not return to the Netherlands until the autumn of 1754, when he was favored with the command of four rather large ships. In 1766 he decided to give up the seagoing life and settled at The Hague. His will of 1772 revealed a sum of fl.5,000 for Boreel, as a financial token of gratitude.[53]

The case of De Beer illustrates that officers were eager to leave naval service for temporary positions with the East India Company. Most officers returned to their admiralties after a couple of years, although some later decided to leave the navy permanently. The situation could be awkward for those officers who were completely dependent on their naval incomes and did not enjoy sufficient and lasting patronage. The Company offered them better opportunities for sources of income beyond the monthly wage. Another category of naval officers did not really mind the lack of active employment. After all, many captains and flag officers lived in a patrician canal house in one of the major cities, or on a country estate or manor, and rode about in a coach-and-four. These officers owed their life-style to their wealthy family backgrounds or to inheritances, or perhaps to "good" marriages into the circle of regents, merchant princes, and bankers. The lists of income assessment compiled in 1742 reveal the great variety of officers' earnings. Captains at Amsterdam, Delft, Enkhuizen, Gorinchem, Gouda, Hoorn, Leiden, Medemblik, and Rotterdam were assessed at an annual income of either 600 to 1,200 guilders or 2,500 to 3,500 guilders. The group of captains in-between was the smallest in number.[54]

It was a feature of the eighteenth century that some naval officers retired at an early age and filled official government positions in their hometowns or provinces. Such a step was the hallmark of an élite officers' corps. In Amsterdam alone, five captains resigned between 1729 and 1740: four, in order to become members of the city councils of Haarlem, Utrecht, Zutphen, and Amsterdam, and one, to represent the nobility in the States of the province of Utrecht. In 1740, this former captain, Van Hardenbroek, succeeded Van Lockhorst on the board at Amsterdam, representing Utrecht. Lieutenant Petrus Alexander Boreel de Mauregnault gave up his naval career at Amsterdam in 1772. During that career—which he had begun only ten years earlier, in 1762—he had not only studied the solar system but had also learned, on a number of trips to the Mediterranean, how to make proper descriptions of coast lines. Making his new home in Goes in Zeeland, and having taken with him all his notes and logs, he was soon admitted to the city council there.[55] Other captains, while still in naval service, held well-paying subsidiary offices which they might sometimes allow to be filled by substitutes; others were rentiers.

Jan Raye had a very interesting career. In 1718, as a midshipman of twenty years of age, he was appointed auctioneer at the Great Fish Market of Amsterdam. His annual income was fl.925, plus two-and-a-half percent of the fish sold—a minimum of fl.500 monthly—a sum generous enough to allow him to hire a substitute to do the actual work. In 1724, Raye was promoted to captain. He commanded two ships during years in the navy, one of which was lost off the Shetland Islands in 1729. Because of his position as auctioneer, Raye had to ask the city government for permission to sail on any voyage. In 1735 he resigned the auctioneership and was appointed governor of Surinam. His brother, a famous diarist, took over his former job at Amsterdam.[56]

There were, of course, great differences in the navigational experience acquired by members of the same officers' corps. The admiralties at Amsterdam and Rotterdam provided many more opportunities than the other three. Each year, they fitted out a number of vessels—a statement that could not be made about the others. A telling example of navigational ineptitude is Jan Linklaan, who was a gin distiller and who had for unknown reasons been appointed a captain in the Frisian admiralty in 1723. His first command was in 1740, but the board at Harlingen soon realized that this man badly needed support from more experienced Amsterdam officers and petty officers. In some periods, the annual escort vessel for the East India Company fleet was the only naval vessel in Zeeland. The candidates drew lots for the command. The British commander of the squadron which was sent in 1747 in support of the Republic observed that the ships from Amsterdam and Rotterdam were better officered and manned than those of Zeeland.[57] It goes without saying that there were at Amsterdam officers who behaved incompetently or who were regularly inebriated, but their number was small. From 1714 till 1751, the Amsterdam admiralty fitted out no fewer than 257 ships, only four of which were lost in shipwrecks.[58]

During their careers, most captains learned a good deal concerning the whereabouts of the Barbary corsairs and became familiar with the ports of the Iberian peninsula. Some captains and junior officers were employed on specific routes. Simon Versteveren (1713–1749) had been on board the first convoy vessel to the West Indies in 1737. He then married a girl from Curaçao but had to leave his new wife behind. Versteveren was promoted to captain in 1738 and was immediately appointed second captain on board warship equipped for the West Indies. Versteveren thereafter became a well-known face in the streets of Willemstad, to which he returned at least six times. The admiralty apparently exploited his knowledge of the local West Indian conditions, as did some others: merchants in Versteveren's city of residence, Edam, used him in business transactions in cheese for Curaçao, for instance. His wife and her family eventually joined him in Edam in 1741.[59] Another example of a captain whose special knowledge of an area was exploited is Jacob Andreas van den Velden, who became a captain at Amsterdam in 1770 when he was thirty years old. As a junior officer, he had been in the Caribbean a few times. In 1766 he married the daughter of the public prosecutor who later served as governor of Surinam Jan Nepveu (1769–1779). Between 1770 and 1779, Van den Velden made three long voyages to the West Indies.[60]

The general conditions in which the officers' corps had to function during this period were not very inspiring, but the officers did learn how to cope with the customs of the ruling élite, a group to whom they either belonged or were closely connected. The founding of the Zeemanscollege at Amsterdam around 1750 was doubtless an uplifting development for naval personnel. And not only did the so-called "auxiliary squadron" of 1744 make promotions more readily available, but the war of 1747 generated even more. Van Aerssen had, from 1713 till his death in 1740, been the last vice admiral at Amsterdam. Yet in 1744, when he was almost seventy-four years old, Hendrik Grave—the only flag officer in Holland—was appointed lieutenant admiral. The three traditional positions of flag officers (lieutenant admiral, vice admiral, and rear admiral) at Amsterdam and Rotterdam were in that year filled once again. During the years from 1747 to 1750, in addition, a number of almost perennial captains were finally promoted to flag officers, for to improve morale among the officers, William IV expanded the flag officers' corps enormously. In 1750, the Amsterdam admiralty, for instance, appointed two lieutenant admirals, three vice admirals, and four rear admirals. While the officers concerned were undoubtedly pleased with their new positions and, of course, were satisfied with their increased monthly salaries (fl.100, fl.200, fl.300 for the three ranks respectively), the opportunities for active employment did not improve. In both 1750 and 1751, only three ships were fitted out. It is no surprise that young, energetic officers like Dedel asked permission in 1752 to join the British navy temporarily, attracted by the reputation of Admiral George Anson.[61]

One of the perennial captains finally to be promoted was Cornelis Schrijver, whose father had also suffered slow advancement and was often disappointed at being passed over for a rear admiralship. Although his appointment as a captain dated from 1711, it was not until 1744 that Cornelis became a vice admiral, and four years later, a lieutenant admiral. Schrijver certainly was the most distinguished naval officer in the first half of the eighteenth century, following the Peace of Utrecht—distinguished not only due to his professional skills but also due to his extensive publishing activities. His concern with innovations in shipbuilding and his activities with regard to the Barbary corsairs have been mentioned already. Schrijver was in frequent contact with the British and was *au fait* with new developments in hydrography, artillery, the art of navigation, naval discipline, and, of course, ship design. To his utter disappointment, his operations in the rank of lieutenant admiral in 1748 ended adversely. The crew of his flagship *Haarlem* (seventy-two guns) became so terribly ill that he had to leave the joint Anglo-Dutch operation and take refuge in Lisbon, where he became involved in diplomatic arguments over the execution of deserters on his vessel. Schrijver was not of a very pliant nature, a trait which did him harm and made him less effective in other circumstances too. In 1747, for instance, he was on good terms with Stadholder William IV, who was interested in his ideas about reforms. It was mainly Schrijver's ideas which caused the admiralty to participate in the Zeemanscollege. Soon, however, he was at loggerheads with William IV's representative Hasselaer, perhaps with good reason, but the dispute undermined Schrijver's other efforts for reform of the navy. He subsequently could only resort to writing memoranda on causes to be redressed and to launching public attacks on those he considered "black sheep." He gradually lost influence, and in 1768, he died embittered, as had his father fifty-seven years earlier.

Schrijver inspired a number of young officers to take their profession seriously, and he had cooperated with the like-minded officers Van Aerssen, Hendrik Lijnslager, and Willem baron van Wassenaer. He collected around him many of the most promising midshipmen and lieutenants, including Joris de Visscher, Gaspar Bost, and Lodewijk graaf van Bylandt. De Visscher, who died young in 1740, was in 1738 the first Dutch naval officer to use Hadley's marine octant. This navigation instrument, invented in 1730, had first been described in a Dutch publication in 1736. Bost was also quick to grasp the advantages of the octant for the determination of latitude.[62]

It was not only an unaccommodating personality that hampered Schrijver in his endeavors to improve the navy. His good connections with councillor Torck were in certain respects very fruitful but also, for reasons discussed above, detrimental. Moreover, he was often outspoken when it came to revealing the misconduct of the board or its individual members—a stance which was not viewed kindly by the councillors, particularly since they considered Schrijver an outsider. His father, Philips, had been an ordinary naval captain, and his mother a captain's daughter. Cornelis's elder brother became a regent in a small provincial town in Holland. In 1728, Cornelis married Maria le Pla, whose father had been a captain in the Dutch army and a man of little means. In 1753, Cornelis's elder daughter married a banker who later became a member of the city council of Amsterdam. Schrijver himself, who rented a house along the Kloveniersburgwal, could afford to live the life of a well-to-do citizen of Amsterdam. He had inherited some money from his father and a few other relatives, enjoyed ten naval commands during the years from 1711 through 1748, and was well rewarded financially for his successes against the Barbary corsairs. In addition, from 1748 onward, the salary of a lieutenant admiral furnished him with fl.300 per month.

What makes Schrijver's finances interesting are his careful investments in English stock and in loans to German princes. He and his wife kept a keen eye also on the reinvestment of interest and dividends. Like his colleagues Van Wassenaer and Van Bylandt, Schrijver also bought the life annuities and bonds sold by the admiralty at Rotterdam in 1748–1749. In 1758 he bought a small country seat just outside Amsterdam. Maria le Pla continued her late husband's financial policy, and on her death in 1784, their two daughters inherited fl.470,000.[63]

During the last part of his life, Schrijver must have noticed that young officers were increasingly better educated. Another striking change from the previous decades was the total number of officers in admiralty service. By 1740 the number of commissioned officers, from the lieutenants to the flag officers, was 170. Thirty years later, around 1770, the total had increased to 280. More junior officers had been appointed, but also more captains. From the 1750s onward, the admiralties at Amsterdam and Rotterdam had begun to appoint captains in numbers well above the previous level. This policy was continued during the rest of the century. The total number of captains at Rotterdam had more than doubled by the late 1780s, and the total at Amsterdam had almost doubled by then. The policy of expanding the size of the officers' corps was also carried out within the junior ranks. By 1790, there were 375 officers altogether at the Amsterdam and Rotterdam admiralties.

The growth of the officers' corps was, for most of the period, not connected with any expansion in the fleet or with increased annual commands. It was *sui generis*. Young men were, of course, attracted by the fact that, once they had become naval lieutenants, their chances of obtaining a captain's position were better than twenty-five percent. But after the Fourth Anglo-Dutch War, the status of a captaincy and also of a flag officer had become rather overinflated. In the wake of the general empathy for the navy after the battle of Dogger Bank, all existing rear and vice admirals were promoted. Moreover, a large number of captains were appointed extraordinary rear admirals. The matching financial rewards, however, were not provided, and the newly promoted flag officers continued to receive their captain's wages.

The number of ordinary captaincies with permanent pay was still restricted. The implication is that most of the captains were only paid when on active service. At Amsterdam in 1784, for instance, only five out of forty-five captains were on permanent pay, while up till about 1750, it had been the custom to have half of the captains (the ordinaries) on permanent pay and half of them (the extraordinaries) on "incidental" pay.

Thus the enlarged officers' corps had only superficial benefits. An officer desiring steady income or frequent service at sea was better off asking permission to enter the East India Company's service. About seventy of them did so during the second half of the century, most of whom were re-engaged by the Company at the end of their term of leave from the navy. Others found employment elsewhere. It has been calculated that about half of those who enrolled as midshipmen in the period 1750–1795 had completely vanished from the admiralties' administration within ten years' time, and after twenty years, two-thirds of them were gone—due either to death, leave, or resignation. The turnover of officers, which had been high during the numerous wars of the seventeenth century, certainly did not lessen during the eighteenth, although the causes of the turnover were now quite different. Flag officers did continue to serve for a very long time, however. Usually appointed at an advanced age—well into their fifties—most of them died in their sixties and seventies while still in office. Only two flag officers died in battle: Rear Admiral Willem Crul, on February 4, 1781, near St. Eustatius in an attack by an English force; and his colleague Jan Gerrit Baron Bentinck, who died eighteen days after the battle of Dogger Bank, having just been promoted to rear admiral for bravery.[64]

Reviewing the different changes with regard to the naval officers' corps during the latter half of the eighteenth century, we can make three observations. First, the corps was considerably increased in numbers, but that increase was in no way related to the actual size of the navy itself. Second, the average young officer was now much better educated in that, regardless of his social background, he had to attend classes and sit for an exam. Third, the responsible authorities realized that an enlarged corps of officers possessing a far superior theoretical education also needed more opportunities for practical training. In 1788 the Department for the Navy at The Hague decided to organize annual training squadrons in the North Sea. The first one, commanded by Van Kinsbergen, took place in 1789 and was followed by another in 1790. The squadrons were a success, but a lack of funds prevented their being continued in 1791, and after that time, the French revolutionary wars created other priorities.[65]

The changes must have had an impact on the recruitment pattern of officers for the Dutch navy. Although detailed research has yet to be done on this, one may reasonably assume that the increase in numbers and the high standards set by the exams resulted in a widening of the circles from which the midshipmen were attracted. And this assumption itself suggests that more middle-class youngsters were becoming naval officers. But it certainly does not imply that the younger sons from the upper classes disappeared from the navy. The careers of three late eighteenth-century naval officers may illustrate the prevailing differences in social backgrounds and in attendant attitudes towards the naval profession: Sebastiaan Rauws, Vaillant, and Van Kinsbergen.

Sebastiaan Rauws was born in the small city of Woudrichem on the river Meuse in 1742. His father was a member of the local ruling élite. As a younger son (the fifth), Sebastiaan had to find employment outside Woudrichem, and in 1759 he became a midshipman of the admiralty at Rotterdam. Between his frequent trips, he attended the compulsory classes of the admiralty's mathematician Laurens Praalder. For health reasons, he asked to resign in 1775, while still a lieutenant. He was able to buy a bailiff's position in the countryside not far from Woudrichem, but two years later, he returned to the navy. His advancement to a captainship occurred in 1779. From then on, he commanded a number of ships, mainly operating in Dutch coastal waters. In 1784, a week after he had finished the log of his last command, he again handed in his resignation, this time for good. He withdrew to the neighborhood of Bergen op Zoom, also in the province of Brabant, where he had bought a country estate for fl.19,000. Two other naval officers, P. H. van Pelt and A. D. van der Gon, lived there as well. Rauws thereafter engaged in real estate and, in 1804, married the forty-seven-year-old daughter of a burgomaster. Rauws died in 1811.[66]

Jan Olphert Vaillant came from the same social background that Rauws did. Born at Enkhuizen in 1750, Vaillant was the second son of an important leader in Enkhuizen and The Hague and in the East India Company. In 1762, Jan Olphert entered the naval service at Amsterdam. He became Dedel's midshipman, and other postings that followed in due course culminated in his captain's commission at Amsterdam in 1781. He then went on to command several ships on voyages to the Mediterranean and also, in 1789, to the East Indies. Vaillant had the same kind of scientific interest in naval affairs as Van Kinsbergen and reported his experiences, mostly with regard to the art of navigation, in a number of publications. This member of the ruling élite of Enkhuizen felt strong ties to the navy and never considered leaving it. He also remained loyal to William V until the very end, January 1795, and not only joined him in exile but also entered the service of the Russian navy. Vaillant died unmarried at Riga in 1800.[67]

Jan Hendrik van Kinsbergen played more or less the same prominent role in the navy during the 1780s and 1790s as Cornelis Schrijver had a half-century earlier. Van Kinsbergen did not have an impressive pedigree: his father was from Germany and a non-commissioned officer in the Dutch army. Jan Hendrik was the first son, born in 1735 at Doesburg, a garrison town in Gelderland. He joined his father for some time in the army and learned to appreciate military discipline, later taking courses in engineering. Through the patronage of the Frisian nobleman who commanded his father's regiment, Jan Hendrik was made a midshipman in 1756. The position was on board a ship of the Amsterdam admiralty under command of Lodewijk graaf van Bylandt, one of the most able captains in the entire navy.

Van Kinsbergen's career followed the normal pattern, but he gained the notice of his colleagues and superiors with his publications. When promotion from commander to captain did not come quickly, he accepted in 1771 an invitation to join the Russian navy. Granted a leave of absence from the Dutch navy, he was simultaneously promoted to captain. Van Kinsbergen stayed in Russia until 1775 and became well known for a number of successful battles against the Turks in the Black Sea. Moreover, he earned good money while in the Russian service—something that was important for any Dutch office lacking private means. Back in the United Provinces, Van Kinsbergen returned to the admiralty at Amsterdam. Soon given commands of ships, he distinguished himself both in skirmishes and in negotiations with the Moroccan corsairs. His star began to rise even more quickly when he became William V's confidant. From then on, Van Kinsbergen was involved in all major naval discussions, and promotions through the ranks to flag officer steadily followed. On a few occasions, foreign rulers—Catharina II the Great, the empress of Russia, for instance—offered him high positions, but he declined them. Active naval service ended for Van Kinsbergen in 1795, but he remained in touch with most naval affairs until his death.

Van Kinsbergen was a vain but generous person who was generally appreciated for his great skills. He remained single until 1786, when at the age of fifty-one, he married a very rich Amsterdam widow, the daughter of burgomaster Henrik Hooft, mentioned above. From then on, Van Kinsbergen enjoyed the lifestyle of the Amsterdam upper classes, living either on the Keizersgracht at Amsterdam or at Castle Adrichem, north of Haarlem. After his wife died in 1795, Van Kinsbergen moved to the countryside in Gelderland, where he died in 1819, leaving almost fl.1,400,000 to friends and to charitable organizations that are still drawing on the principal today.[68]

In 1787, with civil strife rending the Republic, Van Kinsbergen thought it wise to leave his country for some time. Traveling with his new family through Germany and Austria, he returned when William V had been restored to power. The Republic's civil upheaval also penetrated and fragmented the officers' corps, a situation unprecedented in the history of the navy. Officers like Captain Adriaan Braak, who had been publicly disloyal to the stadholder and his party, were dismissed. Braak and others with the same political views—Lieutenant Jan Willem de Winter, for example—voluntarily left the country and went to France, as did Pieter Paulus, advocate fiscal of the admiralty at Rotterdam.[69] These exiles returned in 1795 to direct the centralization of the Dutch navy.

Naval Seaman, a Poor Man's Job

During many previous periods, the navy was able to provide its men with regular employment. Many thousands had been on the annual payroll during the great wars, but those days ended with the War of the Spanish Succession. Now, no more than a few thousand seamen annually were required to carry on the typical peacetime pattern of naval activities, although occasionally the international situation demanded the fitting out of more ships. The admiralty at Amsterdam was responsible for three quarters of all vessels, mainly the lowest-rated ships of the line and frigates. No problems in recruiting for the comparatively few seamen needed were anticipated. But, in fact, the task of adequately manning the ships was soon to prove difficult. By 1725, there were already too few petty officers available, a shortage leading the admiralty at Amsterdam to increase their pay to encourage enlistments.

In 1731, Captain Schrijver suddenly fulminated against the general lack of experience in the armed forces and declared that there was a shortage of both seamen and soldiers. In April of that year, he had had difficulty in manning even two ships of war. Though ultimately he was able to secure the full quota of men, their lack of shipboard know-how delayed sailing and led to accidents. Once at sea, many of the men—far more than usual—were laid low for a long time by seasickness. Although Dutch warships had always operated in South European waters, almost half of Schrijver's crew had never before passed the Berlingas, the small island off the coast near Lisbon where seamen usually underwent their initiation as full-fledged sailors. Later, in the Mediterranean roadstead of Malaga, it became clear that only a few of these men were capable of even rowing a boat in calm water. But Schrijver's observation that the navy's standards were declining from year to year was not taken seriously by the Amsterdam board of admiralty.

The board decided to attach sailors, particularly petty officers, more permanently to the admiralty than it had previously done. Those who had made at least two voyages in a warship and could furnish a certificate from their captains testifying to their good conduct and fitness for their duties were given priority from then on. They received jobs as dock hands or watchmen on the wharf or in the stores—at least, when there were vacancies and the men declared themselves prepared to sign on again for future sea duty. The board also took certain measures to insure the greater retention of mates and gunners. At Rotterdam, the same kind of measures were taken, but at both admiralties, the new program was so short-lived that it had no real effect.

Such half-hearted attempts to improve the quality of sailors and petty officers were overtaken by a typhus epidemic that began in 1731. The large number of victims aboard one ship in that year, some 170 to 180 of them, might have been considered an isolated and chance occurrence if the disease had not spread to thousands of other seamen by 1733. By the start of the next decade, ships throughout the Dutch navy were struggling to withstand the sickness. Probably spotted typhus, its first symptoms were fever, trembling, headache, and back pains, swiftly followed by feelings of listlessness and depression. The face swelled, and vision was affected. Vomiting, diarrhea, and bleeding from the nose and mouth ensued. Often the patient became delirious. Within a day or two, pink spots appeared on the skin. Later, the spots turned to brown. The crisis usually came at the end of the second and third week. There were degrees in the seriousness of the disease; it was certainly not always fatal. Yet the spotted typhus infection continued to spread and claimed new victims daily. Often it would rage on a ship for one or two months, affecting two-thirds of the personnel, from the highest ranks to the lowest. Then, most of the men would make something of a recovery and return to their duties. But at some point, there might be a new outbreak, or an attack of dysentery would seize the crew, their weakened bodies having no resistance left. The East India Company and foreign navies were also confronted by the disease, which intermittently raged throughout the remainder of the century.

At the height of the epidemic, sailing became impossible; ships lay at anchor in the sea routes and harbors. The sick, ensconced in their hammocks in their quarters and tended by those free of the malady, received medicine and, if it was available, fresh food. In addition, the men's quarters were cleaned out, sprinkled with vinegar and then, with hatches and portholes closed, fumigated by burning sulphur, juniper berries, or gunpowder to drive out the "foul air."[70] For in the eighteenth century, it was believed—indeed, there was no reason to think otherwise—that the air transported the contamination. Although the authorities ashore were usually reluctant to give their permission for contagious men to be brought to the land, if it were at all possible, infected seamen were taken to a house or a hospital. Sometimes, they were set up in an old ship. On the isle of Texel, an old fortification called the Schans was also used for this purpose.

Cleanliness received greater attention than before, with new recruits and all clothing being more regularly inspected—uniforms, however, were not introduced. In some ways, this kind of preventive measure had positive effects, but the source of the evil remained unknown. Not until the nineteenth century would the term "spotted typhus" come into being and the cause of fresh outbreaks of the disease be seen in the connection between the cramped and filthy living conditions—particularly during the cold and wet autumn and winter months—and the fact that one or more members of the crew had already been infected with the virus. Only in 1909 did the Frenchman Charles Nicolle discover that the virus was transmitted by body lice that also inhabit the clothing.[71] Why spotted typhus should have become such a general hazard in the eighteenth century, when it had not been so for the seamen of a century earlier, is difficult to determine. There may have been a combination of factors at work—a situation perhaps created by the recruiting of seamen from foreign countries who had unusual habits with regard to clothing and diet. Or perhaps it was simply that a more virulent strain of the virus had developed over the years.

There were other infectious diseases to contend with as well: in many coastal districts, malaria; and on Curaçao, yellow fever—a disease already known to the British and French navies and first experienced by the Dutch when West Indian convoy vessels arrived at the island. As it was with the connection between lice and spotted typhus, mosquitos were not recognized as the source of these infectious diseases, so neither the naval authorities nor the medical profession was able to establish proper methods of treatment. The same situation was largely true with both typhoid fever, caused by a bacterium, and scurvy, caused by a vitamin C deficiency—indeed, it was only by chance that foods high in this vitamin were ever taken aboard a vessel. During the eighteenth century, the navies as well as the merchant skippers of Europe suffered from epidemic diseases on a scale greater than ever before. At times, whole squadrons belonging to France, Britain, and the Dutch Republic were immobilized; the same was true for the ships of the East India Company.[72]

The admiralty at Amsterdam finally became so disquieted by the persistence of disease and the high mortality figures that in 1741 it decided to institute a number of compulsory preventive measures. These policies covered little more, however, than the procedures that many captains had already been following on their own initiative: extra cleaning of living quarters and eating utensils, airing of hammocks, more frequent changes of clothing, and issues of jenever (gin) for the preservation of the health and pepper to make the bacon more palatable. Each crew was split into three watches instead of two so that the men could have longer rest periods. Unfortunately, the admiralties dictated few precautions that were truly effective. New crew members were, for example, neither quarantined nor deloused. In the succeeding years, therefore, spotted typhus in particular was responsible for real slaughter amongst seamen. All the admiralties had to wrestle with the problem of disease, and many ships became floating hospitals.

The physical condition in which the men came on board was often very bad. Several captains blamed the lodginghouse keepers, who in the eighteenth century were the main suppliers of personnel for the navy and the East India Company, for not lodging and feeding their guests properly and for fitting them out insufficiently. Strict selection might have prevented unfit seamen from being enlisted, but just as the epidemics reached an alarming scale during the 1740s, so did a shortage of qualified seamen for both skilled and unskilled shipboard jobs. At Amsterdam in 1744, barely the required number of four thousand men could be recruited for the auxiliary squadron to Portsmouth. For the first and also the last time in the Dutch navy, even convicts were enlisted. Too few seamen were gathering to the drum, and the lodginghouse keepers had not enough people available for the navy, perhaps because they had already given priority to the East India Company. The other admiralties faced the same shortage, and then, when ships were finally manned, a contagious disease all too regularly broke out in the roadstead.

The scarcity of seamen became most acute during the latter part of the eighteenth century. For naval operations in 1780, for instance, more than 8,000 men were needed immediately, but it was only with great effort that 3,000 men were recruited for the fleet that fought at Dogger Bank in August 1781. Merchant shipping and the East India Company's activities had almost reached a complete standstill because hardly any vessel dared to sail without escort unless under a neutral flag. The regulation requiring the delivery of the so-called "third man" as in the seventeenth century was imposed. In 1782, when 31,000 men were actually needed, the admiralties were able to gather only 19,000 for all their vessels, from small to large. The lack of manpower, particularly during the Fourth Anglo-Dutch War kept the pamphleteers active. Yet the higher wages being offered were not sufficiently attractive to induce more enlistments.[73] The shortage of men was a steady aggravation to the naval administration. There were delays in departures, and immobilized ships in overseas ports—situations due directly to the sheer lack of numbers or the high numbers on the sick list.

In addition to the other hygienic measures taken by the admiralties to curb the spread of disease, ventilation of ships' galleys and areas further below decks was also improved, a change initially seen in the English-designed ships at Amsterdam. In 1725, the Amsterdam board also introduced free medical treatment by the surgeon (except in affairs of "Venus" or "Mars"—in other words, venereal diseases or wounds from fighting). For this purpose, half a stuiver per guilder was deducted from each man's wage. For a long time, the other boards hesitated to adopt this measure. Captains were, however, instructed to keep a closer eye on the surgeon's activities and to report on them to the boards. Former surgeon Abraham Titsingh gave instructions to young surgeons and published some textbooks on medical care at sea.[74] Dutch seamen had, until the 1780s, always been treated in local hospitals or on board hospital ships. But during the war of 1780–1784, the treatment of patients was improved by the creation of two naval hospitals ashore at Hellevoetsluis and Enkhuizen, both offering accommodation for more than 500 people. The first was built of timber, and later rebuilt in brick; the other was a former gun-foundry. By 1754, the British navy had already built a hospital at Plymouth and another at Haslar (Portsmouth), the latter being for many years the largest brick building in Britain.[75]

Such measures were intended to attract better-qualified surgeons to the navy and to improve the treatment of patients. There were moves also to try to attract a higher quality of mates and to encourage them to develop their professional skills aboard ship.

Beginning in 1720, first mates were charged with training midshipmen on board, for which instruction the midshipmen paid two guilders per month. In this way, a mate's salary was made more attractive. The first mate on the *Brunswijk* in 1769, for example, earned an extra six guilders above his monthly fl.36. Before the mates were enlisted, their skills and knowledge were tested in more or less the same way as those of the young officers.[7]

More substantial plans to guarantee a permanent reservoir of seamen were put forward by a number of interested people. Van Kinsbergen, for example, was very much in favor of the creation of a permanent corps of naval seamen. Since 1665, the marines had been generally regarded as serving that purpose, but their corps disappeared at the end of the War of the Spanish Succession. When in 1763–1764 a corps of volunteers from the Dutch army suppressed slave riots in the West Indies, it was decided to keep one regiment of these volunteers in permanent service as a regiment of marines. The regiment remained in Surinam well into the 1770s. In 1781, Van Kinsbergen saw an opportunity to rekindle his old idea of a "corps de marine," and even used some documents from 1665 to support his initiative. The result was an official plan, endorsed by William V, for a corps of 6,000 men. But wartime circumstances and the ensuing political turmoil prevented the concept from being realized. Discussions around this theme resumed in 1788, however. And, finally, the year 1792 saw the founding of a permanent corps of naval artillerists, a group composed of six companies of 840 men each, commanded by naval (flag) officers. This major reform, introduced on the eve of the Republic's collapse, was accompanied with provisions stipulating fixed annual wages for all officers and for a restricted number of senior petty officers. Thirty-six masters and an equal number of mates would earn 180 guilders annually when not in active service. The assumption that good petty officers would also attract better ratings went untested.[77] Indeed, the French attack of 1793 made every man most welcome, no matter what his qualifications were.

Thus the Dutch navy was never able to rely upon a fixed pool of naval servicemen. Each captain had to start from scratch when given the command of a ship. Supported by his purser, he had to find his own men and, in most cases, could recruit only seamen who had never before sailed under his command and were accommodated in bad lodginghouses. The breaks between voyages prevented the natural growth of loyalty to captain or ship, so there was no tradition in this respect—a circumstance like that in the Georgian navy, which Nicholas Rodger has so well described in his seminal work *The Wooden World.* [78] In 1747–1748 and during the Fourth Anglo-Dutch War, official recruiting agents were appointed by the admiralties and sent abroad to find the necessary men.

Why was the navy so unpopular, and why did it have such difficulty manning its ships? In any enterprise, of course, a high level of wages can be a mighty instrument for attracting employees. The wages paid by the Dutch navy in the eighteenth-century are recorded in muster rolls and payrolls which, unlike those of earlier periods, have survived the ravages of time as well as the devastating fire in the Department of the Navy at The Hague in 1844. Table 6 (below) gives a few examples of such wages, paid at Amsterdam, Zeeland, and the Noorderkwartier. The examples portray a rather consistent level of payment to the individual personnel, except for the typical craftsmen—the ship's carpenter, the sailmaker, and the cooper, who were apparently very difficult to enlist. The earnings of the seamen did not fluctuate very much but were in general lower than in the second half of the seventeenth century, when they varied between twelve and fifteen guilders.

The level of naval wages bears some connection to the shortage of manpower. It is generally assumed that there was no increase in the nominal wages in the United Provinces after the last quarter of the seventeenth century, while the cost of living became lower. From 1740 onwards, however, and certainly by 1770, living expenses were definitely higher. For a laborer still earning the same wage, this development meant declining purchasing power. So much the worse for naval seamen, who earned less than they did before. It seems obvious that naval service must have lost its attraction for anybody who had other options for employment. In 1770, ordinary seamen, who earned fl.10 monthly, were paid sums of between fl.12 and fl.66 when they were signed off at the end of a voyage of nine months; seamen earning fl.12 collected sums of between fl.22 and fl.84. The differences in the totals stemmed from personal expenses on board and from fines.[79]

The boards of admiralty faced problems each year when their ships had to be fitted out. Their recruiting problems appeared to be solvable, however. In due time, they had always been able to recruit the relatively small number of new men required—because the lack of skills and the poor physical condition of these prospective employees were not taken seriously into account.

Table 6
Monthly Rates of Pay during the Eighteenth Century (in Guilders)

	Amsterdam from 1725 on	*At Zeeland, ca. 1770*	*At the Noorderkwartier, ca. 1775*
master	30	28	28
first mate	36	36	42
second mate	30	30	36
third mate	18	30	32
purser	16	36	24
boatswain	22	22	22
boatswain's mate	16	16	17
second boatswain	18	20	20
second boatswain's mate	15	14	18
quarter-master	15	14	16
chief surgeon	32	30	32
surgeon	30	30	24
surgeon's mate	15	16	18
trumpeter	18	—	20
steward	18	20	20
steward's mate	14	14	16
cook	18	20	20
cook's mate	14	14	16
master gunner	22	20	26
gunner	18	16	20
gunner's mate	15	14	16
carpenter	28	30	40
carpenter's mate	15	20	26
sailmaker	18	25	22
sailmaker's mate	14	16	16
provost	12	14	14
cooper	12	15	18
commander soldiers	14	18	16
seaman	11	9–12	?
soldier	10	10	—
boy	4–7	6–7	7

SOURCES: J. R. Bruijn, *De admiraliteit van Amsterdam in rustige jaren 1713–1751* (Amsterdam, 1970), 147; The Hague, General State Archives, Admiralties Archives 2843 (*Brunswijk*, 1769–1770); and 3126 (*Dieren*, 1775–1777).

There was no reason, therefore, for the boards to take further action, except under such extraordinary circumstances as those in 1747 and 1780. An enlistment bounty was then an easy measure: in 1747, it was first fl.25, and later fl.40. During the Fourth Anglo-Dutch War, the bounties were increased from fl.50 to fl.100 and the wages for able seamen temporarily upgraded to fl.14 and fl.16. William V even offered an extra bonus out of his own pocket. But as soon as the situation returned to normal, such measures were withdrawn.[80] Only the insistent clamoring of people like Van Kinsbergen finally led to the creation of a permanent corps of artillerists in 1792.

The law of supply and demand of course ruled the labor market and the level of wages. The directors of the East India Company were also able to lower their seamen's wages from fl.16 to fl.14, and even to fl.12 as soon as the war was over in 1783 and sailing and recruiting restrictions had been lifted. The monthly wage of fl.14 had been generally accepted by the Company after 1753.[81] Meanwhile, the admiralties were still operating with seamen's wages of fl.12. They had become the least attractive employers in the Republic, having finally taken over that dubious distinction from the Company.

The conditions offered by the navy are reflected in the sort of people it recruited. Striking changes had taken place in the geographical origins of those on board Dutch warships. There was a clear shift both from the Republic to nations abroad as well as from the Dutch countryside to the Dutch urban centers. The samples offered in Table 7 (below) deal with the admiralties at Amsterdam, Zeeland, and the Noorderkwartier.

One can assume that during the seventeenth century, the majority of sailors on board warships were Dutch (see also Tables 1 and 3 above), and this was perhaps also true well into the eighteenth century. Around 1730–1740, however, the balance definitively tipped toward foreigners. There had always been large groups of seamen from the Scandinavian and Baltic countries and from Germany on board; in Zeeland, moreover, recruits came from the Southern Netherlands. Columns II and III in Table 7 illustrate how small the numbers of Dutch seamen had become,[82] and a glance at the 1750–1760 payrolls of the admiralty at Amsterdam confirms this picture. But the Germans, as well as the Scandinavians and others, no longer came predominantly from port cities like Hamburg, Bremen, Copenhagen, Danzig, and their environs but from tiny villages and towns in inland areas.

The old and very detailed *Andrees Allgemeiner Handatlas* is indispensable for identifying specific geographical locations. It suggests that naval personnel aboard Dutch ships largely originated from areas with no maritime tradition, regions with underdeveloped economies and wage levels lower than those offered by the navy and the East India Company. The other foreigners came from all parts of the world, notably from Italy and Corsica, and they came, too, from Dutch overseas settlements. The man

Table 7
Geographical Origins of Petty Officers and Seamen in the Eighteenth Century

	Amsterdam Warships, 1720–1733			*Two Zeeland Warships, 1769–1772*			*Two Noorderkwartier Warships, 1772–1775*		
	petty officers	seamen	%	petty officers	seamen	%	petty officers	seamen	%
Amsterdam	78	228	25	5	21	10	13	36	13
rest of Holland	29	132	13	16	36	19	17	22	11
rest of the Netherlands	20	127	12	7	13	7	15	20	9
Flushing				1	1				
rest of Zeeland				8	5				
Germany	40	199	19	12	70	31	20	109	35
Scandinavia/ Baltic	29	271	24	13	29	16	17	67	23
others	10	45	4	7	21	10	2	26	7
unknown, but foreign	14	21	3		3	1	2	7	2
total	220	1023	100	69	199	100	86	287	100

SOURCES: J. R. Bruijn, *De admiraliteit van Amsterdam in rustige jaren 1713–1751 (Amsterdam, 1970), 144–45; The Hague, General State Archives, Admiralties Archives 2843 (payroll of the Brunswijk*, 1769–1770); 2849 (*payroll of St. Maartensdijk*, 1772); 3125–26 (payrolls of the *Dieren*, 1772–1774 and 1775–1777).

from Salem in New England serving on board a Zeeland ship in 1772 had surely made a mistake; his local merchant vessels would have offered him better pay. Seamen from the British Isles and the Southern Netherlands who had been so evident on board the "old" navy had virtually disappeared.

Rather more confusing is the shift within the United Provinces themselves. It is obvious that fewer men from the countryside, particularly that of Holland, joined the navy. Naval wages were no attraction at all, and those Dutch who enlisted hailed from the cities—Amsterdam in particular, but also Rotterdam, Haarlem, Leiden, and Gouda. Whole groups from one city were sometimes registered in the rolls, one man after another. Most apparently they belonged to the urban populace; others probably came from orphanages. The fact, however, that the admiralties of Zeeland and the Noorderkwartier were hardly able to recruit seamen in their own cities is confusing. The populations of cities like Middelburg, Flushing, Hoorn, and Enkhuizen are known to have suffered from poverty, yet the absence of Flushingers in the navy is very marked.

The "foreigning" and "impoverishing" of the navy are more striking when one takes into account that nearly all soldiers, if on board, came from abroad, mainly Germany. The only aspect which slightly changes the picture concerns the petty officers: most of them were Dutch. Lodginghouse keepers played a prominent role in the navy's recruiting efforts as well as those of the East India Company, which required many thousands of seamen and soldiers each year. It is likely that the drain on manpower caused by the enormously high rate of mortality on board the Company's ships and overseas in Asia also aggravated the recruiting problems of the admiralties. The merchant marine and the whaling trade were not faced with the same manning problems because of their totally different recruiting areas and traditional practices, and their higher wages.[83]

The naval authorities placed no restrictions on the geographical origin, language, race, or religion of its seafaring personnel. Supplementary seamen could be recruited in foreign ports. While it was rather uncommon for blacks or Asians to enlist, a few names on the payrolls do suggest that such men were sometimes on board. Larger numbers of blacks were recruited only in the West Indies when a captain was confronted with a great deal of sickness in his original crew. In these cases, it was normal procedure that the black seamen be entitled to free transport back to, for instance, Curaçao. The East India Company operated in the same way with its Chinese crew members. An interesting episode was the effort in 1781 to associate the Jewish element of the Dutch population with the navy. The lack of manpower in those days made Van Kinsbergen and some notable persons in Amsterdam become inventive in that respect. The leaders of the Jewish community, however, could not be persuaded to give dispensation for the rules governing observance the Sabbath, daily prayers, and the preparation of the food. The argument advanced by the navy that its employing the Jewish poor would "alleviate the pressure upon their relief funds" was not sufficiently convincing.[84] Consequently, no Jews at all were ever enlisted, although they represented almost ten percent of the total Amsterdam population.

To complete the rather negative picture of the eighteenth-century navy, it is necessary to include a description of life on board, particularly with regard to the matters of discipline and desertion. One of the main objectives behind the navy's assigning extra officers to its vessels might have been that of control—the maintenance of order among the new, largely unskilled and unruly, crew members. Many so-called seamen did not know what to expect from seafaring. It meant living in rather crowded quarters with a fixed daily routine of six watches and predictable menus three times a day.[85] One might assume, therefore, that not only was discipline aboard ship a common problem but also that many landlubbers tried to desert the navy as soon as possible. It is difficult for us to trace the numbers of men who managed to escape after they had received their first-month earnest money, and possibly a bounty, but before they had actually embarked. Some captains took their own measures to prevent desertion when in port. In 1755, Captain Lodewijk graaf van Bylandt gave his men shore leave, but only in small groups.[86] When two soldiers took to their heels at Genoa, Van Bylandt withdrew the privilege of shore leave altogether. By and large, however, the numbers of deserters were lower than might be expected, and the thirty-six men out of a crew of 216 to desert the *Dieren* of the Noorderkwartier in 1763–1764 were probably an exceptionally high percentage. In any event, the low numbers indicate either that the measures taken by the navy to prevent desertion must have been effective or that the majority of the men were not too unhappy with their new living and working conditions.

Available figures show that in the 1770s and 1780s, desertion did slowly increase. Captain H. B. L. graaf van Bylandt lost two lower-ranking seamen and two petty officers out of a crew of 149 during a voyage to Algiers in 1769–1770. Only one of the 116 men aboard deserted from a frigate briefly cruising in the North Sea in 1772. Captain Willem Rietveld of the Noorderkwartier, however, reported the desertion of seventeen men out of 195 petty officers and ratings.[87] Between 1783 and 1789, no less than fourteen percent of the 2,169 men on board twelve ships of Rotterdam deserted. Most of the deserters were ratings and soldiers. Desertion was particularly high when the ship was in port or anchored in a roadstead for extended periods—and was obviously an aspect of shipboard life which required constant attention from a captain and his officers during those times. Extra guards were put near the hawseholes and the places where the rowing boats and the sloops were moored to the ship. Although deserters who were caught routinely declared themselves to have been drunk when they jumped ship, they were usually thoughtful enough not to have more than three months' salary in credit—money that was always confiscated by the admiralty.[88] The Articles of War prescribed the death sentence for deserters who were caught. In practice, however, the punishment was generally restricted to a ducking three times from the yardarm and fifty lashes.

The ships' logs and the captains' letters covering the journeys of three vessels of the Rotterdam admiralty in the 1760s, 1770s, and 1780s provide us with a general view of how the rules on board were observed and of the kinds of offenses that took place—although one must keep in mind that the more minor offenses were probably not registered. The eighteen-gun frigate *'t Welvaren van 't Land*, under the command of Captain Andries de Bruijn and manned by a crew of 125, cruised in the North Sea from April 1 till October 11, 1760. Its main task at that time was to wait near the Shetland Islands for homeward-bound East Indiamen and then to escort them on their final leg to the Dutch ports. Nothing particular happened during the first trip of De Bruijn as a captain, and discipline was only rarely a problem. On May 31, a quartermaster got drunk and was put in irons. The next day, he was released under his promise of better behavior in future. The same scenario was repeated with an ordinary seaman on July 1. The steward's mate was put in irons for five days (July 9–14) for neglect of duty. The same quartermaster had fallen back into his old ways and on July 21 received some light corporal punishment. More serious was the impertinent behavior of a lieutenant towards his captain on August 17; he refused to carry out an order. De Bruijn intended to hold a council of war with the commanders of the other convoy vessels, but Lieutenant Sonnemans's timely apology saved him from punishment. A drunken seaman was put in irons on August 29 and, two days later, was ordered to walk through the ship with his hands in cuffs. De Bruijn's authority was apparently not very convincing: another lieutenant and the purser behaved badly on September 4 and 6, but both were released on the 7th after making the familiar promise. A council of war was held on September 8. It had been discovered that the drunken seaman had threatened and injured the boatswain's mate on August 29, and had stabbed a soldier six weeks before that. He was ducked three times from the yardarm, lashed, and put ashore "as a rogue." Seven out of 125 men broke the rules during this voyage of six months.[89]

Captain Justus van Gennep commanded the thirty-two-gun frigate *Jason* on two voyages to the Mediterranean from November 22, 1776, to July 10, 1778. Merchantmen had to be convoyed, and the *Jason* participated in operations on the Moroccan coast. The crew consisted of 199 men on the first trip but was enlarged to 230 men on its return to the Mediterranean in June 1777. Van Gennep, having held earlier commands, was an experienced captain. Each month, he had the Articles of War read to the crew, and he regularly ordered drills in handling the guns and rifles. His ship also took part in some maneuvers in order for the crew to learn to sail in line properly and to retreat without confusion. Van Gennep's practical mind was responsible for the construction of a fence near the *Jason* when it was still in port at Hellevoetsluis. Desertion was thus prevented, not least due to the three guards stationed near the fence. Only a few offenses were recorded in the log. On February 15, 1777, the cooper, the carpenter and his mate, and another man got drunk and were put in irons for one night. The same thing happened with the boatswain on April 10. The second purser, who injured himself with a knife when he got drunk on April 12, was held in irons for the next six days. Remaining fond of alcohol, he was again in irons in June, this time for almost two weeks. One deserter was arrested on shore and brought back to the *Jason*. The last offense registered in the log took place on October 23, 1777: the "schieman's" mate (second boatswain) was caught trying to sell some wine which had been smuggled on board with the cooperation of the cook's mate. Each of the junior petty officers suffered only one day in irons. A total of nine men violating the rules during a shipboard life of nineteen months cannot be considered a very serious affair. Six deaths were suffered on board in the same period.[90]

Carrying fifty-four guns and a crew of 300, the ship of the line *Maarten Harpertszoon Tromp* was commanded by Cornelis van Gennep from September 6, 1781, until November 25, 1782. Although the Dutch were at war, it was April before the *Tromp*—the first man-of-war the Dutch navy named in honor of the admiral, though the East India Company had done so earlier with one of its vessels—could finally depart from the roadstead of Goeree (near Hellevoetsluis). The ship sailed to Texel, joined two very short cruises of the Grand Fleet into the North Sea, and was then ordered to pick up three East Indiamen at Bergen in Norway and escort them safely to Flushing. Cornelis faced more problems on board than had Justus van Gennep. Scurvy was raging during the last three months of the voyage, and twenty-one men died as a result. Furthermore, the petty officers behaved badly—eighteen of them being put in irons for one or two days because of drunkenness, insolence, or neglect of duty; six of them repeated their misdemeanors. Yet only two seamen and one soldier were impertinent or discovered stealing or drunk. Mainly, their penalties were light, just one night's imprisonment. Three petty officers were broken in rank. Two mates were also amongst the offenders, while a few midshipmen were made familiar with a ration of bread and water for one or more days. In September, nine seamen did not keep their word when they received permission to go ashore in Norway and as "honest men" had promised to return. They deserted, but four of them were caught and punished with ducking and lashing. During his next command, Cornelis van Gennep again had several problems with incompetent and insolent petty officers.[91] The frequent complaints about the poor quality of the petty officers in the navy that had been initiated by Schrijver and his colleagues during the 1730s were proving to be still warranted in the early 1780s, according to many ships' logs. For the execution of his orders, a captain had to rely on his petty officers in particular, so the increase in the number of these officers on board was not a luxury in this respect.

The great influence, either positive or negative, that petty officers could have on the behavior of ratings is illustrated by one of the rare mutinies to take place in the Dutch navy. In 1779, several crew members of the Amsterdam frigate *Venus* at anchor off Texel requested that they be discharged. Probably, certain promises made to them as to such a leave were either unfulfilled by their superiors or unclear to begin with. The precise reason for the mutiny, however, was the recent introduction of an enlistment bounty, to which crew members would be entitled only if they were to sign on again. A group of sixteen petty officers, headed by the "schieman," were the main instigators of the mutinous behavior and subordination by a great number of seamen and soldiers. It took a month before the mutiny was ended. The rather severe sentences given to the mutineers were repealed by William V, the admiral general, who granted all the men pardons. Once again, one gets the impression that the penalties inflicted upon the offenders of the Articles of War were mild, whatever the offense might have been.[92] Perhaps the captains themselves did not dare to be too severe, lest they further damage the reputation of the service. It was an atmosphere in which, for example, the wives of seamen could send an anonymous letter to the admiralty board reminding its members that their wearing of expensive wigs was made possible only by the fact that these wives had nothing but cabbage stalks to eat ("want voor ons geld soo draegen de heeren pruijke en wij moeten eete koolstruijke").[93]

There are no indications that the situation on board the ships of the Dutch navy improved in the mid-1780s and the 1790s; on the contrary, it deteriorated. It is telling that from 1784 onward, the East India Company had no problems in recruiting sufficient manpower and was even able to lower its monthly wages from fourteen to twelve guilders. The support Van Kinsbergen received for his reforms with regard to the establishment of a standing corps of petty officers and the attention given to his book on naval discipline, however, point to the fact that both naval officers and admiralty authorities must have realized that something had to be done to make the navy's situation less grim. The foundation of the "Kweekschool voor de Zeevaart" at Amsterdam in 1785 was an attempt to educate young boys for seafaring employment—one which soon proved to be rather successful. And aboard ships, the introduction of sauerkraut improved the food.

The daily distribution of a certain quantity of jenever (gin) to the naval crews of the 1760s had been considered a preventive measure against the West Indian diseases and had been reported to be effective. Soon, therefore, jenever was distributed daily on a general scale, and since it was cheap, the authorities made no objections. Only the board at Rotterdam refused to institute the measure. But in 1781, even that admiralty gave in: its captains had complained that their crews were envious when the bells on the other ships in the roadstead were chimed for the daily jenever ration when they were getting nothing.[94] It is noteworthy that many instances of insolence and neglect of duty were connected with drunkenness. And the rather grim situation became even worse after 1795. Political unrest and the appointment of a whole group of new officers also resulted initially in disorder and mutinies in naval bases and on board ships.

The overall picture of the eighteenth-century Dutch navy can hardly be called positive, at least from a seventeenth-century perspective. It was surely a second-rate navy in comparison with the other European powers of the present day and at times even a third-rate one. The process of adjustment after the exhausting period around 1700 required much time and was accompanied by great financial and professional problems for naval officers. By the 1730s, however, the process of adjustment had been completed. The two major admiralties at Amsterdam and Rotterdam had reconstructed their fleets, and their finances were apparently in rather good order. They were again able to demonstrate Dutch naval power to the states on the Barbary coast, and to introduce their convoy service to the West Indies. In contrast, the three other admiralties had not only lost their former strength and but were now fallen into deep decay.

By the 1740s, the Republic was unexpectedly unmasked as an impotent naval power. An auxiliary squadron of twenty vessels could not be properly fitted out in 1744, and three years later, British naval forces were badly needed to help defend the Dutch frontiers. Though a great number of ships were struck by outbreaks of epidemic diseases—against which naval authority in those days was powerless—this problem could not divert attention from the fact that the Republic was no longer capable of exerting any substantial influence at sea. In the next conflicts in Europe and in the western hemisphere, the Dutch tried to remain neutral but were always at the whim of the British navy and French foreign policy. No Dutch man-of-war again entered the Baltic. The maintenance or restoration of peace with the Barbary states now demanded intensive and annual attention from the States of Holland and the States General.[95] The Fourth Anglo-Dutch war was a political disaster for the Dutch; their navy had become a completely insignificant factor in the international naval balance.

Within the Republic itself, the navy was no longer a matter of obvious concern to the nation's administrators. In 1770, for the first time since the War of the Spanish Succession, the States General voted that some money for the navy be collected by the seven provinces themselves rather than being drawn from special funds. The public's neglect of, and lack of interest in, naval affairs during the latter part of the eighteenth century was largely due to the conflicting opinions about Dutch foreign policy amongst the seven provinces and the stadholder—a situation alluded to earlier in part three of this study. Another element, however, was the lack of unanimity among the nineteen members of the States of Holland. The discrepancies in their political and economic interests were great, and the city of Amsterdam was unable to play the dominant role as it had often done before. And in maritime affairs, that city's regents apparently abstained from direct involvement, as was demonstrated by the independent role played by the Directie van de Oostersche Handel en Reederijen.

By and large, the decision-making process in the States General had become more time-consuming than in the previous century. The number of committees grew extensively. Moreover, there was no commanding person available to push plans through—neither the stadholder nor the grand pensionary, who seldom voiced the opinion of a unanimous Holland. The weakness of that province's finances was another obstacle when plans for strengthening the navy and/or the army were discussed. Thus, during the greater part of the century, the admiralties had to depend on their own declining sources of income and some subsidies out of special funds. Put briefly, there was no general political will to reorganize and maintain a strong navy. Mismanagement and corruption made the situation deteriorate even faster.

For the first part of the eighteenth century, the history of the Dutch navy is no different from that of the other European powers. The British and French fleets also declined and went through the same process of adjustment after the long series of naval wars. In the 1770s, the British navy also faced great political problems. In general, however, most countries expanded their naval forces during the second half of the century, the two Bourbon kingdoms of France and Spain in particular. In the north, the Danish navy had been modernized and enlarged. Viewed within such a context, the fate of the former first-rank Dutch navy becomes all the more striking, from both the international as well as the national perspective.

The eighteenth-century Dutch navy did not lag behind in all respects, however. Its warship design and construction incorporated applicable British concepts, though the greater ships of the line were not built. Most of the new frigates proved successful in skirmishes with the Barbary corsairs. The knowledge and skills of the naval officers had greatly improved and, on the whole, met the accepted standards of the day. Indeed, the quality of a man like Van Kinsbergen was appreciated abroad. Part of the officers' corps did suffer from a lack of seafaring practice due to the small number of vessels generally in service. The corps had been doubled in number and more opportunities for promotion created. The manning of ships was a troublesome task for the Dutch. The navy became the worst-paying employer in the Republic and never considered a permanent increase in wages for any category of its seafaring personnel. The quality of the ratings and petty officers deteriorated as recruiting thus became more and more difficult. Yet apart from the Fourth Anglo-Dutch War, the situation never reached the crisis level.

A few signs of a slight revival of the Dutch navy were noticeable after the Fourth Anglo-Dutch War. A construction program was started, and more vessels were annually fitted out, including even special training squadrons. Naval contingents now also operated in Asia. Existing port facilities were improved and new ones created at Den Helder. Some steps were made along the path to a more centralized direction for the navy. And at long last, a corps of gunners was created—the first group of petty officers and seamen in permanent service. This measure would show its effects on board ship only in the long run, however. The political dissent and turmoil of the 1780s, with its impact on the naval officers and the crews, and the first stages of the French revolutionary wars are factors that tended to overshadow these signs of revival. It would remain for Napoleon himself to recognize the true potential of the Dutch navy.

AFTERMATH

The overthrow of the old Republic of the Seven United Provinces by French revolutionary armies in 1795 had far-reaching consequences for its political structure and for Dutch society at large. The sovereignty of the provinces was ended and the direction of the government centralized at The Hague. The old political leaders, the stadholder, and the Orangistic regents were replaced by new leaders recruited from classes other than the traditional ruling élite. Many reforms that affected both public and private life were introduced during the Napoleonic period. In 1810, the Dutch territory was annexed by the French empire and its independence completely lost. For the Netherlands, the downfall of Napoleon resulted in the restoration of the House of Orange in November 1813. The Netherlands became a monarchy under King William I, the eldest son of William V, who had died in exile. From 1815 to 1830, the Southern Netherlands also belonged to William's kingdom, but in 1830 a brief revolution led to the creation of an independent Belgian kingdom. The Dutch were thrown back again into the position of being a small power. Only the possession of a large colonial empire in Indonesia and some other smaller territories provided the Netherlands with additional political and economic importance in world affairs.

The so-called "Batavian and French Period," from 1795 to 1813, did considerable harm to Dutch overseas trade and shipping. British dominance at sea was such that maritime activities under Dutch colors were almost impossible. Dutch entrepreneurs again exploited their traditional skills in the use of other, neutral flags and documents. British blockades and captures, together with French economic retaliation, resulted, however, in a downward trend for the Dutch merchant trade. In 1811 and 1812, shipping came almost to a complete standstill. A major change in Dutch overseas activities was the dissolution of the East India

Company. Asia was now open to private enterprise, and during the first half of the nineteenth century, Dutch maritime affairs were increasingly centered in Indonesia. Another significant change was the decline in the Dutch Baltic trade.

Dutch naval activity, of course, was also affected by these new developments. The overriding conditions under which the navy operated during this time were the lack of full independence and the British blockade of Dutch ports. The French annexed Flushing in 1795 and curtailed the freedom of Dutch foreign policy through a number of treaties. The Dutch navy was now considered an instrument of French warfare. Hundreds of its small craft, for instance, were involved in Napoleon's British invasion schemes during the years from 1803 to 1805. And from 1810 to 1813, the Dutch navy was actually incorporated into the French navy. Yet Napoleon valued the Dutch navy more highly than had the leaders of previous revolutionary regimes. He started a great construction program and had the works at the Den Helder naval base completed.

During most of the Revolutionary and Napoleonic Wars—in a situation analogous to what had occurred during the Fourth Anglo-Dutch War of 1780–1784—Dutch warships were locked in the roadsteads of Texel and Goeree by the British blockading squadrons. The Dutch forces could rarely escape the British net, and even when they did, their voyages often ended in disaster. In 1796, for example, a squadron set off to Asia but was almost completely annihilated by the British in the Saldanha Bay, north of Cape Town. The next year, the Grand Fleet, under the command of Admiral De Winter, was severely defeated off Camperdown, close to Den Helder, and De Winter was imprisoned in Britain. In 1799, a sizable portion of the Dutch navy was captured at anchor east of Den Helder; the loyalty of most of the crews lay with the former stadholder, and they offered no resistance.

After the Napoleonic Wars had ended, the new royal navy of King William I of the Netherlands was able to concentrate its attention mainly on the Dutch colonies, a rather new field of activities. For the Barbary corsairs had ceased to be a threat soon after a successful American-Anglo-Dutch attack on Algiers in 1815–1816. Merchant shipping in general had thus become safer than ever before and no longer required protection by great numbers of convoy vessels. With the exception of the skirmishes during the Belgian Revolution of 1830–1831, the role of the Dutch navy was now restricted to the protection of its own nation's neutrality and to the exercise of colonial power in Indonesia.

The five boards of admiralty had all been dissolved in 1795. Former advocate fiscal Pieter Paulus was able to organize the direction of naval affairs from The Hague. One single person, called either the secretary or the minister of the navy, then operated as the chief of naval administration—with the exception of one brief period, from 1801 to 1805, when a council of three persons was responsible. Centralizing the five naval administrations proved to be quite a complex task. The closing down of naval establishments was especially difficult. Vested local interests were strong, and arguments about the negative effect on local employment were often used successfully. A long time passed before naval facilities in cities like Hoorn, Enkhuizen, Medemblik, Harlingen, and Veere were abolished. Van der Hoop, who before 1795 had been William V's confidant in naval affairs, was still in charge of many of the old establishments as he was responsible for the navy under William I until 1824. It was not until 1850 that a number of the redundant establishments were closed down. Centralization did, of course, have direct consequences for the navy's funding. A small annual central budget had already been introduced in 1792, but the fall of the old Republic finally resulted in the navy's financing being made a part of the annual state budget. The management of the naval administration became uniform, as did the rules for everybody in the naval service. Provincial particularism was wiped out, for instance, by a policy of transfer of personnel.

The officers' corps suffered badly from the political upheavals. This fact had already become apparent by 1787, but seven years later, the split between the adherents of the old and the new regimes reflected the exclusion of a very substantial part of the corps from active service. It was a long time before the wounds were healed. To fill the open positions, the navy had to enlist several officers from the merchant marine—a category of seafarers which had been absent from naval service since the seventeenth century. Van der Hoop's policy of making careful appointments to the officers' corps finally ended the split after 1813. The naval officer continued to be one of the best educated professionals of that era. His education was greatly improved by the introduction of stricter rules concerning the requirements for examination. From 1803 onward, the teaching was provided by a navy cadets' institute—first housed aboard a laid-up war vessel, later in buildings ashore. In 1828, entry into the naval officers' corps was restricted to those midshipmen who had followed the courses of the institute and passed the exams. One is inclined to assume that until 1828 the social background of the officers did not differ much from that of those in service at the end of the old regime. Yet patronage, so prevalent during the earlier time, had now diminished. The centralization of victualing in 1808 also created a major change in the financial position of commanding officers. The traditional provisioning pennies were abolished, and thus a naval anomaly came to an end. The monthly wages of the officers involved, however, were raised accordingly.

Little was changed with regard to the petty officers and the crew. The rather grim situation on board the ships of the Dutch navy during the 1780s continued after 1795. And many instances of mutinous behavior occurred in the years before 1800. Penal regulations, however, were now officially milder than they were before, corporal punishment being abolished. In 1814, however, corporal punishment was reintroduced. The professional skills of the ratings did not improve, wage levels remaining very low: around 1820, the able seaman still earned from thirteen to fifteen guilders per month, while his colleague in the merchant marine typically received about twenty guilders. The naval crews continued to be recruited in the great urban centers of Holland and in Friesland and Zeeland or abroad. There was no real difference between the geographical origins of naval personnel around 1770 and, for example, in 1825.

In sum, the turn of the century brought centralization to the naval administration, new duties for the fleet, in the East Indies in particular, and institutional education for the officers. For the petty officers and ratings, however, no major changes took place before the mid-nineteenth century with regard to schooling, terms of employment, wages, and social and geographical backgrounds. At that time, the Dutch navy was also on its way to becoming a steam-driven entity.

IN RETROSPECT

The history of the Dutch Republic and its navy is indeed quite astonishing. A small country squeezed between the North Sea and the two great territorial powers of France and the German Empire, and populated by fewer than two million people, it nonetheless played the role of a major political and military power during the seventeenth century. And its navy was particularly impressive, a force respected by its contemporaries and by present-day historians as well. The rise of the Republic as a naval power at the end of the sixteenth century was almost as rapid as its decline at the end of the War of Spanish Succession in the early eighteenth century. In the first part of this hundred-year period, naval operations supported the struggle for the Republic's freedom and its maritime expansion into European waters and beyond. The Baltic was an area of the utmost importance; naval forces were sent several times into that sea to protect Dutch shipping and trading interests. The second part of the period, however, saw a navy whose major functions had changed. It was now primarily a tool in the hands of grand pensionary John de Witt for maintaining or restoring peace in Europe, peace being considered beneficial to the economy of Holland in particular. Next, the stadholder-king William III used both the navy and the army in his long struggle against Louis XIV to preserve a balance of power in Europe. This foreign policy forced the Republic to live well above its means, with predictable results. The navy like the Republic found itself with largely insoluble financial problems.

In the eighteenth century, the operations of the Dutch navy were more closely in accord with the resources of the country. The Republic, soon proving to be only a minor European power, left the navy with no tasks other than protecting the mercantile marine on a restricted number of routes and keeping the Barbary corsairs under some kind of control. Yet at times, it was barely equal to these duties. While Dutch merchants and skippers were only slightly hampered by the British seizures of their ships during the Seven Years' War, their enterprises suffered greatly during the Fourth Anglo-Dutch War of 1780–1784—a war waged as part of a world-encompassing conflict whose roots lay in the American Revolution. Before, during, and after that conflict, a naval armament race was being run in Europe. The Dutch Republic, unwilling to remain a bystander, developed a rather impressive naval shipbuilding program, which seemed likely to make the Dutch navy once again a factor of some importance in the balance of naval power between Britain on the one side and France with Spain on the other. The building program had little enduring effect, however, because in 1795, Revolutionary France succeeded in taking over the Dutch navy. Never again would the Netherlands play a significant role in European naval politics. The navy found new tasks for itself, but they were elsewhere in the world: in the East Indies (Indonesia), where it took on the duties of being an instrument in the expansion of the Dutch colonial empire. Much later, in the twentieth century, the Dutch navy was to serve something of a similar purpose: it figured as an element, though a minor one, in the policy of the Western powers regarding Japan's expansion.

In early modern Europe, a nation's expenditures were closely related to the cost of its army and navy. Armies invariably required more resources than navies. Even in the seafaring Dutch Republic of the seventeenth century, the portion of the budget allocated for the army was double that for the navy—a discrepancy that was in the next century to become a quadruple one.[1] Regular expenses for the Dutch navy were covered mostly by revenues from duties on trade and shipping. Special subsidies for war expenditures were voted by the States General, the monies being taken largely out of taxes collected on consumer goods. Such was in general the situation at a time when the maritime economy was in good shape and local as well as national authorities were convinced of the necessity of spending heavily on naval power. Later in the eighteenth century these advantages would not continue, however. Then the admiralties had much smaller budgets.

The organizational system of the Dutch navy, with its five separate admiralties, has been considered an anomaly in an era in which most countries were able to set up centralized bodies to govern affairs of such national importance. One has, however, to keep in mind that a more centralized navy would not have been easily accommodated by a federation of seven sovereign provinces, each with a different government structure. Admiralties did not function simply as naval institutions; they also handled economic affairs. Separate admiralties best suited the interests of the three sovereign maritime provinces. And, as matters turned out, a unified effort in the output of ships and the supply of manpower could be demonstrated when it was needed. Gifted leaders such as John de Witt and Michiel de Ruyter played important roles in such circumstances. Virtually no serious thought was given to more centralization, neither when some admiralties could barely pay the salaries of their permanent staff out of ordinary revenues nor when the Fourth Anglo-Dutch War proved the weakness of the navy as a armed force.

The Dutch navy lacked both a central policy-making institution and a structure for long-term planning. Each policy was therefore the outcome of discussions by admiralty boards with many members. Nevertheless now and then a few able individual persons with well-defined views on the use of the navy in wartime put their mark on Dutch naval policy. Leading naval officers, however, such as M. H. Tromp, De Ruyter, and Van Kinsbergen were only incidentally asked for their opinions on matters of national naval importance. By comparison, the British integrated seafaring experience and knowledge into naval administration on an extremely broad scale, particularly during the eighteenth century.

The Dutch navy did not introduce any new ideas into general naval warfare after it developed its policy of providing convoys on dangerous routes for its lightly armed and unarmed mercantile marine. It held on, as long as possible, to the cheap policy of hiring and arming merchant vessels instead of constructing a sizeable fleet of permanent warships. The victory at the Downs in 1639 against the Spaniards proved the success of that policy most impressively. Only in a very late stage (about 1652) did Dutch naval authorities follow the English example and start building a standing navy. Dutch ships of the line had no innovative features in proportions and armament. Constraints on ship design were always set by the shallowness of the waters in the Netherlands. Vast supplies of shipbuilding materials guaranteed quick construction in the yards of the five admiralties or by private shipbuilders. Line tactics were probably not a Dutch invention. Admiral De Ruyter and his colleague Banckert, however, introduced the tactics of concentration of forces and breaking through the enemy's line—the latter of which was merely developed further by Rodney and Nelson at the end of the eighteenth century. That audacity was one of the features of Dutch naval fighting is a fact well demonstrated by campaigns far into the Baltic and, above all, by the raid on the Medway in 1667.

The Dutch navy in general had no great difficulty in manning its vessels during the seventeenth century. No fixed procedures—like the registration systems in Spain, France, and Sweden—existed in the Republic for the recruitment of naval personnel. It was all arranged on an ad hoc basis, with the primary responsibility for collecting a crew resting with the captain of each warship, large or small. Only an embargo on the departure of merchant and whaling vessels could help him if he were in immediate need of substantial manpower. Of more general consequence was the fact that the Republic's labor market attracted a constant influx of foreigners in search of employment: the vessels of the Dutch navy were largely manned by multinational crews, creating conditions very much unlike those in the navy of England or France. Also important was the fact that the admiralties were located in the main centers of maritime activities. Due to the fact that recruitment was done by individual captains and that a relative abundance of seamen were available, no specific qualifications were required of naval personnel. In the eighteenth century, however, the situation changed. The navy was no longer a regular employer of numerous seamen. Its reputation was now rather tarnished, and eventually, it became the worst-paying employer in the seafaring business. Most seamen were then enlisted from the lowest strata of the urban population and from among unqualified, foreign job-seekers.

Dutch naval officers and admirals have often been described as "tarpaulins," a label normally used in reference to common seamen and petty officers. There is little validity to that charge. With only a few exceptions, Dutch naval officers, certainly those reaching the rank of captain, belonged either to the higher or to the highest social classes in the cities and the countryside. When the aristocratization process of the ruling classes started in the second quarter of the seventeenth century—a process which was completed later in that century—the changes throughout the officer corps were broadly similar in that respect. Striking examples of this process are provided in the sons of the admirals Tromp and De Ruyter. As regents customarily did, both of these men left their urban homes in the 1670s and moved to country estates. In the eighteenth century, the social background of the naval officers' corps remained the same. Many regent-class families committed their sons, often almost by tradition, to the officer corps. So too did the nobility, although they supplied the navy on a much smaller scale than they did the army. According to a recent study, sixty percent of those eighteenth-century army officers who achieved ranks comparable to that of naval commander and higher were of noble birth; one third of them belonged to foreign nobility.[2]

For a very long time, absolutely no official program for the education of future naval officers existed. The naval administration, therefore, had no real influence upon the professional knowledge of its officers. Established customs were the forces that ruled both the recruitment and the training of young boys for naval service , and ready employment provided them with the practical experience. Much later than all the other navies did the Dutch subject their officers to any sort of examination, let alone to an education in an institute ashore. The numerous expeditions made by the navy during the seventeenth-century wars, in addition to its many regular commitments, served as its means not only of keeping its officers well trained but also of creating opportunities for them to receive promotions. From the mid-eighteenth century onwards, more regulations concerning a naval officer's education and career were introduced. The ultimate product of this process was a naval officer who could successfully compete with any other educated Dutchman in technical, cultural, and social skills.

The history of the Dutch navy is full of logic and illogic, success and defeat, innovation and decline. As such, it is a fascinating and surprising story—one that also provides an excellent example of developments in Europe in the armed forces and in the bureaucracy in the early modern period.

NOTES

INTRODUCTION

1. J. D. Tracy, *Holland under Habsburg Rule, 1506–1566: The Formation of a Body Politic* (Berkeley, 1990), esp. 1–8.

2. J. P. Sigmond, *Nederlandse zeehavens tussen 1500 en 1800* (Amsterdam, 1989), chaps. 2–3.

3. For the institutions of the Dutch Republic, see R. Fruin and H. T. Colenbrander, *Geschiedenis der staatsinstellingen in Nederland tot den val der Republiek* (The Hague, 1922); for the admiralties, see S. J. Fockema Andreae, *De Nederlandse staat onder de Republiek* (Amsterdam, 1962), 26–29, 114–16, 203–9.

4. J. W. Koopmans, *De Staten van Holland en de Opstand* (The Hague, 1990), 155.

5. J. R. Bruijn, *De admiraliteit van Amsterdam in rustige jaren 1713–1751 (Amsterdam, 1970), 71.*

6. J. S. Bartstra, *Vlootherstel en Legeraugmentatie, 1770*–1780 (Assen, 1952).

7. The Hague, General State Archives, Admiralties Archives XXXI, 20 (Aug. 9, 1664). P. M. van der Padt of The Hague kindly gave me this reference.

8. J. Th. H. Verhees-van Meer, *De Zeeuwse kaapvaart tijdens de Spaanse Successieoorlog, 1702–1713* (Middelburg, 1986).

9. The Hague, General State Archives, Collection Dassevael 4.

10. J. van der Poel, "Het particularisme van Zeeland en de convoyen en licenten," in *Archief Zeeuwsch Genootschap der Wetenschappen* 1929, 1–113, esp. 15.

11. See J. K. Oudendijk, *Johan de Witt en de zeemacht* (Amsterdam, 1944).

PART ONE: THE "OLD" NAVY, LATE 1500s–1652

1. R. Fruin, *Tien jaren uit den Tachtigjarigen oorlog, 1588–1598* (The Hague, 1861).

2. J. I. Israel, *Dutch Primacy in World Trade, 1585–1740* (Oxford, 1989), chaps. 3–5. For the best general survey of the Dutch navy in this period, see R. E. J. Weber, "Met smakzeilen en spiegelschepen tegen den Spanjaard: de organisatie van een oorlogsmarine," in J. Romein et al., *De Tachtigjarige oorlog* (Amsterdam, 1941), 132–58.

3. F. Pollentier, *De Admiraliteit en de oorlog ter zee onder de Aartshertogen (1596–1609)* (Brussels, 1972), 78–90.

4. J. E. Elias, *Schetsen uit de geschiedenis van ons zeewezen*, vol. 1, *1568–1652* (The Hague, 1916), 47–48.

5. W. Troost, "Capiteynen te water (2): Gerrit Pietersz. de Witte," *Marineblad* 80 (1970): 516–32, esp. 523, 528–29; and "Capiteynen te water (7): Jan Allertsz.," *Marineblad* 83 (1973): 67–87, esp. 71–84.

6. Troost, "Capiteynen te water (3): Jan Claesz. Spiegel," *Marineblad* 80 (1970): 697–716, esp. 705–7; A. G. van der Steur, "Johan van Duvenvoirde en Woude (1547–1610), heer van Warmond, admiraal van Holland," *Hollandse Studiën* 8 (1975): 179–273, esp. 195–99; S. and E. Usherwood, *The Counter-Armada 1596: The Journall of the "Mary Rose"* (London, 1983).

7. Troost, "Capiteynen te water (2)," 529–30; "Capiteynen te water (3)," 708–13; "Capiteynen te water (1): Loth Steyn," *Marineblad* 80 (1970): 239–57, esp. 248–55; and "Capiteynen te water (8): Jan Allertsz.," *Marineblad* 83 (1973): 469–511, esp. 471–501.

8. J. K. J. de Jonge, *De oorsprong van Neerland's bezittingen op de kust van Guinea* (The Hague, 1871), 205; C. Ligtenberg, *Willem Usselinx* (Utrecht, 1914), 17, 20; A. de Booy, *De derde reis van de VOC naar Oost-Indië onder het beleid van admiraal Paulus van Caerden uitgezeild in 1606*, Werken Linschoten-Vereeniging, vol. 70 (The Hague, 1968), 22.

9. J. E. Elias, *De vlootbouw in Nederland in de eerste helft der 17e eeuw, 1596–1655* (Amsterdam, 1933), 27–31; A. Bijl Mz., *De Nederlandse convooidienst* (The Hague, 1951), 52–62.

10. Elias, *Schetsen* 1:71–78.

11. Elias, *De vlootbouw*, 7–33.

12. R. E. J. Weber, *De beveiliging van de zee tegen Europeesche en Barbarijsche zeeroovers 1609–1621* (Amsterdam, 1936), 27–47; C. Senior, *A Nation of Pirates: English Piracy in Its Heyday* (Newton Abbot, 1976).

13. Weber, *De beveiliging*, 87–156.

14. J. K. J. de Jonge, *De oorsprong*, 15–16, 40–43.

15. C. de Jong, *Geschiedenis van de oude Nederlandse walvisvaart* (Pretoria, 1972), 1:203–7.

16. P. Geyl, *Christofforo Suriano: Resident van de Serenissime Republiek van Venetië in Den Haag, 1616–1623* (The Hague, 1913), 224–60.

17. Elias, *De vlootbouw*, 35–36; W. Voorbeijtel Cannenburg, *De reis om de wereld van de Nassausche vloot, 1623–1626*, Werken Linschoten-Vereeniging, vol. 65 (1964), XXII–XXXIV and 4–5.

18. H. Winkel-Rauws, *Nederlandsch-Engelsche samenwerking in de Spaansche wateren, 1625–1627* (Amsterdam, 1946).

19. M. G. de Boer, *Tromp en de Armada van 1639* (Amsterdam, 1941); C. R. Boxer, *The Journal of Maarten Harpertsz. Tromp, Anno 1639* (Cambridge, 1930); C. Rahn Phillips, *Six Galleons for the King of Spain: Imperial Defense in the Early Seventeenth Century* (Baltimore, 1986), 206–22.

20. J. C. de Jonge, *Geschiedenis van het Nederlandsche zeewezen* (Haarlem, 1858), 1:238, 263–67; Israel, *Dutch Primacy*, chap. 5.

21. R. Baetens, "The Organization and Effects of Flemish Privateering in the Seventeenth Century," in *Acta Historiae Neerlandicae: Studies on the History of the Netherlands* 9 (The Hague, 1976), 48–75, esp. 62–63.

22. Bijl, *De Nederlandse convooidienst*, 64–71.

23. J. C. de Jonge, *Geschiedenis . . . zeewezen* 1:255–58, 262, 374; Elias, *Schetsen* 1:116, 118–22, 142–43.

24. G. W. Kernkamp, *De sleutels van de Sont: Het aandeel van de Republiek in den Deensch-Zweedschen oorlog van 1644–1645* (The Hague, 1890), 74–75, 188, 193–94.

25. W. J. van Hoboken, *Witte de With in Brazilië, 1648–1649* (Amsterdam, 1955).

26. S. Groenveld, "The English Civil Wars as a Cause of the First Anglo-Dutch War, 1640–1652," *The Historical Journal* 30 (1987): 541–66.

27. The Hague, General State Archives, Admiralties Archives 119–20, Rotterdam minutes of 1625. Retired Vice Admiral A. de Booy at The Hague has made transcripts of these minutes and kindly put them at my disposal.

28. For favors to fellow citizens at Amsterdam, see M. G. de Boer, "Een kwarteeuw admiraliteitsleven," *Tijdschrift voor Geschiedenis* 56 (1941): 113–51, esp. 115n.

29. The Hague, General State Archives, Admiralties Archives 133, Rotterdam minutes of 1638.

30. De Boer, "Een kwarteeuw," 122–26 and 143.

31. W. F. H. Oldewelt, "De Hoeffijserse schuld (1616–1681)," *Jaarboek Amstelodamum* 51 (1959): 37–52.

32. Van der Poel, "Het particularisme," 50–58.

33. Elias, *Schetsen* 1:93–94.

34. P. Geyl, "De dateering van Vondel's Roskam," *Tijdschrift Nederlandsche Taal-en Letterkunde* 30, n.s., 22 (1911), 308–20; A. Th. van Deursen, *Het kopergeld van de Gouden Eeuw* (Assen, 1979), 3:10–23.

35. The Hague, General State Archives, Admiralties Archives 119, Rotterdam minutes of Sept. 8, 1625.

36. W. Troost, "Capiteynen te water (5): Jan Claesz. Breet," *Marineblad* 81 (1971): 891–909, esp. 903–6.

37. I. Kuyper, "Pieter Jansz. Liorne en de Nederlandse scheepsbouw," *West-Frieslands Oud en Nieuw* 24 (1957): 60–75; Elias, *De vlootbouw*, 15, 17–25.

38. H. Terpstra, *Jacob van Neck: Amsterdams admiraal en regent* (Amsterdam, 1950), 108–71.

39. C. Schmidt, *Om de eer van de familie: Het geslacht Teding van Berkhout 1500–1950, een sociologische benadering* (Amsterdam, 1986), 22–28.

40. The Hague, General State Archives, Admiralties Archives 119, Rotterdam minutes of Feb. 2, 1625; Admiralties Archives 120, minutes of Dec. 14 and 31, 1625; Admiralties Archives 122, minutes of Feb. 20, 1627; E. A. Engelbrecht, *De vroedschap van Rotterdam, 1572–1795* (Rotterdam, 1973), 151–52; R. Bijlsma, *Rotterdams welvaren, 1550–1650* (The Hague, 1918), 174–75, 184.

41. Elias, *De vlootbouw*, 122n.

42. Elias, *Schetsen* 1:124–39.

43. See also G. Teitler, *De wording van het professionele officierscorps* (Rotterdam, 1974), chaps. 5–9.

44. J. C. A. de Meij, *De Watergeuzen en de Nederlanden, 1568–1572* (Amsterdam, 1972), 154–56.

45. A. van der Moer, "Willem Bloys van Treslong (ca. 1529–1594)," *Marineblad* 95 (1985): 524–31.

46. Van der Steur, "Johan van Duvenvoirde en Woude," 185–207.

47. See the articles by W. Troost previously cited, and also his "Een Amsterdams kapitein uit het einde der 16de eeuw: Joachim Pietersz. Cleynsorghe," *Mededelingen Nederlandse Vereniging voor Zeegeschiedenis* 22 (1971): 20–28.

48. Troost, "Capiteynen te water (3)"; De Meij, *De Watergeuzen*, 178.

49. G. Kolleman, "Admiraal Swartenhondt en zijn vrouw Lysbeth Bas," *Ons Amsterdam* 19 (1967): 57–62; Weber, *De beveiliging*, 146–49, 188.

50. J. C. de Jonge, *Levensbeschrijving van Johan en Cornelis Evertsen, luitenant-admiralen van Zeeland* (The Hague, 1820), 1–18; Elias, *Schetsen* 1:66–67.

51. C. A. Davids, *Zeewezen en wetenschap: De wetenschap en de ontwikkeling van de navigatietechniek in Nederland tussen 1585 en 1815* (Amsterdam, 1986), 294, 299; J. C. de Jonge, *Geschiedenis . . . zeewezen* 1:289–90.

52. Weber, *De beveiliging*, 186–87; D. F. Scheurleer, ed., *Van varen en van vechten* (The Hague, 1914), 1:148–50.

53. De Jonge, *Geschiedenis . . . zeewezen* 1:246; Elias, *Schetsen* 1:96.

54. F. Graefe, *De kapiteinsjaren van Maerten Harpertszoon Tromp* (Amsterdam, 1938), 36n.

55. E. C. M. Huysman, ed., *Particuliere notulen van de vergaderingen der Staten van Holland 1620–1640 door N. Stellingwerff en S. Schot*, 3 (1625–1628), Rijks Geschiedkundige Publicatiën, Grote Serie 206 (The Hague, 1989), 481; Winkel-Rauws, *Nederlandsch-Engelsche samenwerking*, 63; Rahn-Phillips, *Six Galleons*, 3, 77.

56. J. C. M. Warnsinck, *Drie zeventiende-eeuwsche admiraals: Piet Heyn, Witte de With, Jan Evertsen* (Amsterdam, 1943), 13–54; A. van der Moer, "Pieter Pieterszoon Heyn (1577–1629)," *Marineblad* 96 (1986): 556–64; Huysman, ed., *Particuliere notulen*, 320.

57. M. G. de Boer, *Het proefjaar van Maarten Harpertsz. Tromp, 1637–1639* (Amsterdam, 1946), 11–36; and *Tromp en de Duinkerkers* (Amsterdam, 1949), 81.

58. J. K. Oudendijk, *Maerten Harpertszoon Tromp* (The Hague, 1952), 80–82.

59. Schmidt, *Om de eer*, 28–48, 204; De Boer, *Het proefjaar*, 79; and *Tromp en de Armada*, 198–99; J. E. Elias, *De vroedschap van Amsterdam, 1578–1795*, vol. 1 (Haarlem, 1903), 392.

60. J. C. de Jonge, *Geschiedenis . . . zeewezen* 1:265–66; G. J. A. Raven, "De Banckerts," *Marineblad* 92 (1982): 518–26.

61. The Hague, General State Archives, Collection Evertsen 4; Warnsinck, *Drie admiraals*, 121–66.

62. The Hague, General State Archives, States General Archives 3199, minutes of Nov. 2, 1640.

63. J. R. Bruijn, "Voeding op de Staatse vloot," *Spiegel Historiael* 2 (1967): 175–83.

64. *Rotterdamsche Historiebladen* 3 (1880): 83–84.

65. De Boer, *Het proefjaar*, 13–16.

66. The most up-to-date biographies are Oudendijk, *Maerten Harpertszoon Tromp*, and A. Doedens and L. Mulder, *Tromp: Het verhaal van een zeeheld* (Baarn, 1989).

67. Loenen aan de Vecht, Teding van Berkhout, Family Archive 187.

68. The Hague, General State Archives, States General Archives 9403 (Feb. 5, 1653); Elias, *De vlootbouw*, 92n; Elias, *Schetsen*, vols. 2–5, passim.

69. The Hague, General State Archives, Admiralties Archives, the sections of the various admiralties; Middelburg, State Archives in Zeeland, Rekenkamer Archives.

70. De Meij, *De Watergeuzen*, 157–64.

71. J. C. de Jonge, *Geschiedenis . . . zeewezen* 1:749, 751, 754.

72. J. R. Bruijn, "Mercurius en Mars uiteen: De uitrusting van de oorlogsvloot in de zeventiende eeuw," in *Bestuurders en geleerden*, ed. S. Groenveld et al. (Amsterdam, 1985), 97–106, esp. 99.; De Boer, "Een kwarteeuw," 141–42.

73. Davids, *Zeewezen*, 74, 119–20.

74. Elias, *Schetsen* 1:59–61; Weber, *De beveiliging*, 191–93.

75. W. Voorbeijtel Cannenburg, *De Groene Draeck: Het snelle schip van Maerten Harpertsz. Tromp* (Amsterdam, 1957), 21–22 (examples for 1625); J. C. de Jonge, *Geschiedenis . . . zeewezen* 1:246–48.

76. A. Th. van Deursen, "Holland's Experience of War during the Revolt of the Netherlands," in *Britain and The Netherlands*, vol. 6 (War and Society), ed. A. C. Duke and C. A. Tamse (The Hague, 1977), 19–53, esp. 40–47; E. Stols, *De Spaanse Brabanders of de handelsbetrekkingen der Zuidelijke Nederlanden met de Iberische wereld, 1598–1648* (Brussels, 1971), 301–3; The Hague, General State Archives, Admiralties Archives 137, minutes of Nov. 26, 1642.

77. A. Th. van Deursen, *Het kopergeld* 3:96–97.

78. G. Valk, "Oproeren, onlusten en rellen in Alkmaar gedurende de Republiek," *Holland* 13 (1981): 230–47, esp. 236.

79. For instance, G. L. Grove, ed., *Journalen van de admiralen Van Wassenaer-Obdam (1658/59) en De Ruyter (1659/60)*, Werken Historisch Genootschap 3e serie, no. 23 (Amsterdam, 1907), 166.

80. T. H. Milo, "Het Nederlands hulpeskader voor Portugal [1641]," in *Varia Historica aangeboden aan Professor doctor A. W. Byvanck* (Assen, 1954), 165–76; P. J. Blok, *Michiel Adriaanszoon De Ruyter* (The Hague, 1930), 33–44.

81. Van Hoboken, *Witte de With*, 192–208.

82. Voorbeijtel Cannenburg, *De Groene Draeck*, 7, 15, 35.

83. Elias, *De vlootbouw*, 36–80.

84. Bruijn, "Mercurius en Mars uiteen," 98–100.

PART TWO: THE "NEW" NAVY, 1652–1713

1. See also S. Schama, *The Embarrassment of Riches: An Interpretation of Dutch Culture* (New York, 1987).

2. Israel, *Dutch Primacy*, chaps. 6–8.

3. J. A. Faber et al., "Population Changes and Economic Developments in the Netherlands: A Historical Survey," *A. A. G. Bijdragen* 12 (1965): 47–110, esp. 60, 110.

4. B. Capp, *Cromwell's Navy: The Fleet and the English Revolution, 1648–1660* (Oxford, 1989), 42–60.

5. Elias, *De vlootbouw*, 80–83.

6. Capp, *Cromwell's Navy*, 66–78.

7. R. E. J. Weber, "The Introduction of the Single Line Ahead as a Battle Formation by the Dutch, 1665–1666," *Mariner's Mirror* 73 (1987): 5–19, esp. 7–8.

8. Elias, *De vlootbouw*, 84–91.

9. J. C. de Jonge, *Geschiedenis . . . zeewezen* 1:403–520; Capp, *Cromwell's Navy*, 78–86.

10. Elias, *De vlootbouw*, chaps. 9–12.

11. Elias, *Schetsen* 6:113–24.

12. Oudendijk, *Johan de Witt*, 3–56.

13. Oudendijk, *Johan de Witt*, 50–53; Elias, *Schetsen* 2:54, 81–87; Blok, *De Ruyter*, 107–8.

14. Elias, *De vlootbouw*, 157–60.

15. H. H. Rowen, *John de Witt, Grand Pensionary of Holland, 1625–1672* (Princeton, 1978), 170–90.

16. F. Muller van Brakel, "Amsterdamse admiraliteitsheren actief achter de schermen," *Marineblad* 66 (1956), 226–43; J. P. Sigmond, *Nederlandse zeehavens tussen 1500 en 1800* (Amsterdam, 1989), 88–89.

17. Oudendijk, *Johan de Witt*, 86–89; Rowen, *John de Witt*, 460–63.

18. N. F. Noordam, *De Republiek en de Noordse oorlog 1655–1660* (Assen, 1940), 164.

19. P. A. Leupe, ed., "Aanbevelingen voor scheepskapiteins enz. ingekomen bij den raadpensionaris Johan de Witt, 1653–1672," *Kroniek Historisch Genootschap* 29 (1873): 603–54.

20. Blok, *De Ruyter*, 253.

21. Oudendijk, *Johan de Witt*, 96–178.

22. Noordam, *De Republiek*; Grove, ed., *Journalen*.

23. J. C. de Jonge, *Geschiedenis . . . zeewezen* 1:541–48, 589–97; Blok, *De Ruyter*, 120–33, 136–54, 180–208; see also F. Binder, "Die Zeeländische Kaperfahrt," in *Archief Koninklijk Zeeuwsch Genootschap der Wetenschappen* 1976, 40–92, esp. 40–71.

24. C. Wilson, *Profit and Power: A Study of England and the Dutch Wars* (London, 1957); C. R. Boxer, *The Anglo-Dutch Wars of the 17th Century, 1652–1674* (London, 1974).

25. J. C. M. Warnsinck, "De laatste tocht van Wassenaer van Obdam. Voorjaar 1665," in *Van vlootvoogden en zeeslagen* (Amsterdam, 1940), 242–300; see also his *De retourvloot van Pieter de Bitter (Kerstmis 1664–Najaar 1665)* (The Hague, 1929).

26. H. A. van Foreest and R. E. J. Weber, *De Vierdaagse Zeeslag 11–14 Juni 1666* (Amsterdam, 1984).

27. R. Ollard, *Man of War: Sir Robert Holmes and the Restoration Navy* (London, 1969), chap. 13.

28. J. R. Bruijn, "Dutch Privateering during the Second and Third Anglo-Dutch Wars," in *The Low Countries History Yearbook 1978: Acta Historiae Neerlandicae 11* (The Hague, 1979), 79–93, esp. 86–90; Israel, *Dutch Primacy*, 278; F. Snapper, *Oorlogsinvloeden op de overzeese handel van Holland, 1551–1719* (Amsterdam, 1959), 150, 178, 311.

29. See R. Ollard, *Pepys: A Biography* (London, 1974), chap. 12; P. G. Rogers, *The Dutch in the Medway* (London, 1970); C. J. W. van Waning and A. van der Moer, *Dese Aengenaeme Tocht: Chatham 1667 herbezien door zeemansogen* (Zutphen, 1981); J. C. M. Warnsinck, *Abraham Crijnssen: De verovering van Suriname en zijn aanslag op Virginië 1667* (Amsterdam, 1936).

30. T. H. Milo, "Michiel Adriaenszoon de Ruyter als tacticus," *Onze Vloot* 46 (1957): 89–92; Weber, "The Introduction of the Single Line Ahead," 9–18.

31. J. C. M. Warnsinck, *Admiraal De Ruyter: De Zeeslag op Schooneveld Juni 1673* (The Hague, 1930); R. Fruin, *De oorlog van 1672* (Groningen, 1972); J. R. Bruijn, *De oorlogvoering ter zee in 1673 in journalen en andere stukken* (Groningen, 1966), 209.

32. D. G. Shomette and R. D. Haslach, *Raid on America: The Dutch Naval Campaign of 1672–1674* (Columbia, S.C., 1988); Bruijn, "Dutch Privateering," 90–93.

33. Blok, *De Ruyter*, 391–419; see also A. van der Moer, *Michiel Adriaenszoon de Ruyter* (n.p., 1990), 23–48.

34. J. C. de Jonge, *Geschiedenis . . . zeewezen* 2:513–740. See also J. Römelingh, *De diplomatieke betrekkingen van de Republiek met Denemarken en Zweden, 1660–1675* (Amsterdam, 1969).

35. J. C. de Jonge, *Geschiedenis . . . zeewezen* 3:8–21.

36. A. van der Kuijl, *De Glorieuze overtocht:De expeditie van Willem III naar Engeland in 1688* (Amsterdam, 1988), 41, 57, 73–74.

37. J. R. Bruijn, "William III and His Two Navies," *Notes and Records of the Royal Society of London* 43 (1989): 117–32, esp. 117–20.

38. J. C. M. Warnsinck, *De vloot van den Koning-Stadhouder, 1689–1690* (Amsterdam, 1934). For the French navy, see G. Symcox, *The Crisis of French Sea Power, 1688–1697: From the Guerre d'Escadre to the Guerre de Course* (The Hague, 1974).

39. For more details, see J. C. de Jonge, *Geschiedenis . . . zeewezen* 3:240–532, 749. The English navy has been studied in great detail by J. Ehrman in *The Navy in the War of William III, 1689–1697* (Cambridge, England, 1953).

40. J. C. de Jonge, *Geschiedenis . . . zeewezen* 3:730–34.

41. Verhees-van Meer, *De Zeeuwse kaapvaart*, 138–42.

42. N. A. M. Rodger, "The British View of the Functioning of the Anglo-Dutch Alliance, 1688–1795," in *Navies and Armies: The Anglo-Dutch Relationship in War and Peace, 1688–1988*, ed. G. J. A. Raven and N. A. M. Rodger (Edinburgh, 1990), 12–32, esp. 12–16; P. C. van Royen, *Zeevarenden op de koopvaardijvloot omstreeks 1700* (Amsterdam, 1987), 59–70; J. B. Hattendorf, *England in the War of the Spanish Succession: A Study of the English View and Conduct of Grand Strategy* (New York, 1987), 91–92, 155–60, 318–22.

43. J. C. de Jonge, *Geschiedenis . . . zeewezen* 3:545–718, 4:1–93; A. N. baron De Vos van Steenwijk, "Gibraltar," *Marineblad* 78 (1968): 907–23, 1064.

44. There is no biographical study of De Wildt. For scattered information, see Elias, *De vroedschap*, 1: 392–93; Muller van Brakel, "Amsterdamse admiraliteitsheren"; J. C. de Jonge, *Geschiedenis . . . zeewezen* 3:73, 109–11; A. J. Veenendaal, ed., *De briefwisseling van Anthonie Heinsius, 1702–1720*, vol. 1, Rijks Geschiedkundige Publicatiën, Grote Serie 158 (The Hague, 1976), 88; vol. 2, no. 163 (1978), 24, 517; vol. 3, no. 169 (1980), 18. The quotation is found in *De briefwisseling*, vol. 3, letter of Jan. 15, 1704.

45. A. L. van Schelven, *Philips van Almonde: Admiraal in de gecombineerde vloot, 1644–1711* (Amsterdam, 1947), 94. See also Veenendaal, ed., *De briefwisseling*; the letters have been edited up to 1712 (vol. 12, 1990).

46. J. C. de Jonge, *Geschiedenis . . . zeewezen* 3:85–94.

47. H. E. Becht, *Statistische gegevens betreffende den handelsomzet van de Republiek der Vereenigde Nederlanden gedurende de 17e eeuw (1579–1715)* (The Hague, 1908), 147–48; J. C. de Jonge, *Geschiedenis . . . zeewezen* 3:739.

48. C. W. J. Schaap, "De admiraliteit van Friesland: haar vlagofficieren en schepen," in *Fries Scheepvaart Museum en Oudheidkamer, Jaarboek 1982*, 43–77, esp. 53, 61; J. C. de Jonge, *Geschiedenis . . . zeewezen* 3:732–34.

49. M. van der Bijl, *Idee en Interest: Voorgeschiedenis, verloop en achtergronden van de politieke twisten in Zeeland en vooral in Middelburg tussen 1702 en 1715* (Groningen, 1981), 21, 29, 44.

50. P. M. van der Padt, "De admiraliteit van Zeeland in drukke jaren: Logistiek en agrarisatie van de admiraliteit van Zeeland tijdens de overwintering van de vloot in Spanje, 1694–1695" (Master's thesis, University of Leiden, 1989); Verhees-van Meer, *De Zeeuwse kaapvaart*, 121–25; J. de Witte van Citters, *Contracten van Correspondentie en andere bijdragen tot de geschiedenis van het ambtsbejag in de Republiek der Vereenigde Nederlanden* (The Hague, 1873), 276–78.

51. Verhees-van Meer, *De Zeeuwse kaapvaart*, 125–35.

52. The report appears *in extenso* in *Hollandsche Mercurius verhalende de voornaemste saken van staat . . . in het jaer 1688* (Haarlem, 1689), 123–49. K. W. Swart indirectly refers to it; see *Sale of Offices in the Seventeenth Century* (The Hague, 1949), 76.

53. Elias, *De Vroedschap*, 1: 481, 494–95; J. R. Bruijn, "Cornelis Tromp (1629–1691): een niet-gewaardeerd dienaar van de heren," *Tijdschrift voor Geschiedenis* 96 (1983): 179–92, esp. 192. At Harlingen, the advocate-fiscal ranked tenth in the local financial hierarchy, the secretary twenty-third (T. Marseille, *Harlingen de vermaerde zeestad* [Harlingen, 1984], 111).

54. Elias, *Schetsen* 6:45–47.

55. Oudendijk, *Johan de Witt*, 133.

56. Bruijn, *De oorlogvoering*; see on May 17; June 14, 16, 28; August 25.

57. S. Groenveld, *"Evidente factiën in den Staet": Sociaal-politieke verhoudingen in de 17e-eeuwse Republiek der Verenigde Nederlanden* (Hilversum, 1990), 63–64.

58. A summing-up of the discussion on the regents' class appears in J. de Jong's *Een deftig bestaan: Het dagelijks leven van regenten in de 17de en 18de eeuw* (Utrecht, 1987); and in L. Kooijmans's "Patriciaat en aristocratisering in Holland tijdens en zeventiende en achttiende eeuw," in *De bloem der natie: Adel en patriciaat in de Noordelijke Nederlanden*, ed. J. Aalbers and M. Prak (Meppel, 1987), 93–103.

59. J. R. Bruijn, "In een veranderend maritiem perspectief: het ontstaan van directies voor de vaart op de Oostzee, Noorwegen en Rusland," *Tijdschrift voor Zeegeschiedenis* 9 (May 1990): 15–25.

60. See, e.g., Teitler, *De Wording*, 6–9. On Van Rechteren, see J. F. van Dulm, "Het Memoriaal van Johan Willem baron van Regteren," in *Jaarverslag Vereeniging Nederlandsch Historisch Scheepvaartmuseum*(Amsterdam, 1971–1972), 80–82.

61. J. C. de Jonge, *Geschiedenis . . . zeewezen* 1:675–84.

62. Davids, *Zeewezen*, 297–99.

63. Van Foreest and Weber, *De Vierdaagse Zeeslag*, 89–91.

64. Schaap, "De admiraliteit van Friesland," 50–53; J. C. de Jonge, *Geschiedenis . . . zeewezen* 3:188n.

65. J. C. de Jonge, *Geschiedenis . . . zeewezen* 3:280–549.

66. Leupe, ed., "Aanbevelingen voor scheepskapiteins enz.," *Kroniek Historisch Genootschap* 29 (1873): 640–42; Bruijn, ed., *De oorlogvoering*, 16–18.

67. P. Holck, *Cort Adeler* (Copenhagen, 1934), 17, 82–85; J. H. Barfod, *Niel Juel: A Danish Admiral of the 17th Century* (Copenhagen, 1977), 10–13; Leupe, ed., "Aanbevelingen voor scheepskapteins enz. ingekomen bij," *Kroniek Historisch Genootschap* 29 (1873): 604–5; J. C. de Jonge, *Geschiedenis . . . zeewezen* 1:678–79; Blok, *De Ruyter*, 323.

68. Warnsinck, *De vloot van den Koning-Stadhouder*, 137–38; G. van Alphen, *De stemming van de Engelsen tegen de Hollanders in Engeland tijdens de regeering van den Koning-Stadhouder Willem III* (Assen, 1938), 147, 217n; Van Schelven, *Philips van Almonde*, 61n; Blok, *De Ruyter*, 324.

69. The Hague, General State Archives, Collection De Ruyter 115; *Groot Placaetboeck vervattende de placaten, ordonnantiën en de edicten van de Staten-Generael der Vereenigde Nederlanden . . .*, 3:206.

70. Bruijn, "Voeding," 180–83; J. R. Bruijn and E. S. van Eyck van Heslinga, eds., "Aan 'Wijffje lief,' Brieven van zeekapitein Eland du Bois aan zijn vrouw (1669–1674)," *Nederlandse Historische Bronnen* 5 (1985): 111–44, esp. 123.

71. Rotterdam, Municipal Archive, Notarial Records 931, f.632–43; E. Wiersum, *Egbert Meussen Cortenaer* (Assen, 1939), 31; "Inventaris van den boedel van den Luitenant Admiraal Tjerk Hiddes de Vries, 2 Januarij 1667," *Friesche Volks-*

almanak (1889): 112–27. See also Schama, *The Embarrassment*, 304–6, 314–25, 425–29.

72. W. F. H. Oldewelt, "De beroepsstructuur van de bevolking der Hollandse stemhebbende steden volgens de kohieren van de familiegelden van 1674, 1715 en 1742," *Economisch-Historisch Jaarboek* 24 (1950): 80–161, esp. 120, 134–35.

73. Rotterdam, Municipal Archive, Notarial Records 1216, acts 30 and 62 (February 5, 1700); P. J. Blok, "Inventaris van De Ruyter's inboedel, opgemaakt 22–24 maart 1677," *Bijdragen en Mededelingen Historisch Genootschap* 49 (1928): 187–213, esp. 194–95, 205; W. Martin, "Een en ander uit den inventaris der nalatenschap van Cornelis Tromp," *Oud-Holland* 19 (1901): 65–76.

74. Bruijn and Van Eyck van Heslinga, eds., "Aan 'Wijffje lief,'" passim.

75. Grove, ed., *Journalen*, 212; C. E. Warnsinck-Delprat, ed., *Reyse gedaen bij Adriaen Schagen aen de croonen van Sweden ende Polen in den jaere 1656*, Werken Linschoten-Vereeniging, vol. 69 (The Hague, 1968), 159, 163–64.

76. See, e.g., The Hague, General State Archives, Admiralties Archives 1839–60 (1661–1682).

77. *Groot Placaetboeck* 3:223–25; J. C. de Jonge, *Geschiedenis . . . zeewezen* 2:200; J. Belonje, "Het oorlogsschip 'De Alkmaar' en zijn wapenfeit bij Kijkduin in 1673," *Mededelingen Nederlandse Vereniging voor Zeegeschiedenis* 24 (1972): 11–14.

78. Bruijn and Van Eyck van Heslinga, eds., "Aan 'Wijffje lief,'" 120; Bruijn, "Cornelis Tromp," 181–82.

79. The Hague, General State Archives, Collection De Ruyter 179, 184, and 189, no. 20; Blok, "Inventaris," 198–203; and *De Ruyter*, 325–26, 432. See also S. Hart, "Michiel Adriaanszoon de Ruyter en de Noortcaepse Compagnie," in *Geschrift en Getal* (Dordrecht, 1976), 247–54.

80. The Hague, General State Archives, Admiralty Archives XXXI:7 (Nov. 18, 1662); Oudendijk, *Johan de Witt*, 174.

81. Warnsinck, *Admiraal De Ruyter*, 62, 120; Rowen, *John de Witt*, 875–81.

82. Bruijn and Van Eyck van Heslinga, eds., "Aan 'Wijffje lief,'" medical report, 142–44.

83. See also A. Hallema, *Cornelis Maartenszoon Tromp, 1629–1691* (The Hague, 1941).

84. F. L. Diekerhoff, ed., *Journael gehouden op 's landts schip d'Eendracht door de heer Aert van Nes lt. admrl. van Holland ende Westvriesland in den jaere 1667*, Bijdrage Geschiedenis Zeewezen Bureau Maritieme Historie Marinestaf, vol. 2 (1967), 11; J. C. de Jonge, *Geschiedenis . . . zeewezen* 3:31n.

85. Warnsinck, *De vloot van den Koning-Stadhouder*, 139–41; J. C. de Jonge, *Geschiedenis . . . zeewezen* 3:410.

86. Warnsinck, *Van vlootvoogden*, 212; B. J. Slot, *Archipelagus turbatus: Les Cyclades entre colonisation latine et occupation Ottomane, c. 1500–1718* (Leiden, 1982), 22, 199.

87. Leupe, ed., "Aanbevelingen voor scheepskapteins enz. ingekomen bij," *Kroniek Historisch Genootschap* 29 (1873): 630, 639–40, 643–50; Veenendaal, ed., *De briefwisseling* 2:289.

88. P. A. Leupe, ed., "Voordracht tot aanstelling van Stachhouwer, Vlugh enz. tot kapiteins, door het Noorder-Kwartier aan H. H. M., 19 Februarij 1665," *Kroniek Historisch Genootschap* 22 (1866): 291–97, esp. 295; "Aanbeveling van vlagofficieren enz.," *Kroniek Historisch Genootschap* 26 (1870): 286–301, esp. 295; "Aanbevelingen van kapiteins bij het Noorder Kwartier, 1667," *Kroniek Historisch Genootschap* 29 (1873): 165–79, esp. 167–74; "Aanbevelingen voor scheeps-

kapteins enz. ingekomen bij," *Kroniek Historisch Genootschap* 29 (1873): 638; and "Aanbevelingen voor scheepskapiteins enz.," *Kroniek Historisch Genootschap* 31 (1875): 504–13, esp. 510.

89. See R. B. Prud'homme van Reine, "Willem Bastiaensz. Schepers (1619–1704), een veelzijdig Rotterdams koopman en reder," *Tijdschrift voor Zeegeschiedenis* 7 (1988): 14–41.

90. F. P. de Boer, "Gerard Callenburgh," *Marineblad* 90 (1980): 292–304, esp. 296; Bruijn, *De admiraliteit*, 114.

91. Van Schelven, *Philips van Almonde*; L. L. M. Eekhout, "Philips van Almonde: Admiraal in de schaduw," *Marineblad* 95 (1985): 404–11.

92. The Hague, General State Archives, Collection Evertsen 14.

93. Veenendaal, ed., *De briefwisseling* 2:289.

94. Hoorn, Westfries Museum, Collection VerLoren, 44; Bruijn, *De admiraliteit*, 120–21; see also J. C. de Jonge, *Geschiedenis . . . zeewezen*, vols. 3–4, passim; Veenendaal, ed., *De briefwisseling* 2:289.

95. T. Marseille, *Harlingen*, 111.

96. Oudendijk, *Johan de Witt*, 99; Elias, *Schetsen* 5:128–29.

97. The Hague, General State Archives, States of Holland Archives, minutes of April 16, 1672; General State Archives, Aanwinsten 1888, 25 (muster roll, *Gouden Leeuw*, 1673).

98. Noordam, *De Republiek*, 158–59; Grove, ed., *Journalen*, 170; J. C. de Jonge, *Geschiedenis . . . zeewezen* 1:663–66.

99. J. C. de Jonge, *Geschiedenis . . . zeewezen* 3:737–55, 4:755–57; J. R. Bruijn and J. Lucassen, eds., *Op de schepen der Oost-Indische Compagnie: Vijf artikelen van J. de Hullu* (Groningen, 1980), 14.

100. Ph. M. Bosscher, *De Nederlandse mariniers* (Bussum, 1966), chaps. 4–9; J. C. de Jonge, *Geschiedenis . . . zeewezen* 1:668–73, 3:545–47.

101. Oudendijk, *Johan de Witt*, 99; Elias, *Schetsen* 5:128–29.

102. Q. Rian, "State and Society in Seventeenth-century Norway," *Scandinavian Journal of History* 10 (1985): 337–60, esp. 350–52.

103. Warnsinck-Delprat, ed., *Reyse*, 147, 156; Grove, ed., *Journalen*, 33, 75; J. C. M. Warnsinck, ed., *Reisen van Nicolaus de Graaff gedaan naar alle gewesten des werelds beginnende 1639 tot 1687 incluis*, Werken Linschoten-Vereeniging, vol. 33 (The Hague, 1930), 79–80, 96; Elias, *Schetsen* 3:76–77.

104. Rotterdam, Municipal Archive, Notarial Records 778, f. 177, 1021, f.221–55; Grove, ed., *Journalen*, 51.

105. S. Haagsma, *Eenige bladzijden uit Friesland's zeegeschiedenis* (n.p., ca. 1895), 100; Diekerhoff, ed., *Journael*, 3.

106. Bosscher, *De Nederlandse mariniers*, chaps. 4–9; J. C. de Jonge, *Geschiedenis . . . zeewezen* 1:668–73, 3:545–47.

107. The Hague, General State Archives, Admiralties Archives 1839–54; Middelburg, State Archives in Zeeland, Rekenkamer Archives 703.

108. Davids, *Zeewezen*, 297–98.

109. L. Noordegraaf, *Daglonen in Alkmaar, 1500–1800* (n.p., 1980), 21, 24–25, 45–47; and *Hollands welvaren? Levensstandaard in Holland, 1450–1650* (Bergen, 1985), 60–61; G. Groenhuis, *De predikanten: De sociale positie van de gereformeerde predikanten in de Republiek der Vereenigde Nederlanden voor ± 1700* (Groningen, 1977), 65–66. Ship carpenters earned higher wages (twenty-six to thirty-three stuivers); see R. W. Unger, *Dutch Shipbuilding before 1800* (Assen, 1978), 99–100.

110. J. de Vries, *The Dutch Rural Economy in the Golden Age, 1500–1700* (New Haven, 1974), 183; J. A. Faber, "De Noordelijke Nederlanden van 1480 tot 1780: Structuren in beweging," in *Algemene Geschiedenis der Nederlanden* (Haarlem, 1980), 5:196–250, esp. 203; see also J. Lucassen, *Migrant Labour in Europe, 1660–1900: The Drift to the North Sea* (London, 1987).

111. J. de Vries, *The Dutch Rural Economy*, 183–84.

112. See Bruijn, "Voeding."

113. The Hague, General State Archives, Collection De Ruyter 94 (1666); Haagsma, *Eenige bladzijden*, 138, 140.

114. C. Allard, *Nieuwe Hollandsche scheepsbouw* (Amsterdam, 1695), 54–55.

115. A. E. Leuftink, *De geneeskunde bij 'slands oorlogsvloot in de 17e eeuw* (Assen, 1953), 68, 84, 90, 118–21, 126; C. E. Warnsinck-Delprat, ed., *Reyse*, 151n.4. See also *Groot Placaetboeck* 5:288–89.

116. Grove, ed., *Journalen*, 33–70; Diekerhoff, ed., *Journael*, 72; The Hague, General State Archives, Admiralties Archives 2518 (March 12, 1695). P. M. van der Padt gave me this reference.

117. Warnsinck-Delprat, ed., *Reyse*, 146, 149, 166; Warnsinck, *De vloot van den Koning-Stadhouder*, 70; Warnsinck, ed., *Reisen*, 55, 83.

118. The Hague, General State Archives, Aanwinsten 1896, 151; Warnsinck, ed., *Reisen*, 92–93; Bruijn, ed., *De oorlogvoering*, 162; Warnsinck, *De vloot van den Koning-Stadhouder*, 116–18.

119. *Groot Placaetboeck* 3:219–22, 5:275–90.

120. Haagsma, *Eenige bladzijden*, 118; Warnsinck, *De vloot van den Koning-Stadhouder*, 176; The Hague, General State Archives, Collection De Ruyter 192 (August 1674).

121. C. A. Davids, *Wat lijdt den zeeman al verdriet: Het Nederlandse zeemanslied in de zeiltijd (1600–1900)* (The Hague, 1980), 41, 47, 49.

122. Warnsinck, *De vloot van den Koning-Stadhouder*, 193; Warnsinck, ed., *Reisen*, 97; Grove, ed., *Journalen*, 294; Warnsinck-Delprat, ed., *Reyse*, 42, 120; H. Hardenberg, ed., *Tussen zeerovers en christenslaven* (Leiden, 1950), 21.

123. Haagsma, *Eenige bladzijden*, 128, 178; Diekerhoff, ed., *Journael*, 45, 68. See also S. W. P. C. Braunius, "Het leven van de zeventiende-eeuwse zeeman: valse romantiek of werkelijkheid?" *Mededelingen Nederlandse Vereniging voor Zeegeschiedenis* 40–41 (1980): 11–21.

124. Groenhuis, *De predikanten*, 147; Warnsinck, *De vloot van den Koning-Stadhouder*, 168n; Warnsinck-Delprat, ed., *Reyse*, 145–64; C. R. Boxer, *The Dutch Seaborne Empire, 1600–1800* (London, 1965), 73–74.

PART THREE: A SECOND-RATE NAVY, 1714–1795

1. Veenendaal, ed., *De briefwisseling* 9:4.

2. A. C. Carter, *Neutrality or Commitment: The Evolution of Dutch Foreign Policy, 1667–1795* (London, 1975), chaps. 7–8. Israel, *Dutch Primacy*, chaps. 9–10.

3. Bruijn, *De admiraliteit*, 7, 79–82.

4. A. A. van der Houwen, "De Directie Oostersche Handel en Reederijen en het Oostzee-eskader van 1715," *Tijdschrift voor Zeegeschiedenis* 9 (May 1990): 77–88. See also J. Glete, "Sails and Oars: Warships and Navies in the Baltic during the 18th Century (1700–1815), in *Les Marines de guerre Européennes XVII–XVIIIe siècles*, ed. M. Acerra et al. (Paris, 1986), 369–401.

5. Bruijn, *De admiraliteit*, 12–18, 20.

6. Bruijn, *De admiraliteit*, 26–30.

7. Bruijn, *De admiraliteit*, 76–92.

8. J. R. Bruijn, "Protection of Dutch Shipping: The Beginning of Dutch Naval Presence in the Caribbean, 1737–c. 1775," in *Global Crossroads and The American Seas*, ed. C. G. Reynolds (Missoula, 1988), 127–33, esp. 127–28.

9. Bruijn, *De admiraliteit*, 18–21, 32–37, 92–98; Rodger, "The British View," 20–24; Bartstra, *Vlootherstel*, chap. 1.

10. J. C. de Jonge, *Geschiedenis . . . zeewezen* 4:302–13, 353–77.

11. J. C. de Jonge, *Geschiedenis . . . zeewezen* 4:314–52; A. C. Carter, *The Dutch Republic in Europe in the Seven Years War* (London, 1971), 125–28.

12. See D. A. Miller, *Sir Joseph Yorke and Anglo-Dutch Relations, 1774–1780* (The Hague, 1970); Bartstra, *Vlootherstel*, chaps. 5–7; Rodger, "The British View," 25–27.

13. R. B. Prud'homme van Reine, *Jan Hendrik van Kinsbergen (1735–1819): Admiraal en filantroop* (Amsterdam, 1990), 108–20, 132–34.

14. E. S. van Eyck van Heslinga, "De vlag dekt de lading: De Nederlandse koopvaardij in de Vierde Engelse oorlog," *Tijdschrift voor Zeegeschiedenis* 1 (1982): 102–13.

15. J. C. de Jonge, *Geschiedenis . . . zeewezen* 4:440–683.

16. J. C. de Jonge, *Geschiedenis . . . zeewezen* 4:471–74, 5:1–5; Modelski and Thompson, *Seapower*, 70; J. M. F. Fritschy, *De patriotten en de financiën van de Bataafse Republiek* (The Hague, 1988), 62–64, 93.

17. J. C. de Jonge, *Geschiedenis . . . zeewezen* 4:684–752; J. R. Bruijn et al., eds., *Dutch-Asiatic Shipping in the 17th and 18th Centuries*, Rijks Geschiedkundige Publicatiën, Grote Serie 165 (The Hague, 1979-87), 1:246–49.

18. J. C. de Jonge, *Geschiedenis . . . zeewezen* 5:65–120.

19. Prud'homme van Reine, *Jan Hendrik van Kinsbergen*, 306–14. The 's Lands Zeemagazijn was restored in 1793.

20. Bruijn, *De admiraliteit*, 40–43.

21. The Hague, General State Archives, Admiralties Archives 782, f. 36.

22. Bruijn, *De admiraliteit*, 55–59.

23. Bruijn, *De admiraliteit*, 52–55; see also O. Vries, "Geschapen tot een ieders nut: Een verkennend onderzoek naar de Noordnederlandse ambtenaar in de tijd van het Ancien Régime," *Tijdschrift voor Geschiedenis* 90 (1977): 328–49, esp. 337–49.

24. Elias, *De vroedschap*, 2:576–78; Bruijn, *De admiraliteit*, 62.

25. The Hague, General State Archives, Admiralties Archives XXXVII:427.

26. Marseille, *Harlingen*, 112; see also Part Two, note 53.

27. The Hague, General State Archives, Admiralties Archives XXXVII:319 (the Maze in 1746); General State Archives, Collection Van Wassenaer V, O[2].

28. The Hague, General State Archives, Admiralties Archives 1739 and XXXIX:104. See also F. S. Gaastra, "Arbeid op Oostenburg: Het personeel van de kamer Amsterdam van de Verenigde Oostindische Compagnie," in *Van VOC tot Werkspoor: Het Amsterdamse industrieterrein Oostenburg* (Utrecht, 1986), 65–80, esp. 78–80.

29. J. Hovy, *Het voorstel van 1751 tot instelling van een beperkt vrijhavenstelsel in de Republiek (Propositie tot een gelimiteerd porto-franco)* (Groningen, 1966), 107 and passim.

30. Bruijn, *De admiraliteit*, 43–48.

31. Bruijn, *De admiraliteit*, 63–68; Hovy, *Het voorstel*, 242, 252, 258, 395; Davids, *Zeewezen*, 350–51, 465–68.

32. Bartstra, *Vlootherstel*, 167–68; A. J. C. M. Gabriëls, *De heren als dienaren en de dienaar als heer: Het stadhouderlijk stelsel in de tweede helft van de 18de eeuw* (The Hague, 1990), 157.

33. Gabriëls, *De heren*, 97, 124, 453; Prud'homme van Reine, *Jan Hendrik van Kinsbergen*, 190, 193–94; J. C. de Jonge, *Geschiedenis . . . zeewezen* 4:597–99.

34. J. C. de Jonge, *Geschiedenis . . . zeewezen* 5:60–64; Fruin and Colenbrander, *Geschiedenis*, 356–60.

35. J. R. Bruijn, "Engelse scheepsbouwers op de Amsterdamse admiraliteitswerf in de achttiende eeuw: enkele aspecten," *Mededelingen Nederlandse Vereniging voor Zeegeschiedenis* 25 (1972): 18–24.

36. E. Crone, *Cornelis Douwes, 1712–1773, zijn leven en zijn werk* (Haarlem, 1941), chaps. 3–4.

37. J. C. de Jonge, *Geschiedenis . . . zeewezen* 4:297; 5:17–19, 82–85.

38. F. J. A. Broeze and W. M. Jansen, "Den Helder en het Nieuwe Diep (1770–1822)," *Mededelingen Nederlandse Vereniging voor Zeegeschiedenis* 22 (1971): 5–19; Sigmond, *Nederlandse zeehavens*, 150–52.

39. Davids, *Zeewezen*, 298–300, 309, 320.

40. Davids, *Zeewezen*, 184–86, 202–3, 209–10, 224–26, 306–7.

41. Prud'homme van Reine, *Jan Hendrik van Kinsbergen*, 43–51, 159–84.

42. Amsterdam, Rijksmuseum Nederlands Historisch Scheepsvaartmuseum, Collection Dedel, BI, 895.

43. Bruijn, *De admiraliteit*, 109–12.

44. M. Gijswijt-Hofstra, *Wijkplaatsen voor vervolgden: Asielverlening in Culemborg, Vianen, Buren, Leerdam en IJsselstein van de 16de tot eind 18de eeuw* (Dieren, 1984).

45. See D. A. Baugh, *British Naval Administration in the Age of Walpole* (Princeton, 1965), 102–8.

46. Amsterdam, Rijksmuseum Nederlands Historisch Scheepsvaartmuseum, Collection Dedel; The Hague, General State Archives, Generaliteits Rekenkamer 571–96; Elias, *De vroedschap*, 2:754, 828, 881.

47. A. J. Veenendaal, Sr., *Matthijs Sloot: een zeeman uit de achttiende eeuw ± 1719–1779* (The Hague, 1975).

48. The Hague, General State Archives, Admiralties Archives XXXIX:112, ff. 203, 229, 234.

49. Bruijn, *De admiraliteit*, 112–18; Veenendaal, *Matthijs Sloot*, 47–49.

50. The Hague, General State Archives, Admiralties Archives XXXI:7.

51. The Hague, General State Archives, Admiralties Archives XXXI:104–8.

52. Middelburg, State Archives in Zeeland, Collection Boreel van Mauregnault 4.

53. P. Dekker, "Der 'Admiral' Nis de Bombell (1706–1772): Ein Nordfriese in niederländischen Seediensten," *Nordfriesisches Jahrbuch* Neue Folge 13 (1977): 107–33.

54. W. R. H. Oldewelt, "De beroepsstructuur," *Economisch-Historisch Jaarboek* 24 (1950): 80–161; and *Kohier van de Personeele Quotisatie te Amsterdam over het jaar 1742* (Amsterdam, 1945).

55. Middelburg, State Archives in Zeeland, Collection Boreel van Mauregnault, 1, 2, and 4; Bruijn, *De admiraliteit*, 119.

56. Bruijn, *De admiraliteit*, 120. See also F. Beijerinck and M. G. de Boer, *Het dagboek van Jacob Bicker Raye, 1732–1772* (Amsterdam, n.d.).

57. By courtesy of John Montagu, Dr. N. A. M. Rodger of the Public Record Office at London kindly gave this quotation from the private Sandwich Papers (Mapperton Manor near Beaminster, Dorset).

58. Bruijn, *De admiraliteit*, 124–25.

59. Bruijn, "Protection," 129.

60. The Hague, General State Archives, Admiralties Archives XXVII:1–20.

61. Bruijn, *De admiraliteit*, 99–100.

62. Davids, *Zeewezen*, 176, 199, 320.

63. J. R. Bruijn, "Cornelis Schrijver (1687–1768)," in *Vier Eeuwen Varen: Kapiteins, kapers, kooplieden en geleerden*, ed. L. M. Akveld et al. (Bussum, 1973), 161–75; Bruijn, *De admiraliteit*, 120–22.

64. G. J. A. Raven, "Blijven of weggaan? De perspectieven voor marineofficieren tijdens de nadagen van de Republiek, 1751–1795," *Mededelingen Nederlandse Vereniging voor Zeegeschiedenis* 40–41 (1980): 23–50.

65. Prud'homme van Reine, *Jan Hendrik van Kinsbergen*, 277–82, 288–290.

66. H. Winkel-Rauws, *Wel en wee van het geslacht Rauws* (Zutphen, 1979), 80–105.

67. S. Dörr, *De kundige kapitein: Brieven en bescheiden betrekking hebbend op Jan Olphert Vaillant kapitein-ter-zee (1751–1800)* (Zutphen, 1988). See also Prud'homme van Reine, *Jan Hendrik van Kinsbergen*, for some corrections.

68. See Prud'homme van Reine's biography of Van Kinsbergen.

69. J. C. de Jonge, *Geschiedenis . . . zeewezen* 5:92–105.

70. Bruijn, *De admiraliteit*, 153–58.

71. See H. Zinsser, *Rats, Lice and History* (Boston, 1935), chap. 9.

72. A. E. Leuftink, *Harde heelmeesters: Zeelieden en hun dokters in de 18e eeuw* (Zutphen, 1991), chaps. 6–7.

73. G. J. A. Raven, "'Aanhoudend sukkelen om bootsvolk': Een keerpunt in het personeelsbeleid van de marine, 1775–95," *Tijdschrift voor Zeegeschiedenis* 1 (1982): 132–42.

74. Bruijn, *De admiraliteit*, 150–51; Leuftink, *Harde heelmeesters*, 29–36 and 182-86.

75. J. C. de Jonge, *Geschiedenis . . . zeewezen* 5:21–22; N. A. M. Rodger, *The Wooden World: An Anatomy of the Georgian Navy* (London, 1986), 109–12.

76. Davids, *Zeewezen*, 298–300; The Hague, General State Archives, Admiralties Archives 2843.

77. J. C. de Jonge, *Geschiedenis . . . zeewezen* 4:359, 5:27–34; Prud'homme van Reine, *Jan Hendrik van Kinsbergen*, 159–63, 288–90.

78. See chap. 4 of *The Wooden World*.

79. The Hague, General State Archives, Admiralties Archives 2843; Noordegraaf, *Daglonen*, 45–47.

80. Bruijn, *De admiraliteit*, 161–62; J. C. de Jonge, *Geschiedenis . . . zeewezen* 4:475–77.

81. I. G. Dillo, *De nadagen van de Verenigde Oostindische Compagnie, 1783–1795: Schepen en Zeevarenden* (Amsterdam, 1992), chap. 4; Bruijn et al., eds., *Dutch-Asiatic Shipping* 1:210–13.

82. See The Hague, General State Archives, Admiralties Archives 1960, 1961, 1963, and 1965, for example.

83. Bruijn et al., *Dutch-Asiatic Shipping* 1:163; P. C. van Royen, *Zeevarenden*, chap. 3.

84. Bruijn, "Protection," 128–29; E. van Biema, "Het Nederlandsche zeewezen en de Amsterdamsche Joden in het einde der 18e eeuw," *Amsterdamsch Jaarboekje* 5 (1901): 76–91.

85. On this aspect, see also Davids, *Wat lijdt*, 30–38.

86. The Hague, General State Archives, Admiralties Archives XXVII:46, f.115 (Sept. 20, 1755).

87. The Hague, General State Archives, Admiralties Archives, 2843, 2849, 3123, 3126.

88. The Hague, General State Archives, Admiralties Archives, 842, 844, 846, 849–57. Mrs. M. Höfkens at The Hague kindly provided these figures. N. A. M. Rodger mentions a seven-percent desertion rate in the British navy during the Seven Years' War (*The Wooden World*, 203).

89. The Hague, General State Archives, Admiralties Archives 1157.

90. The Hague, General State Archives, Admiralties Archives 1173, no. 3.

91. The Hague, General State Archives, Admiralties Archives 1193, 1205.

92. J. R. Verbeek, "Muiterij op het fregat de 'Venus,' 1779," *Mededelingen Nederlandse Vereniging voor Zeegeschiedenis* 38 (1979): 19–39.

93. The Hague, General State Archives, Admiralties Archives XXXVII:427.

94. The Hague, General State Archives, Admiralties Archives XXXI:7.

95. Bartstra, *Vlootherstel*, 145–47, 170–71.

IN RETROSPECT

1. Fritschy, *De patriotten*, 81–82. Detailed and systematic research on the admiralities' finances has not yet been done.

2. H. L. Zwitzer, *"De militie van den staat": Studies over het leger van de Republiek der Verenigde Nederlanden* (Amsterdam, 1991), chap. 6.

BIBLIOGRAPHY

MANUSCRIPT SOURCES

Amsterdam. Rijksmuseum Nederlands Historisch Scheepvaartmuseum. Collection Dedel.
The Hague. General State Archives. Aanwinsten. 1888, 1896.
The Hague. General State Archives. Admiralties Archives.
The Hague. General State Archives. Collection Dassevael.
The Hague. General State Archives. Collection De Ruyter.
The Hague. General State Archives. Collection Evertsen.
The Hague. General State Archives. Collection Van Wassenaer.
The Hague. General State Archives. Generaliteits Rekenkamer.
The Hague. General State Archives. States General Archives.
The Hague. General State Archives. States of Holland Archives.
Hoorn. Westfries Museum. Collection VerLoren.
Loenen aan de Vecht. Teding van Berkhout Family Archive.
Middelburg. State Archives in Zeeland. Collection Boreel van Mauregnault.
Middelburg. State Archives in Zeeland. Rekenkamer Archives.
Rotterdam. Municipal Archive. Notarial Records.

PUBLISHED SOURCES

Allard, C. *Nieuwe Hollandsche scheepsbouw*. Amsterdam, 1695.

Alphen, G. van. *De stemming van de Engelsen tegen de Hollanders in Engeland tijdens de regeering van den Koning-Stadhouder Willem III*. Assen, 1938.

Anderson, M. S. *War and Society in Europe, 1618–1789*. London, 1988.

Andrees Allgemeiner Handatlas. Bielefeld, 1903.

Backer Dirks, J. J. *De Nederlandsche zeemagt in hare verschillende tijdperken geschetst*. 4 vols. Rotterdam, 1865–1876.

Baetens, R. "The Organization and Effects of Flemish Privateering in the Seventeenth Century." In *Acta Historiae Neerlandicae: Studies on the History of the Netherlands* 9, 48–75. The Hague, 1976.

Barfod, J. H. *Niels Juel: A Danish Admiral of the 17th Century*. Copenhagen, 1977.

Bartstra, J. R. *Vlootherstel en legeraugmentatie, 1770–1780*. Assen, 1952.

Baugh, D. A. *British Naval Administration in the Age of Walpole*. Princeton, 1965.

Becht, H. E. *Statistische gegevens betreffende den handelsomzet van de Republiek der Vereenigde Nederlanden gedurende de 17e eeuw (1579–1715)*. The Hague, 1908.

Beijerinck, F., and M. G. de Boer. *Het dagboek van Jacob Bicker Raye, 1732–1772.* Amsterdam, n.d.

Belonje, J. "Het oorlogsschip 'De Alkmaar' en zijn wapenfeit bij Kijkduin in 1673." *Mededelingen Nederlandse Vereniging voor Zeegeschiedenis* 24 (1972): 11–14.

Biema, E. van. "Het Nederlandsche zeewezen en de Amsterdamsche Joden in het einde der 18e eeuw." *Amsterdamsch Jaarboekje* 5 (1901): 76–91.

Bijl, M. van der. *Idee en Interest: Voorgeschiedenis, verloop en achtergronden van de politieke twisten in Zeeland en vooral in Middelburg tussen 1702 en 1715.* Groningen, 1981.

Bijl Mz., A. *De Nederlandse convooidienst.* The Hague, 1951.

Bijlsma, R. *Rotterdams welvaren, 1550–1650.* The Hague, 1918.

Binder, F. "Die Zeeländische Kaperfahrt, 1654–1662." In *Archief Koninklijk Zeeuwsch Genootschap der Wetenschappen* 1976, 40 –92.

Blok, P. J. "Inventaris van De Ruyter's inboedel, opgemaakt 22–24 maart 1677." *Bijdragen en Mededelingen Historisch Genootschap* 49 (1928): 187–213.

______. *Michiel Adriaanszoon De Ruyter.* The Hague, 1930.

Boer, F. P. de. "Gerard Callenburgh." *Marineblad* 90 (1980): 292–304.

Boer, M. G. de. *Tromp en de Armada van 1639.* Amsterdam, 1941.

______. "Een kwarteeuw admiraliteitsleven." *Tijdschrift voor Geschiedenis* 56 (1941): 113–51.

______. *Het proefjaar van Maarten Harpertsz. Tromp, 1637–1639.* Amsterdam, 1946.

______. *Tromp en de Duinkerkers.* Amsterdam, 1949.

Booy, A. de. *De derde reis van de VOC naar Oost-Indië onder het beleid van admiraal Paulus van Caerden uitgezeild in 1606.* Werken Linschoten-Vereeniging, vol. 70. The Hague, 1968.

Bosscher, Ph. M. *De Nederlandse mariniers.* Bussum, 1966.

Boxer, C. R. *The Journal of Maarten Harpertsz. Tromp, Anno 1639.* Cambridge, England, 1930.

______. *The Dutch Seaborne Empire, 1600–1800.* London, 1965.

______. *The Anglo-Dutch Wars of the 17th Century, 1652–1674.* London, 1974.

Braunius, S. W. P. C. "Het leven van de zeventiende-eeuwse zeeman: valse romantiek of werkelijkheid?" *Mededelingen Nederlandse Vereniging voor Zeegeschiedenis* 40–41 (1980): 11–21.

Broeze, F. J. A., and W. M. Jansen. "Den Helder en het Nieuwe Diep (1770–1822)." *Mededelingen Nederlandse Vereniging voor Zeegeschiedenis* 22 (1971): 5–19.

Bruijn, J. R. "Voeding op de Staatse vloot." *Spiegel Historiael* 2 (1967): 175–83.

______. *De admiraliteit van Amsterdam in rustige jaren, 1713–1751.* Amsterdam, 1970.

______. "Engelse scheepsbouwers op de Amsterdamse admiraliteitswerf in de achttiende eeuw: enkele aspecten." *Mededelingen Nederlandse Vereniging voor Zeegeschiedenis* 25 (1972): 18–24.

______. "Cornelis Schrijver (1687–1768)." In *Vier Eeuwen Varen: Kapiteins, kapers, kooplieden en geleerden*, edited by L. M. Akveld et al., 161–75. Bussum, 1973.

______. "Dutch Men-of-War: Those on Board c. 1700–1750." In *Acta Historiae Neerlandicae: Studies on the History of the Netherlands* 7, 88–121. The Hague, 1974.

_____. "Dutch Privateering during the Second and Third Anglo-Dutch Wars." In *The Low Countries History Yearbook 1978: Acta Historiae Neerlandicae* 11, 79–93. The Hague, 1979.

_____. "Cornelis Tromp (1629–1691): een niet-gewaardeerd dienaar van de heren." *Tijdschrift voor Geschiedenis* 96 (1983): 179–92.

_____. "Mercurius en Mars uiteen: De uitrusting van de oorlogsvloot in de zeventiende eeuw." In *Bestuurders en geleerden*, edited by S. Groenveld, 97–106. Amsterdam, 1985.

_____. "Protection of Dutch Shipping: The Beginning of Dutch Naval Presence in the Caribbean, 1737–c. 1775." In *Global Crossroads and the American Seas*, edited by C. G. Reynolds, 127–33. Missoula, 1988.

_____. "William III and His Two Navies." *Notes and Records of the Royal Society of London* 43 (1989): 117–32.

_____. "The Dutch Navy in Its Political and Social-Economic Setting of the Seventeenth Century." In *1688: The Seaborne Alliance and Diplomatic Revolution*, edited by C. Wilson and D. Proctor, 45–58. London, 1989.

_____. "In een veranderend maritiem perspectief: het ontstaan van directies voor de vaart op de Oostzee, Noorwegen en Rusland." *Tijdschrift voor Zeegeschiedenis* 9 (May 1990): 15–25.

_____, ed. *De oorlogvoering ter zee in 1673 in journalen en andere stukken.* Groningen, 1966.

Bruijn, J. R., and J. Lucassen, eds. *Op de schepen der Oost-Indische Compagnie: Vijf artikelen van J. de Hullu.* Groningen, 1980.

Bruijn, J. R., and E. S. van Eyck van Heslinga, eds. "Aan 'Wijffje lief': Brieven van zeekapitein Eland du Bois aan zijn vrouw (1669–1674)." *Nederlandse Historische Bronnen* 5 (1985): 111–44.

Bruijn, J. R., F. S. Gaastra, and I. Schöffer, eds. *Dutch-Asiatic Shipping in the 17th and 18th Centuries.* 3 vols., Rijks Geschiedkundige Publicatiën, Grote Serie 165 –67. The Hague, 1979–1987.

Bruin, G. de. *Geheimhouding en verraad: De geheimhouding van staatszaken ten tijde van de Republiek, 1600–1750.* The Hague, 1991.

Capp, B. *Cromwell's Navy: The Fleet and the English Revolution, 1648–1660.* Oxford, 1989.

Carter, A. C. *The Dutch Republic in Europe in the Seven Years War.* London, 1971.

_____. *Neutrality or Commitment: The Evolution of Dutch Foreign Policy, 1667–1795.* London, 1975.

Crone, E. *Cornelis Douwes, 1712–1773, zijn leven en zijn werk.* Haarlem, 1941.

Damsteegt, B. C. *Nieuwe Spiegel der Zeevaart: Nederlandse namen op zeekaarten uit de 16e en 17e eeuw.* Amsterdam, 1942.

Davids, C. A. *Wat lijdt den zeeman al verdriet: Het Nederlandse zeemanslied in de zeiltijd (1600–1900).* The Hague, 1980.

_____. *Zeewezen en wetenschap: De wetenschap en de ontwikkeling van de navigatietechniek in Nederland tussen 1585 en 1815.* Amsterdam, 1986.

Davies, J. D. *Gentlemen and Tarpaulins: The Officers and Men of the Restoration Navy.* Oxford, 1991.

Dekker, P. "Der 'Admiral' Nis de Bombell (1706–1772): Ein Nordfriese in niederländischen Seediensten." *Nordfriesisches Jahrbuch* Neue Folge 13 (1977): 107–33.

Deursen, A. Th. van. "Holland's Experience of War during the Revolt of the Netherlands." In *Britain and The Netherlands*, vol. 6, War and Society, edited by A. C. Duke and C. A. Tamse, 19–53. The Hague, 1977.

______. *Het kopergeld van de Gouden Eeuw*. Vol. 3, Volk en Overheid. Assen, 1979.

______. *Plain Lives in a Golden Age: Popular Culture, Religion and Society in Seventeenth-Century Holland*. Cambridge, England, 1991.

Diekerhoff, F. L., ed. *Journael gehouden op 's landts schip d'Eendracht door de heer Aert van Nes lt. admrl. van Holland ende van Westvriesland in den jare 1667*. Bijdrage Geschiedenis Zeewezen Bureau Maritieme Historie Marinestaf, vol. 2. 1967.

Dillo, I. G. *De nadagen van de Verenigde Oostindische Compagnie, 1783–1795: Schepen en Zeevarenden*. Amsterdam, 1992.

Doedens, A., and L. Mulder. *Tromp: Het verhaal van een zeeheld*. Baarn, 1989.

Dörr, S. *De kundige kapitein: Brieven en bescheiden betrekking hebbend op Jan Olphert Vaillant kapitein-ter-zee (1751–1800)*. Zutphen, 1988.

Dulm, J. F. van. "Het Memoriaal van Johan Willem baron van Regteren." In *Jaarverslag Vereeniging Nederlandsch Historisch Scheepvaartmuseum*, 80–82. Amsterdam, 1971–1972.

Eekhout, L. L. M. "Philips van Almonde: Admiraal in de schaduw." *Marineblad* 95 (1985): 404–11.

Ehrman, J. *The Navy in the War of William III, 1689–1697*. Cambridge, England, 1953.

Elias, J. E. *De vroedschap van Amsterdam, 1578–1795*, 2. vols. Haarlem, 1903–1905.

______. *Schetsen uit de geschiedenis van ons zeewezen*. 6 vols. The Hague, 1916–1930.

______. *Het Voorspel van den Eersten Engelschen oorlog*. 2 vols. The Hague, 1920.

______. *De vlootbouw in Nederland in de eerste helft der 17e eeuw, 1596–1655*. Amsterdam, 1933.

Engelbrecht, E. A. *De vroedschap van Rotterdam, 1572–1795*. Rotterdam, 1973.

Eyck van Heslinga, E. S. van. "De vlag dekt de lading: De Nederlandse koopvaardij in de Vierde Engelse oorlog." *Tijdschrift voor Zeegeschiedenis* 1 (1982): 102–13.

Faber, J. A., et al. "Population Changes and Economic Developments in the Netherlands: A Historical Survey." *A. A. G. Bijdragen* 12 (1965): 47–110.

Faber, J. A. "De Noordelijke Nederlanden van 1480 tot 1780: Structuren in beweging." In *Algemene Geschiedenis der Nederlanden* 5:196–250. Haarlem, 1980.

Fockema Andreae, S. J. *De Nederlandse staat onder de Republiek*. Amsterdam, 1962.

Foreest, H. A. van, and R. E. J. Weber. *De Vierdaagse Zeeslag 11–14 Juni 1666*. Amsterdam, 1984.

Fritschy, J. M. F. *De patriotten en de financiën van de Bataafse Republiek*. The Hague, 1988.

Fruin, R. *Tien jaren uit den Tachtigjarigen oorlog, 1588–1598*. The Hague, 1861.

Fruin, R., and H. T. Colenbrander. *Geschiedenis der staatsinstellingen in Nederland tot den val der Republiek*. The Hague, 1922.

Fruin, R. *De oorlog van 1672*. Groningen, 1972.

Gaastra, F. S. "Arbeid op Oostenburg: Het personeel van de kamer Amsterdam van de Verenigde Oostindische Compagnie." In *Van VOC tot Werkspoor: Het Amsterdamse industrieterrein Oostenburg*, 65–80. Utrecht, 1986.

______. *De Geschiedenis van de VOC.* Zutphen, 1991.

Gabriëls, A. J. C. M. *De heren als dienaren en de dienaar als heer: Het stadhouderlijk stelsel in de tweede helft van de 18de eeuw.* The Hague, 1990.

Geyl, P. "De dateering van Vondel's Roskam." *Tijdschrift Nederlandsche Taal-en letterkunde* 30, n.s., 22 (1911): 308–20.

______. *Christofforo Suriano: Resident van de Serenisseme Republiek van Venetië in Den Haag, 1616–1623.* The Hague, 1913.

Gijswijt-Hofstra, M. *Wijkplaatsen voor vervolgden: Asielverlening in Culemborg, Vianen, Buren, Leerdam en IJsselstein van de 16de tot eind 18de eeuw.* Dieren, 1984.

Glete, J. "Sails and Oars: Warship and Navies in the Baltic during the 18th Century (1700–1815)." In *Les marines de guerre Européennes XVII–XVIIIe siècles,* edited by M. Acerra et al., 369–401. Paris, 1986.

Graefe, F. *De kapiteinsjaren van Maerten Harpertszoon Tromp.* Amsterdam, 1938.

Groenhuis, G. *De predikanten: De sociale positie van de gereformeerde predikanten in de Republiek der Verenigde Nederlanden voor ± 1700.* Groningen, 1977.

Groenveld, S. "The English Civil Wars as a Cause of the First Anglo-Dutch Wars, 1640–1652." *The Historical Journal* 30 (1987): 541–66.

______. *"Evidente factiën in den staet": Sociaal-politieke verhoudingen in de 17e-eeuwse Republiek der Verenigde Nederlanden.* Hilversum, 1990.

Groot Placaetboeck, vervattende de placaten, ordonnantiën en de edicten van de Staten-Generael der Vereenigde Nederlanden. . . . Vol. 3. Edited by S. van Leeuwen. The Hague, 1683. Vol. 5. Edited by P. Scheltus. The Hague, 1725.

Grove, G. L., ed. *Journalen van de admiralen Van Wassenaer-Obdam (1658/59) en De Ruyter (1659/60).* Werken Historisch Genootschap 3e Serie, no. 23. Amsterdam, 1907.

Haagsma, S. *Eenige bladzijden uit Friesland's zeegeschiedenis.* N.p., ca. 1895.

Haak, B. *Hollandse schilders in de Gouden Eeuw.* Amsterdam, 1984.

Hallema, A. *Cornelis Maartenszoon Tromp, 1629–1691.* The Hague, 1941.

Hardenberg, H., ed. *Tussen zeerovers en christenslaven.* Leiden, 1950.

Hart, S. "Michiel Adriaanszoon de Ruyter en de Noordcaepse Compagnie." In *Geschrift en Getal,* 247–54. Dordrecht, 1976.

Hattendorf, J. B. *England in the War of the Spanish Succession: A Study of the English View and Conduct of Grand Strategy.* New York, 1987.

Hoboken, W. J. van. *Witte de With in Brazilië, 1648–1649.* Amsterdam, 1955.

Holck, P. *Cort Adeler.* Copenhagen, 1934.

Hollandse Mercurius: verhalende de voornaemste saken van staet . . . in het jaer 1688. Haarlem, 1689.

Houwen, A. A. van der. "De Directie Oostersche Handel en Reederijen en het Oostzee-eskader van 1715." *Tijdschrift voor Zeegeschiedenis* 9 (May 1990): 77–88.

Hovy, J. *Het voorstel van 1751 tot instelling van een beperkt vrijhavenstelsel in de Republiek (Propositie tot een gelimiteerd porto-franco).* Groningen, 1966.

Huysman, E. C. M., ed. *Particuliere notulen van de vergaderingen der Staten van Holland 1620–1640 door N. Stellingwerff en S. Schot.* Vol. 3 , *1625–1628.* Rijks Geschiedkundige Publicatiën, Grote Serie 206. The Hague, 1989.

"Inventaris van den boedel van den Luitenant Admiraal Tjerk Hiddes de Vries, 2 Januarij 1667." *Friesche Volksalmanak* (1889): 112–27.

Israel, J. I. *The Dutch Republic and the Hispanic World, 1606–1661.* Oxford, 1982.

———. *Dutch Primacy in World Trade, 1585–1740.* Oxford, 1989.
Jong, C. de. *Geschiedenis van de oude Nederlandse walvisvaart.* 3 vols. Pretoria, 1972–1979.
Jong, J. de. *Een deftig bestaan: Het dagelijks leven van regenten in de 17de en 18de eeuw.* Utrecht, 1987.
Jonge, J. C. de. *Levensbeschrijving van Johan en Cornelis Evertsen, luitenant-admiralen van Zeeland.* The Hague, 1820.
———. *Geschiedenis van het Nederlandsche zeewezen.* 5 vols. Haarlem, 1858–1862.
Jonge, J. K. J. de. *De oorsprong van Neerland's bezittingen op de kust van Guinea.* The Hague, 1871.
Kepler, J. S. *The Exchange of Christendom: The International Entrepôt at Dover, 1622–1651.* Leicester, 1976.
Kernkamp, G. W. *De sleutels van de Sont: Het aandeel van de Republiek in den Deensch-Zweedschen oorlog van 1644–1645.* The Hague, 1890.
Kolleman, G. "Admiraal Swartenhondt en zijn vrouw Lysbeth Bas." *Ons Amsterdam* 19 (1967): 57–62.
Kooijmans, L. "Patriciaat en aristocratisering in Holland tijdens de zeventiende en achttiende eeuw." In *De bloem der natie: Adel en patriciaat in de Noordelijke Nederlanden,* edited by J. Aalbers and M. Prak, 93–103. Meppel, 1987.
Koopmans, J. W. *De Staten van Holland en de Opstand.* The Hague, 1990.
Kuijl, A. van der. *De Glorieuze overtocht: De expeditie van Willem III naar Engeland in 1688.* Amsterdam, 1988.
Kuyper, I. "Pieter Jansz. Liorne en de Nederlandse scheepsbouw." *West-Frieslands Oud en Nieuw* 24 (1957): 60–75.
Leuftink, A. E. *De geneeskunde bij 's lands oorlogsvloot in de 17e eeuw.* Assen, 1953.
———. *Harde heelmeesters: Zeelieden en hun dokters in de 18e eeuw.* Zutphen, 1991.
Leupe, P. A., ed. "Voordracht tot aanstelling van Stachhouwer, Vlugh enz. tot kapiteins, door het Noorder-Kwartier aan H. H. M., 19 Februarij 1665." *Kroniek Historisch Genootschap* 22 (1866): 291–97.
———. "Aanbevelingen van vlag-officieren enz." *Kroniek Historisch Genootschap* 26 (1870): 286–301.
———. "Aanbevelingen van kapiteins bij het Noorder-Kwartier, 1667." *Kroniek Historisch Genootschap* 29 (1873): 165–79.
———. "Aanbevelingen voor scheepskapiteins enz. ingekomen bij den raadpensionaris Johan de Witt, 1653–1672." *Kroniek Historisch Genootschap* 29 (1873): 603–54.
———. "Aanbevelingen voor scheepskapiteins enz." *Kroniek Historisch Genootschap* 31 (1875): 504–13.
Ligtenberg, C. *Willem Usselinx.* Utrecht, 1914.
Lucassen, J. *Migrant Labour in Europe, 1600–1900: The Drift to the North Sea.* London, 1987.
Maritieme Geschiedenis der Nederlanden. 4 vols. Bussum, 1976–1978.
Marseille, T. *Harlingen de vermaerde zeestad.* Harlingen, 1984.
Martin, W. "Een en ander uit den inventaris der nalatenschap van Cornelis Tromp." *Oud-Holland* 19 (1901): 65–76.
Meij, J. C. A. de. *De Watergeuzen en de Nederlanden, 1568–1572.* Amsterdam, 1972.

Miller, D. A. *Sir Joseph Yorke and Anglo-Dutch Relations, 1774–1780.* The Hague, 1970.

Milo, T. H. "Het Nederlands hulpeskader voor Portugal [1641]." In *Varia Historica aangeboden aan Professor doctor A. W. Byvanck*, 165–76. Assen, 1954.

______. "Michiel Adriaenszoon de Ruyter als tacticus." *Onze Vloot* 46 (1957): 89–92.

Modelski, G., and W. R. Thompson. *Seapower in Global Politics, 1494–1993.* London, 1988.

Moer, A. van der. "Willem Bloys van Treslong (ca. 1529–1594)." *Marineblad* 95 (1985): 524–31.

______. "Pieter Pieterszoon Heyn (1577–1629)." *Marineblad* 96 (1986): 556–64.

______. *Michiel Adriaenszoon de Ruyter.* N.p., 1990.

Mollema, J. C. *Geschiedenis van Nederland ter zee.* 4 vols. Amsterdam, 1939–1942.

Muller van Brakel, F. "Amsterdamse admiraliteitsheren actief achter de schermen." *Marineblad* 66 (1956): 226–43.

Noordam, N. F. *De Republiek en de Noordse oorlog, 1655–1660.* Assen, 1940.

Noordegraaf, L. *Daglonen in Alkmaar, 1500–1800.* N.p., 1980.

______. *Hollands welvaren? Levenssstandaard in Holland, 1450–1650.* Bergen, 1985.

Oldewelt, W. F. H. *Kohier van de Personeele Quotisatie te Amsterdam over het jaar 1742.* 2 vols. Amsterdam, 1945.

______. "De beroepssstructuur van de bevolking der Hollandse stemhebbende steden volgens de kohieren van de familiegelden van 1674, 1715 en 1742." *Economisch-Historisch Jaarboek* 24 (1950): 80–161.

______. "De Hoeffijserse schuld (1616–1681)." *Jaarboek Amstelodamum* 51 (1959): 37–52.

Ollard, R. *Man of War: Sir Robert Holmes and the Restoration Navy.* London, 1969.

______. *Pepys: A Biography.* London, 1974.

Oudendijk, J. K. *Johan de Witt en de zeemacht.* Amsterdam, 1944.

______. *Maerten Harpertszoon Tromp.* The Hague, 1952.

Padt, P. M. van der. "De admiraliteit van Zeeland in drukke jaren: Logistiek en organisatie van de admiraliteit van Zeeland tijdens de overwintering van de vloot in Spanje, 1694–1695." Master's thesis, University of Leiden, 1989.

Parker, G. *The Military Revolution: Military Innovation and the Rise of the West.* Cambridge, England, 1988.

Poel, J. van der. "Het particularisme van Zeeland en de convoyen en licenten." In *Archief Zeeuwsch Genootschap der Wetenschappen*, 1–113. 1929.

Pollentier, F. *De Admiraliteit en de oorlog ter zee onder de Aartshertogen (1596–1609).* Brussels, 1972.

Prud'homme van Reine, R. B. "Willem Bastiaensz. Schepers (1619–1704), een veelzijdig Rotterdams koopman en reder." *Tijdschrift voor Zeegeschiedenis* 7 (1988): 14–41.

______. *Jan Hendrik van Kinsbergen (1735–1819): Admiraal en filantroop.* Amsterdam, 1990.

Rahn Phillips, C. *Six Galleons for the King of Spain: Imperial Defense in the Early Seventeenth Century.* Baltimore, 1986.

Raven, G. J. A. "Blijven of weggaan? De perspectieven voor marineofficieren tijdens de nadagen van de Republiek, 1751–95." *Mededelingen Nederlandse Vereniging voor Zeegeschiedenis* 40–41 (1980): 23–50.

———. "'Aanhoudend sukkelen om bootsvolk': Een keerpunt in het personeelsbeleid van de marine, 1775–95." *Tijdschrift voor Zeegeschiedenis* 1 (1982): 132–42.

———. "De Banckerts." *Marineblad* 92 (1982): 518–26.

Reynolds, C. G. *Command of the Sea: The History and Strategy of Maritime Empires.* New York, 1974.

Rian, Q. "State and Society in Seventeenth-century Norway." *Scandinavian Journal of History* 10 (1985): 337–60.

Robinson, M. S. *The Paintings of the Willem van de Veldes: A Catalogue of the Paintings of the Elder and Younger Willem van de Velde.* 2 vols. Greenwich, 1990.

Rodger, N. A. M. *The Wooden World: An Anatomy of the Georgian Navy.* London, 1986.

———. "The British View of the Functioning of the Anglo-Dutch Alliance, 1688–1795." In *Navies and Armies: The Anglo-Dutch Relationship in War and Peace, 1688–1988,* edited by G. J. A. Raven and N. A. M. Rodger, 12–32. Edinburgh, 1990.

Rogers, P. G. *The Dutch in the Medway.* London, 1970.

Römelingh, J. *De diplomatieke betrekkingen van de Republiek met Denemarken en Zweden, 1660–1675.* Amsterdam, 1969.

Rotterdamsche Historiebladen 3 (1880), 83–84.

Rowen, H. H. *John de Witt, Grand Pensionary of Holland, 1625–1672.* Princeton, 1978.

———. *The Princes of Orange: The Stadholder in the Dutch Republic.* Cambridge, Mass., 1988.

Royen, P. C. van. *Zeevarenden op de koopvaardijvloot omstreeks 1700.* Amsterdam, 1987.

Schaap, C. W. J. "De admiraliteit van Friesland: haar vlagofficieren en schepen." In *Fries Scheepvaart Museum en Oudheidkamer, Jaarboek 1982,* 43–77.

Schama, S. *The Embarrassment of Riches: An Interpretation of Dutch Culture in the Golden Age.* New York, 1987.

Schelven, A. L. van. *Philips van Almonde: Admiraal in de gecombineerde vloot, 1644–1711.* Amsterdam, 1947.

Scheurleer, D. F. *Herinneringsdagen uit de Nederlandsche zeegeschiedenis.* The Hague, 1913.

———, ed. *Van Varen en van Vechten: Verzen van tijdgenooten op onze zeehelden en zeeslagen, lof-en schimpdichten, matrozenliederen.* 3 vols. The Hague, 1914.

Schmidt, C. *Om de eer van de familie: Het geslacht Teding van Berkhout 1500–1950, een sociologische benadering.* Amsterdam, 1986.

Senior, C. *A Nation of Pirates: English Piracy in Its Heyday.* Newton Abbot, 1976.

Shomette, D. G., and R. D. Haslach. *Raid on America: The Dutch Naval Campaign of 1672–1674.* Columbia, S.C., 1988.

Sigmond, J. P. *Nederlandse zeehavens tussen 1500 en 1800.* Amsterdam, 1989.

Slot, B. J. *Archipelagus turbatus: Les Cyclades entre colonisation Latine et occupation Ottomane, c. 1500–1718.* Leiden, 1982.

Snapper, F. *Oorlogsinvloeden op de overzeese handel van Holland, 1551–1719.* Amsterdam, 1959.

Steur, A. G. van der. "Johan van Duvenvoirde en Woude (1547–1610), heer van Warmond, admiraal van Holland." *Hollandse Studiën* 8 (1975): 179–273.

Stols, E. *De Spaanse Brabanders of de handelsbetrekkingen der Zuidelijke Nederlanden met de Iberische wereld, 1598–1648.* Brussels, 1971.
Swart, K. W. *Sale of Offices in the Seventeenth Century.* The Hague, 1949.
Symcox, G. *The Crisis of French Sea Power, 1688–1697: From the Guerre d'Escadre to the Guerre de Course.* The Hague, 1974.
Teitler, G. *De wording van het professionele officierscorps.* Rotterdam, 1974.
Terpstra, H. *Jacob van Neck: Amsterdams admiraal en regent.* Amsterdam, 1950.
Tracy, J. D. *Holland under Habsburg Rule, 1506–1566: The Formation of a Body Politic.* Berkeley, 1990.
Troost, W. "Capiteynen te water (1): Loth Steyn." *Marineblad* 80 (1970): 239–57.
______. "Capiteynen te water (2): Gerrit Pietersz. de Witte." *Marineblad* 80 (1970): 516–32.
______. "Capiteynen te water (3): Jan Claesz. Spiegel." *Marineblad* 80 (1970): 697–716.
______. "Een Amsterdams kapitein uit het einde der 16de eeuw: Joachim Pietersz. Cleynsorghe." *Mededelingen Nederlandse Vereniging Zeegeschiedenis* 22 (1971): 20–28.
______. "Capiteynen te water (4): Lambert Jansz. Verhagen." *Marineblad* 81 (1971): 253–65.
______. "Capiteynen te water (5): Jan Claesz. Breet." *Marineblad* 81 (1971): 891–909.
______. "Capiteynen te water (6): Gerrit Luyten." *Marineblad* 82 (1972): 393–417.
______. "Capiteynen te water (7): Jan Allertsz." *Marineblad* 83 (1973): 67–87.
______. "Capiteynen te water (8): Jan Allertsz." *Marineblad* 83 (1973): 469–511.
Unger, R. W. *Dutch Shipbuilding before 1800.* Assen, 1978.
______. *The Ship in the Medieval Economy, 600–1600.* London, 1980.
Usherwood, S. and E. *The Counter-Armada 1596: The Journall of the "Mary Rose".* London, 1983.
Valk, G. "Oproeren, onlusten en rellen in Alkmaar gedurende de Republiek." *Holland* 13 (1981): 230–47.
Veenendaal, A. J., Sr. *Matthijs Sloot, een zeeman uit de achttiende eeuw ± 1719–1779.* The Hague, 1975.
Veenendaal, A. J., ed. *De briefwisseling van Anthonie Heinsius, 1702–1720.* Vols. 1–12 (1702–1712), Rijks Geschiedkundige Publicatiën, Grote Serie 158, 163, 169, 177, 183, 189, 194, 198, 204, 207, 214, 221. The Hague, 1976–1992.
Verbeek, J. R. "Muiterij op het fregat de 'Venus,' 1779." *Mededelingen Nederlandse Vereniging voor Zeegeschiedenis* 38 (1979): 19–39.
Verhees-van Meer, J. Th. H. *De Zeeuwse kaapvaart tijdens de Spaanse Successieoorlog, 1702–1713.* Middelburg, 1986.
Voorbeijtel Cannenburg, W. *De Groene Draeck: Het snelle schip van Maerten Harpertsz. Tromp.* Amsterdam, 1957.
______. *De reis om de wereld van de Nassausche vloot, 1623–1626.* Werken Linschoten-Vereeniging, vol. 65. The Hague, 1964.
Vos van Steenwÿk, A. N., baron de, "Gibraltar." *Marineblad* 78(1968): 907–23, 1049–64.
Vries, J. de. *The Dutch Rural Economy in the Golden Age, 1500–1700.* New Haven, 1974.
Vries, O. "Geschapen tot een ieders nut: Een verkennend onderzoek naar de Noordnederlandse ambtenaar in de tijd van het Ancien Régime." *Tijdschrift voor Geschiedenis* 90 (1977): 328–49.

Waning, C. J. W. van, and A. van der Moer. *Dese Aengenaeme Tocht: Chatham 1667 herbezien door zeemansogen*. Zutphen, 1981.

Warnsinck-Delprat, C. E., ed. *Reyse gedaen bij Adriaen Schagen aen de croonen van Sweden ende Polen in den jaere 1656*. Werken Linschoten-Vereeniging, vol. 69. The Hague, 1968.

Warnsinck, J. C. M. *De retourvloot van Pieter de Bitter (Kerstmis 1664–Najaar 1665)*. The Hague, 1929.

______. *Admiraal De Ruyter: De zeeslag op Schooneveld Juni 1673*. The Hague, 1930.

______. *De vloot van den Koning-Stadhouder, 1689–1690*. Amsterdam, 1934.

______. *Abraham Crijnssen: De verovering van Suriname en zijn aanslag op Virginië 1667*. Amsterdam, 1936.

______. *Van vlootvoogden en zeeslagen*. Amsterdam, 1940.

______. *Drie zeventiende-eeuwsche admiraals: Piet Heyn, Witte de With, Jan Evertsen*. Amsterdam, 1943.

______, ed. *Reisen van Nicolaus de Graaff gedaan naar alle gewesten des werelds beginnende 1639 tot 1687 incluis*. Werken Linschoten-Vereeniging, vol. 33. The Hague, 1930.

Weber, R. E. J. *De beveiliging van de zee tegen Euroopeesche en Barbarijsche zeeroovers 1609–1621*. Amsterdam, 1936.

______. "Met smakzeilen en spiegelschepen tegen den Spanjaard: de organisatie van een oorlogsmarine." In *De Tachtigjarige Oorlog*, J. Romein et al., 132–58. Amsterdam, 1941.

______. "The Introduction of the Single Line Ahead as a Battle Formation by the Dutch, 1665–1666." *Mariner's Mirror* 73 (1987): 5–19.

Wiersum, E. *Egbert Meussen Cortenaer*. Assen, 1939.

Wilson, C. *Profit and Power: A Study of England and the Dutch Wars*. London, 1957.

Winkel-Rauws, H. *Nederlandsch-Engelsche samenwerking in de Spaansche wateren, 1625–1627*. Amsterdam, 1946.

______. *Wel en wee van het geslacht Rauws*. Zutphen, 1979.

Witte van Citters, J. de. *Contracten van Correspondentie en andere bijdragen tot de geschiedenis van het ambtsbejag in de Republiek der Vereenigde Nederlanden*. The Hague, 1873.

Zinsser, H. *Rats, Lice and History*. Boston, 1935.

Zwitzer, H. L. *"De militie van den staat": Studies over het leger van de Republiek der Verenigde Nederlanden*. Amsterdam, 1991.

INDEX

The following are indexed only when specific characteristics are mentioned: Republic; States General; (States of) Holland; (States of) Zeeland; Amsterdam, Rotterdam, Middelburg, and other cities; the admiralties at Amsterdam, Rotterdam, Zeeland, Noorderkwartier, and Friesland; and the functions of stadholder, grand pensionary, secretary, advocate fiscal, and admiral general.